Charles Mackay

The Founders of the American republic

A History and Biography

Charles Mackay

The Founders of the American republic
A History and Biography

ISBN/EAN: 9783337013912

Printed in Europe, USA, Canada, Australia, Japan

Cover: Foto ©ninafisch / pixelio.de

More available books at **www.hansebooks.com**

THE FOUNDERS

OF

THE AMERICAN REPUBLIC

A HISTORY AND BIOGRAPHY

WITH

A SUPPLEMENTARY CHAPTER ON ULTRA-DEMOCRACY

BY

CHARLES MACKAY

AUTHOR OF 'LIFE AND LIBERTY IN AMERICA,' ETC.

WILLIAM BLACKWOOD AND SONS
EDINBURGH AND LONDON
MDCCCLXXXV

CONTENTS.

THE FOUNDERS

THE AMERICAN REPUBLIC.

———•———

WASHINGTON.

PART I.

It is fortunate for the men who, not being born to such greatness as crowns and sceptres confer upon their inheritors, are destined "to achieve greatness or have it thrust upon them," that they do not come into the world with the marks of their destiny upon them—that no sign upon their foreheads, no nimbus or aureole of glory around their baby faces, proclaims to the generation in which their lot is cast that such little germs of humanity are to become dangerous original thinkers, invincible warriors, or reckless revolutionists, whose deeds are to

A

deflect the current of history. Were it otherwise, many plots would be devised by the Herods of the epoch to nip such buds of promise at their birth, and cut short the days of those who, if permitted to live, might shake old sytems of faith and remove the old boundaries of empires. Such a child came into the world in the year 1732, and lived well on to, or even a step beyond, what Dante calls the *mezzo del cammin di nostra vita*, without exhibiting the possession of any extraordinary qualities of mind, or promising to be anything more than a highly respectable country gentleman—a mere local magnate, to be honoured after death by a stone in the village churchyard, or an obituary eulogium in the county newspaper. Yet this obscure man was the founder of a great and mighty State, without knowing what he did—as much a blind instrument in the hands of Fate as the hammer in the hands of a blacksmith that welds the hot iron into a sword or a ploughshare.

In that year there stood at a place called Bridges Creek, in Virginia, a lonely farmhouse, of which scarcely a vestige now remains. It was of primitive construction and rude materials—had a steep roof and far projecting eaves, so near to the ground that a tall man could touch them if standing underneath. It consisted of four large rooms on the ground - floor, and as many in the attic. Here resided a wealthy and highly respectable planter, Mr Augustine Washington, the owner of many fertile farms within the district between the then little known but now renowned and historical rivers, the Potomac and the Rappahannock. Mr Washington was in his thirty-eighth year, and had been twice married. By his first wife, Jane Butler, whom he had espoused at twenty-one, he had a family of four children, only two of whom—Laurence and Augustine—survived. This lady dying in 1728, he married in 1730 Mary Ball, the reigning belle and toast of Virginia, who in her progress through life manifested the possession of mental virtues and graces more endearing than physical beauty, and was the true friend, adviser, and consoler of her husband.

On a cold wintry morning—the 22d of February 1732—a child was born to this couple in the farm-house at Bridges Creek, whose destiny, if it could have been foreseen by its father and mother, would have caused them to hail its birth with emotions of a higher kind than those which are common to humanity on such interesting occasions. The child received the name of George. The father did not live to see it reach maturity. The mother lived to see its name illustrious, and to acknowledge her son as one of the powers and potentates of the earth.

Soon after the birth of George Washington, his father removed to a better house on an estate in Stafford County, on the bank of the Rappahannock, opposite to the city of Fredericksburg, at that time little better than a village. Here five other children —three sons and two daughters—were born to the wealthy planter, whose days flowed in an equable current, occupied in agriculture, in rural sports, in the care and education of his growing family, and in the small political intrigues of a contented and a prosperous colony. The Washingtons had always held their heads high in Virginia. They were of no plebeian stock, but aristocrats who claimed to be descended from the De Wessingtons of the county of Durham in England, who "came over with the Conqueror." The first of the race who settled in America were two brothers—John and Andrew. John was the grandfather of Augustine Washington, and came to Virginia in 1657. He was an ardent Cavalier, disgusted with English politics, especially with the execution of the King and the triumph of the abhorred and revolutionary Roundheads. He did not come to Virginia empty-handed or by accident, but with money enough to purchase lands and slaves, and with the design of sharing the congenial society of many brother Cavaliers who had quitted England for the same reasons as himself.

He and his descendants, as well as those of his brother Andrew, prospered in the New World, and held rank among what it has since become the fashion to call the F. F. V.'s, or " First Families of Virginia." They hunted, they shot, they fished ; they kept open house for their friends ; they were aristocrats in all their tastes and habits, spoke of England as their " home," sided with the Tory or Royalist party in English politics, and looked with aversion upon Puritanism and the airs which it gave itself both in Old England and in New. Laurence, the elder son of Mr Augustine Washington, and future head of the family—fourteen years older than George—was sent to England when fifteen, to pick up the graces and refinements of English society. He returned to Virginia in the newest gloss of fashion — accomplished in manners and conversation—seven years afterwards. George, by this time a boy of eight, had been sent to acquire the rudiments of education at the common school of the village, kept by one Hobby, his father's

tenant, and sexton of the parish. He never received any higher instruction but such as this, and
a subsequent school of the like character, afforded,
except a few supplementary lessons in the evenings
from his father and mother. He acquired no ac-
complishments,—no Latin, no Greek, not even a
smattering of French; but he made considerable
proficiency in mathematical studies, to which he
took kindly, and to which he continued much attached throughout life. Though little indebted to
schools or schoolmasters, or even to parental teachings, he had an inquisitive and a retentive mind,
and while there was anything to learn, never was
foolish enough to think that his education was
completed. His father dying of a severe attack of
gout in the stomach when George was in his
twelfth year, he was left to the care of his
widowed mother — aided, however, by Laurence,
a young man of high character, towards whom
George entertained not only a brotherly affection,
but a filial deference and respect. Laurence, with
his father's approbation, had, four years previously,
volunteered into a regiment raised in the Colonies
to assist Great Britain in an expedition to the West
Indies to repel the aggressions of the Spaniards and
French upon British commerce. In this regiment

he obtained a captain's commission; and in a short but brilliant military service, made the acquaintance and friendship of the famous Admiral Vernon, the captor of Porto Bello.

It was in honour of this naval hero that the chief residence of the Washington family received the name of Mount Vernon, which it has ever since retained. Two years after his father's death, George came to the conclusion that he was no longer a schoolboy. He longed to play the part of a man, and to commence his career either in the military or the naval service of Great Britain. But his mother objected. She could not spare her first-born; and when he finally decided to enter the navy, she peremptorily refused her consent. Washington was tenderly attached to her, and made it his duty to obey. He consequently returned to his studies— varying them occasionally, as is the fashion with lads when they first feel the impulses of manhood, by falling desperately in love with one or other of the beauties of the neighbourhood. It does not appear that his fits of youthful passion for these fair sirens ever drove the sedate young man into poetry, or even into rhyme—though, if he did not compose verses to his mistress's eyebrows, he copied the verses of other people upon cognate themes into his diary. Even at this early period he was cold and stern; was not at all what the Americans call "demonstrative"; repelled rather than courted intimacy; was slow in forming friendships, though stanch to the few that he made; and as far as the world knew, was without other vices than obstinacy, and occasional fits of violence of temper. He was his mother's darling, his elder brother's pride—a pattern young man; not unamiable, though unsympathetic; a favourite with all old people for the great deference he showed them; and not disliked by the youthful, though they rather tolerated than enjoyed his company. At sixteen years of age he was already a philosopher, and had drawn up for his guidance through life a code of laws or maxims, very methodical, very precise, very (what in our irreverent age would be called) "goody," and very much in the prudent shopkeeping style of Benjamin Franklin. Indeed it seems probable that the 'Poor Richard's Almanack' of that author, first published in the year of George Washington's birth, had fallen under the young man's notice, and given that "canny" turn to his mind which always distinguished him not only in his business transactions, but in the more serious and important events of his life.

Among the most intimate friends of the Washington family was the Honourable William Fairfax, cousin of Thomas Lord Fairfax, agent to and manager of the large estates which that nobleman had inherited from his mother, the daughter of Lord Culpeper, to which latter they had been granted by a charter of King Charles II. In the year of his father's death, Laurence Washington married Anne, this gentleman's daughter, and by this means brought the families into still closer connection. Shortly afterwards, Lord Fairfax himself appeared upon the scene; and although at the time that he and George Washington came into intimate personal relationship he was old enough to be Washington's grandfather, there were so many points of sympathetic contact between them as to lead to as great a degree of friendship as was possible between persons of such different ages.

The wild lands of Lord Fairfax, that had since been completely surveyed, extended far into the glens and valleys of the Alleghany Mountains; and rude squatters from Great Britain and Germany were continually settling upon the choicest corners, where the soil was most fertile, or where there were running streams with water-power sufficient to turn the wheels of saw or corn mills, and claiming them as their own by the sole right of possession, which, in new countries even more than in old, is considered to be nine-tenths of the law. Young Washington had mathematical knowledge enough for making accurate surveys; and his taste as well as talent for this profession induced Lord Fairfax to appoint him his surveyor almost immediately after he had ceased to attend school. In young countries, young men play more prominent parts than in old ones. The struggle for life in the wilderness, with its wild beasts and wilder men; the face-to-face conflict with hardship, privation, and peril which is their usual lot,—hardens their bones and ripens their intellects at a period of life when, in an old country surrounded by law, protection, and security, they would still be under tutelage. If such young men lack experience, they generally possess vigour of body and independence of judgment; and among the rough and hardy people of a frontier-land— where the civilised man and the savage come into contact—vigour is often the next best thing to wisdom, if it be not a part of it.

Lord Fairfax, when he first appointed George Washington to this post, was a tall, gaunt, bony veteran, in the sixtieth year of his age. He was fond of rural life and sports, kept a pack of foxhounds, and aspired to lead the life of an English nobleman in a country where he was the only noble, though by no means the only gentleman. He had in his youth run a brilliant career in English society; was an officer in the "Blues"; had contributed one or two papers to the 'Tatler,' which had been fathered by Sir Richard Steele; and in the height of his popularity and fashion had fallen in love with a young lady of rank, to whom he offered hand, heart, and fortune. He was accepted; the wedding-day was fixed; the bridal trinkets and dresses were bought; and a house furnished in London with all the luxuries appropriate to a young couple of their rank and fortune. Suddenly the fickle fair one changed her mind. She had seen some one since her betrothal whom she liked better than Lord Fairfax. The fortunate "some one" was a duke, and Fairfax was but a baron; and to become a duchess, she broke her word and ceased to be a lady. The unhappy lover, to forget, if possible, the too fascinating flirt who had trifled with the most precious thing in the world,—the affection of a true man's heart,—shook off the dust of London from his feet, and visited for the first time his estates in the New World. He was pleased with Virginia, and liked it so well that he resolved to live and die in it.

" His lordship was a stanch foxhunter. The neighbourhood abounded with sport. But foxhunting in Virginia required bold and skilful horsemanship. He found Washington as bold as himself in the saddle, and as eager to follow the hounds. He forthwith took him into particular favour, and made him his constant hunting companion."[1]

Such was Washington's earliest friend, by whom he was first introduced to the active business of life. The surveyorship was eagerly accepted; and in the month of March 1748, having completed his sixteenth year in February, he set out for the beautiful valley of the Shenandoah in company with George William Fairfax—a young man of two-and-twenty—the son of the Hon. William Fairfax, his lordship's cousin. He was engaged in this expedition about a month, and enjoyed for the first time the hardy delights of " roughing it " in the wilderness,—of sleeping on the bare ground; of waging war against wild animals; of parleying diplomatically with wary, and, it might be, treacherous and hostile Indians; of fording streams when swollen into floods; of braving the wind, the rain, the cold, and of thinking about danger only as a thing to be defied and surmounted. He had no particular

[1] Washington Irving.

taste for the beautiful or the romantic, but he had a very keen eye for the practical and the useful. He was neither poet nor artist, but wholly a surveyor. He detected the best "localities" at a glance; studied the qualities of the soil, of the timber, of the water; knew where to lay out building lots and farm lots to the best purpose; and, young as he was, treasured in his mind, like a true disciple of Poor Richard, the places where, in the immediate neighbourhood of his patron's lands, he could secure from other and smaller proprietors an occasional good bargain for himself. He received for his services on this occasion a doubloon *per diem* —a sum equivalent to about thirty shillings—and performed his duties so greatly to the satisfaction of Lord Fairfax that, through his lordship's influence, aided by that of his own family, he received the valuable appointment of Public Surveyor.

This was rapid advancement for such a youth, even in a new country, and was due as much to his high connections as to his merits. Partly in consequence of the reports made by Washington in his survey, Lord Fairfax laid out a large manor called Greenway Court, containing ten thousand acres of arable, meadow, and forest land, and projected a lordly manor-house fit for the accommodation of a person of his rank and fortune. The manor-house was never even commenced—his lordship contenting himself, until he should find time and money to build such a residence as he required, with a low stone building overshadowed by trees, the former residence of his steward and land-agent. In this house he entertained his friends, but never slept in it, lodging every night in a contiguous "shanty," which he fitted up to suit tastes that had become somewhat eccentric since the luckless day when he was so cruelly jilted, and that became more and more eccentric with his advancing years.

He never lost his love of hunting or of literature ; and as befitted a *quondam* contributor to the ' Tatler ' —and, it was said, to the ' Spectator ' also—he took a lively interest in books both new and old, of which he had a considerable store, all of which he placed at the disposition of the young surveyor. Around the humble dwelling-place in the midst of this splendid domain were numerous wooden outhouses for his retinue of servants, both black and white, with stables for his horses and kennels for his hounds. He kept open house for all comers, whether Indians, half-breeds, or the hardy backwoodsmen who came to carve themselves homes and estates out of the illimitable wilderness. His table was plain but plentiful, and served in the English fashion ; and his conversation—to such as knew how to appreciate it, like the members of the Washington family, and especially George—was highly instructive as well as entertaining. For three years George Washington was a welcome guest at Greenway Court ; and when he could spare a few days from the wandering work of his profession, he preferred to spend them in his lordship's society rather than in his own home. During these years the young man—unknown to himself—under the hands of the Providence that shapes our ends to purposes of which we never dream when we are rough-hewing them, was gradually acquiring the experience and the habits that fitted him in after-life for the great part he was destined to play in the history of America. " His rugged and toilsome expeditions in the mountains, among rude scenes and among rough people, inured him to hardships and made him apt at expedients ; while his intercourse with his cultivated brother and with the various members of the Fairfax family had a happy effect in toning up his mind and manners, and counteracting the careless and self-indulgent habitudes of the wilderness."[1]

In the year 1751, the long-pending disputes

[1] Washington Irving.

between the British and French Governments, on the *quæstio vexata* of the boundaries of the respective possessions of the two countries in North America, reached a point that portended a settlement by arms rather than by negotiation. France claimed all the vast unknown countries that lay to the west of the Ohio, and all the beautiful and fertile valley of that river; and endeavoured, not without success, to enlist the Indian aborigines on the French side of the quarrel. The English Government and the colonists were equally stubborn in the assertion of their rights; and in Virginia more especially, which claimed possession of the whole breadth of the continent in a westerly direction to the Rocky Mountains, the hostility against both the French and Indians daily increased in bitterness and intensity.

The better to prepare for impending war, the whole inhabited province was divided into military or militia districts, each to be governed by an adjutant-general, with the rank of a major in the army, and the pay of £150 per annum. The duties of each adjutant-general were to attend to the organisation and equipment of the militia. Laurence Washington sought and obtained one of these appointments for his brother George. But he never lived to see his brother enter upon the duties of his office. The state of his health had long been delicate, and the symptoms of pulmonary consumption having developed themselves with alarming rapidity, he was advised by his physicians to escape the severity of a Virginian winter by a voyage to the West Indies. Thither he repaired in the autumn of 1751, with his brother George for companion, and arrived in Barbadoes after a voyage of five weeks. Laurence seemed to derive benefit from the change of climate; but George, after he had been fourteen days in the island, was attacked with smallpox. He lay in some danger for three weeks, but finally recovered. The disease left a few traces on his face, but not sufficiently deep to disfigure him, or even to attract the notice of those who conversed with him. The benefit derived by Laurence was but of short duration; and fearing that he might not live to return home, George was commissioned to return to Virginia and escort Mrs Washington to her husband.

After George had taken his departure, his brother's health revived a little, and he determined to proceed to Bermuda, with the intention of passing a year in that island. Ultimately he countermanded the orders sent to his wife to join him in the West Indies, and returned home to die in the bosom of

his family.   He was only in his thirty-fourth year.
In him George Washington lost a true friend and
a second father.   Laurence reposed so much confidence in his brother as to appoint him one of
his executors, and guardian of his only child, an
infant daughter.   After devoting himself, with the
mingled energy and prudence that characterised
him in all his doings, to the settlement of his
brother's affairs—a task which occupied him for
some months, and which was almost wholly left to
him and his co-executors — he entered into the
business of his military appointment; and for six
years, with occasional and often long visits to his
home, was engaged in a series of frontier expeditions against the Indian allies of the French.   Many
and great were the hardships he underwent, but
these he bore cheerfully.   Greater and still more
trying were the annoyances he suffered at the hands
of the raw, ignorant, and insubordinate militiamen
whom it was his fortune to command.   The men
mostly took service for a limited period, and when
that period had expired, refused to serve any longer.
They were generally mutinous; thought themselves
as good as their commander, and perhaps a great deal
better, which is a very common characteristic of the
native-born American to this day, whether he be

sailor or soldier, or a subordinate in civil life; they wasted their provisions, and refused to carry their rations, preferring to subsist on the chance spoils of the way. On the march, when breakfast was wanted, they would knock down the first ox or cow they could find, roast it whole or piecemeal, as their firewood served or their impatience impelled, never caring to whom it belonged, or paying, or even apologising to the unhappy owner. At dinner or supper—to both of which meals they looked forward with as much regularity as if they were at home—if no settler's ox or sheep came in the way or a little out of it, they separated in search of game; and the commander had to halt in spite of himself, to allow the greedy stragglers to return to the rendezvous. "For the want of proper military laws," says Mr Washington Irving, "they were obstinate, self-willed, and perverse. Every individual had his own crude notion of things, and would undertake to direct. If his advice were neglected, he would think himself slighted, and to redress his grievance would depart for his home." Well was it, perhaps, for Washington, that he had much experience of his countrymen in small matters, for it prepared him for a more painful experience in after-times in matters of vital moment. By learning to subdue small evils, he grew hardened enough to be able to subdue great ones.

As Washington was by birth, training, and feeling an aristocrat, he looked upon these democratic vagaries of his soldiers with both personal and professional disgust, and used the influence which his family possessed in the Virginia Legislature to introduce and carry an Act for the better regulation of the militia, the establishment of courts-martial, and the punishment of insubordination. This done, he proceeded to reorganise his little force, to fill up vacancies, and extend the length of service. He was at this time in his twenty-fourth year, still a young man, though matured in mind, and having as yet but little sympathy with the Republican habits and ideas that were springing up around him, though not perhaps so vigorously in his native Virginia as in the colonies of New England. His military duties bringing him in the year 1756 to Philadelphia, then the principal commercial city of the Western World, he sent an order to London for liveries for his servants, which shows how little in unison were his tastes with those which have since prevailed in America, where not even the President dares to introduce a livery-suit to his servants. " Send me," he wrote, " two complete livery-suits for servants, with a spare cloak, and all necessary trimmings for two suits more. I would have you choose the livery by *our* (the Washington) arms; only, as the field of the arms is white, I think the clothes had better not be quite so, but nearly like the enclosed (pattern). The trimmings and facings of scarlet, and a scarlet waistcoat. If livery lace is not quite disused, I should be glad to have the cloak laced — I like that fashion best; and two silver-laced hats for the above servants. One set of horse-furniture, with livery lace, with the Washington crest on the housings, &c. The cloak to be of the same piece and colour of the clothes. Three gold-and-scarlet sword-knots. Three silver-and-blue ditto. One fashionable gold-laced hat."

Proceeding to New York, the young commander—not wholly hardened against female charms by his rough life on the frontier and the cares of command, but with that keen eye to the main chance which had been strengthened by the maxims of Poor Richard — became aware both of the beauty and of the wealth of a certain Miss Mary Philipse, daughter of a great landed proprietor on the banks of the Hudson. A schoolfellow and friend of his early days—one Beverley Robinson, son of John Robinson, Speaker of the Lower House of the Virginia

Legislature—had married the sister and co-heiress of this lady. Washington, while his military duties detained him in New York, was invited to make his early schoolmate's house his home. Here he was thrown every evening into the society of the fair lady, who for a time became dear to his heart, and pleasant in anticipation to his pocket. But somehow or other he did not prosper in his wooing. Either he was not ardent enough or acceptable enough, or the lady's affections had been placed elsewhere; or perhaps, as Mr Washington Irving hints by way of explanation, he was called away by his public duties before he had made sufficient approaches in his siege of her heart to warrant a summons to surrender.

However this may be, his stay at New York was but short, and he had to hurry first to Williamsburg to attend the opening of the Legislature of Virginia, and afterwards to Winchester to oppose the Indians, who, with their French allies, threatened the security of the whole frontier line of the Ohio, and even of Lord Fairfax in his rural domains of Greenway Court. At Winchester, after a few weeks' absence, a letter reached him from a confidential friend in New York, urging him to return thither without delay if he wished to secure the hand and fortune of Miss Philipse; for a formidable rival was in the field—a certain Captain Morris, who was carrying everything before him. The critical state of military affairs generally, and the imminent danger of the city of Winchester, forbade Washington to leave the post of duty; and the lady of his love (and, perhaps, of his calculations) fell a prize to the more fortunate Captain Morris.

Washington was too cool, too busy, and too wise to grieve over the disappointment; and for nearly three years after this time he continued on frontier service, ill supported by the Legislature, worse supported by the militia under his command, but never so greatly discouraged in deed as he was in word, and continually urging plans that were universally acknowledged to be sagacious, even by those who refused to act upon them. He had succeeded, after great difficulty, in having Winchester properly fortified, and in inducing the Legislature to establish a line of forts, fifteen miles apart, all along the line of the Ohio. The key of the frontier was at Fort Duquesne, and it had long been the cherished object of Washington, as it had been that of his superiors in military rank, both in the colonial service and in that of the British army, to expel the French from that position. By the year 1758 the fortunes of

France in America began to wane. The reduction of Louisburg in Nova Scotia by the British, and the capture of the Island of Cape Breton, were the first of the great blows which in no distant time were destined to make an end of French dominion in the northern part of the North American continent,— blows that were rapidly followed up by the crowning victory of General Wolfe on the Heights of Abraham, and the surrender of all Canada to Great Britain.

It was in November 1758, after the disastrous failure of an attack upon Fort Duquesne by Major Grant, a British officer, commanding a regiment of Highlanders and Militia, that Washington found himself at the head of one division of a force that was charged to make a second attack for the dislodgment of the French and Indians. The French did not await the onset. The garrison was without supplies, or the reasonable hope of obtaining any; and when the English and Virginians were within one day's march, with a force against which resistance would have been foolhardy, the French commandant embarked his troops in boats upon the Ohio, blew up his powder-magazine, set fire to the fort, and retreated down the Ohio. Washington, in command of the advanced-guard, took possession on the 25th, and planted the standard of Great Britain amid the ruins of the fort, still smouldering and smoking. The first care of the conquerors was partially to rebuild the fort, restore it to a defensible condition, and change its name to Fort Pitt, in honour of the great English statesman. Upon its site now stands the flourishing manufacturing city of Pittsburg—the Manchester of the Ohio.

Washington now found his occupation gone, and retired to Mount Vernon to rest for a while on his laurels. With that keen eye for the main chance of which mention has already been made, he had looked abroad, after the failure of his attack on the heart and person of Miss Philipse, for another fair one to supply her place in his affections—and his calculations—and had found her in a Mrs Curtis, a rich and buxom widow with two children. She had been a widow three years; was rather below the middle size, but well shaped; had an agreeable countenance, dark hair and eyes, engaging manners, and a quarter of a million of charms in the shape of a quarter of a million of dollars. Washington's wooing was this time prosperous: he was married shortly after his return from Fort Duquesne, at the home of the bride, and retired forthwith from military toils and responsibilities to lead the life of a country squire, after the English fashion—with the sole difference of a more fertile soil and more delicious climate than he would have enjoyed in the home of his ancestors, and with black slaves to cultivate his lands, instead of white labourers to work for wages.

This was the halcyon period of his life,—a period that promised him nothing but its own peaceful continuation—the happy realisation of the juvenile dream of Alexander Pope :—

> " Happy the man whose wish and care
>   A few paternal acres bound,
>   Content to breathe his native air
>   On his own ground."

Mr Washington was himself well-to-do in the world, and by the death of his brother Laurence, had become the actual, if not nominal, head of the family. By his marriage with Mrs Curtis, he acquired a third of her late husband's fortune, which consisted of £45,000 sterling in money, and of large landed possessions in Virginia. He thus became not only comfortable but wealthy— had youth, health, love, leisure, reputation, culture, means, everything that smooths the passage through life and strews its pathway with flowers.

Mount Vernon, where he fixed his abode after his marriage, was a residence entirely to his mind. Writing to a friend, he said,—"No estate in America is more pleasantly situated: in a high and healthy country; in a latitude between the extremes of heat and cold; on one of the finest rivers in the world—a river well stocked with fish at all the various seasons of the year, and in the spring with shad, herrings, bass, carp, sturgeon, &c., in good abundance. The borders of the estate are washed by more than ten miles of tide water. Several valuable fisheries appertain to it; the whole shore, in fact, is one entire fishery." Here the old young man lived *en grand seigneur*. He kept a carriage-and-four for Mrs Washington, with black coachmen, footmen, and postilions in the Washington livery. He had an excellent stud of horses for himself and his friends, for riding, hunting, and driving, including "Magnolia," an Arab, and other costly favourites. He had dogs also for fox-hunting with Lord Fairfax, entering their names in his diary as Ringwood, Sweetlips, Forrester, Music, True-love, Rockwood, and others known in the annals of English sport.

But though fond of recreation, Washington never neglected his business. No detail of management

was too small for his microscopic eye, and no circumstance too trivial for his attention. The planter
in those days was a veritable autocrat in his own
domain ; and his domain supplied him and his slaves
and retainers with all the necessaries, and with some
of the minor luxuries, of life. The greater luxuries
—the plate, the jewelleries, the silks, the velvets,
the liveries, the rare wines—were all imported from
England. The slaves did not consist merely of field-
labourers for the production of tobacco, maize, wheat,
vegetables, fruits, and for the care and propagation
of sheep, cattle, and poultry, but of tailors, shoe-
makers, blacksmiths, wheelwrights, saddlers, bakers,
and other artificers.

Tobacco was the great staple ; and Washington,
unlike other planters who left the reins of government in the hands of overseers (Robert Burns, it may
be remembered, was a candidate for such an office in
Jamaica), superintended the growth, preparation, and
export of this article himself, and regularly corre-
sponded with his consignees in Liverpool, Bristol,
and London on the subject. He was particularly
careful of and attentive to the health of his slaves,
but was a stern foe to idleness. In most respects he
was a model slave-owner ; and by " overseeing " his
overseers, and being his own prime minister in the

management of his little kingdom, he prevented those acts of oppression of which brutal and uneducated slave-drivers were sometimes guilty. The colour of their own skins seemed, in the estimation of too many of those jacks-in-office, to justify them in the commission of cruelty; while the colour of the skins of their victims seemed in like manner to court the stripes, which in the nature of things it was their duty to bear without repining. Washington tolerated no practices of the kind. He exacted from his negroes the fullest amount of work that their strength and age enabled them to perform; and he in return gave them full protection, liberal treatment, and a fair amount of holidays.

For five years his life passed happily and profitably on his estates. Cultivating his plantations, hunting with Lord Fairfax, fishing by himself on the bountiful and beautiful Potomac, shooting canvas-back ducks on the not far-distant bays and inlets of the Chesapeake, and entertaining hospitably the officers of the British ships of war that occasionally made their appearance before Mount Vernon, he had always sufficient to occupy his time. Moreover, he was elected a member of the House of Burgesses of Virginia, of which Assembly he long remained a useful though a silent member. He did not possess the gift of eloquence, which the Americans prize so highly—scarcely ever ventured to address the House, and never made a set speech. It is related that, on his taking his seat for the first time, the Speaker, Mr Robinson, conveyed to him the thanks of the House for the public services he had rendered on the frontier; and that Washington, on rising to reply, was so nervous and confused that he could not utter a word. "Sit down, Mr Washington," said the Speaker; "your modesty equals your valour—and that surpasses the power of any language I possess."

Public affairs beyond the confines of Virginia did not occupy much of the young planter's attention; though the time was rapidly approaching when disputes with the mother-country, small in their origin, were to assume large and formidable proportions, and to put the loyalty of the colonists —both aristocratic and puritanic—to the severest test. The conquest and the surrender of Canada were not events of unmixed good, though they had given very great satisfaction both in England and America. A sagacious statesman, the Count de Vergennes, French Ambassador at Constantinople, uttered a prophecy which, though consolatory to the *amour propre* of the French nation, and intended to be so, betokened a marvellous insight into the arcana of political action. "The triumph of England," he said, "will be fatal to her power in America. The Colonies will no longer need her protection. She will call upon them to contribute towards supporting the burdens they have helped to bring upon her, and they will answer by renouncing their dependence."

No more remarkable prediction was ever made; and peace was no sooner restored to the American continent than events began to shape themselves towards its fulfilment. The question of taxing the Colonies was not a new one. It had been suggested so early as the days of Sir Robert Walpole. That wary Minister, however, would not hear of it. "He will be a bolder man than I am," he said, "and one less friendly to commerce, who will venture on such an expedient. For my part, I would encourage the trade of the Colonies to the utmost; one-half of the profits will be sure to come into the royal Exchequer through the increased demand for British manufactures. This will be to tax them, but far more agreeably to their own constitution and laws." But the sagacious policy of Walpole did not find favour with his successors; and shortly after the close of the war against the French on the North

American continent, the Grenville Administration proposed and carried through the Commons a resolution, that " towards further defraying the expenses, it may be proper to charge certain stamp-duties in the said colonies and plantations " ! Unhappy resolution ! Everybody in England thought it was quite right. Everybody in America thought it was quite wrong. Even Washington was shaken in his faith that the people at home could not err, and began to anticipate evil.

Massachusetts, the focus of Puritanism and Republicanism, was, if not the first of the colonies to take the alarm, the first to give legal expression to its displeasure ; and her Legislature declared authoritatively " that the sole right of giving and granting the money of the people of that colony was vested in themselves, and that the imposition of taxes and duties by the Parliament of Great Britain, upon a people who are not represented in that Parliament, is absolutely irreconcilable with their rights." Here spoke the angry spirit of the sons of the English Commonwealth. The other colonies followed one after the other in drawing up petitions to the King and the Parliament, all in the same sense and spirit ; and Pennsylvania, more energetic than the rest, despatched Benjamin Franklin, the apostle of " number one," as portrayed and deified in 'Poor Richard,' to England, as the agent of the colony, charged with the mission of representing to the British Government the danger as well as the impolicy of the proposed measure—founded on the utterly erroneous idea that the English in America were less sensitive about that sacred place, the pocket, than the English at home.

On Franklin's arrival in London, he was consulted both by the Ministers and the Opposition; and declared, with all the fervour of a shopkeeper against an attempted robbery, that the Americans would resist the imposition, passively and actively, and that they would rather see the disruption of the Empire than submit to imperial taxation. The Ministry were not convinced, and pressed forward their measure, which, however, excited as little interest in the House of Commons as a debate upon Indian finance does in our own day. In vain Colonel Isaac Barré, who in after-years was suspected, and not without reason, of being the author of the Letters of Junius, thundered against the measure, and brought his experience of America, where he had served under the illustrious Wolfe, to bear in support of his arguments; in vain did other and less famous leaders of the Opposition take the same side. The

Bill was passed, and the seeds of disaffection, so soon to expand into revolution, were planted in America. Virginia, most loyal and aristocratic of colonies, was as deeply discontented as puritanical New England ; and Patrick Henry, a young lawyer recently elected as a member of the House of Burgesses, suddenly made himself one of the most popular men in America, by introducing into the Legislature a series of resolutions declaring that the General Assembly of Virginia had the exclusive right and power to tax the people of that colony, and that whoever maintained the contrary ought to be regarded as a public enemy.

Mr Robinson, the Speaker, objected to the resolutions as inflammatory ; but the orator, with all the fervour of his Celtic blood boiling in his veins, defended alike their spirit and their phraseology, and forgot himself so far in the vehemence of his declamation as to warn the Sovereign personally of the danger he incurred by setting himself in opposition to the wishes of his American subjects. "Cæsar," said he, " had his Brutus ; Charles his Cromwell ; and George III. may—— " here the horrified Speaker started on his chair, and a cry of " Treason ! treason !" resounded on all sides. Henry saw with quick perception that his " buncombe " might be dangerous if persisted in; and after a pause and a low bow to the Speaker, deliberately finished his sentence —"and George III. may profit by their example. If this be treason, sir, make the most of it."

The House was not in the mood for violent language; and Henry having agreed to modify his resolutions in form, but retaining their spirit, they were passed by a large majority. The Lieutenant-Governor of the colony unwisely added fuel to this growing fire by dissolving the Assembly and issuing writs for a new election—thus keeping up and intensifying an excitement which it would have been better to have allayed. Washington made no public utterances upon the subject; but in a letter to Mr Dandridge, his wife's uncle, a resident in London, he said "that the *speculative* part of the colonists looked upon this unconstitutional method of taxation as a direful attack upon their liberties." He was somewhat cautious, as became so faithful a disciple of the philosophy of Poor Richard, in expressing his own opinion; but went on to say: "Whatever may be the result of this and of some other (*I think I may add*) ill-judged measures, I will not undertake to determine; but this I may venture to affirm, that the advantage accruing to the mother-country will fall greatly short of the expectation of the Ministry. . . . As to the Stamp Act, regarded in a single view, one of the first bad consequences attending it is, that our Courts of Judicature must inevitably be shut up; for it is impossible, or next to impossible, under our present circumstances, that the Act of Parliament can be complied with, were we ever so willing to enforce its execution. And not to say (which alone would be sufficient) that we have not money enough to pay for the stamps, there are many other cogent reasons which prove that it would be ineffectual."

While Washington was thus privately " venturing to affirm," and timidly thinking that he might call the measures ill-judged, the fiery oratory of Patrick Henry was working to more potent ends on the public mind, not alone in Virginia, but in all the other colonies. On the motion of the General Assembly of Massachusetts, nearly five months after the passing of Henry's modified resolutions, a Congress was held in New York, at which delegates attended from nine out of the thirteen colonies; and after stormy though all but unanimous debates, prepared an address to the King, and petitions to both Houses of Parliament, setting forth the grievances of the American people, and demanding the repeal of the obnoxious Act. Meanwhile riots broke out in several cities; the stamp distributors were hung in effigy; their offices were sacked or levelled with the ground; the stamps were seized and thrown into the flames; while most of the stamp distributors—happy not to be executed in person as well as in effigy—hastened to range themselves on the popular side, by resigning their too dangerous appointments.

On the 1st of November 1765, when the Act was to come into operation, all the ships in the harbour of Boston displayed their colours half-mast high, as a sign of mourning for the departed liberty of America; while the bells of that and other cities rang funereal peals throughout the day. At New York a copy of the Act was fixed upon a pole, surmounted by a death's-head, and a scroll bearing the inscription, "The folly of England and the ruin of America!" and carried through the streets, followed by a clamorous multitude. Colden, the Lieutenant-Governor—who had made himself especially obnoxious to the New Yorkers, by recommending to the British Government the taxation of the Colonies, and the establishment of hereditary instead of elective Assemblies—fearful of personal violence, withdrew into the fort on Governor's Island, in the harbour, and garrisoned it for defence with marines from a British man-of-war. He was barely in time to escape. The mob broke into his stable, took out his carriage, put his effigy into it, paraded it through the streets, with shouts and yells of execration, to the park, where it was hung on a high gallows. In the evening the effigy was cut down, put into the carriage, along with another effigy representing the devil, and drawn by torch-light to the Bowling Green, under the very guns of the fort, where the two effigies, the carriage, and large heaps of stamps, were all committed to the flames.

The news of these and similar events, on arriving in the mother-country, very greatly annoyed the British Ministry, and very greatly astonished the people. By one party, the Americans were accused not only of ingratitude, but of rebellion; by the other, they were supported in their agitation, and urged to persevere, on their own behalf as well as on that of the liberties of Great Britain, which were held on the same tenure as their own. The Grenville Administration had fallen, and been succeeded by that of the Marquis of Rockingham. The new Ministers, not too obstinate to learn wisdom from events, sent instructions to the various lieutenant-governors of the colonies to do their best to allay the rising storm of disaffection, and promised recomsideration of the whole subject in the approaching session of Parliament. They fulfilled their pledge. Mr Grenville and his friends supported the Stamp Act, which they had carried, and were joined by many friends of the new Administration; but the Americans found a powerful ally in Mr Pitt. He declared emphatically that the British Parliament had no right to tax the Colonies; that taxation was no part of the governing or legislative power; that taxes were a voluntary gift and grant of the Commons alone; and that the Commons of Great Britain could only grant what was their own, and not that which belonged to the Commons of America. At the same time, he admitted the authority of King, Lords, and Commons to be suzerain and supreme in all other matters. Warming with his subject, and in reply to Mr Grenville, who had all but accused him by name of fomenting a seditious spirit in the Colonies, he said, addressing the Speaker: " Sir, a charge is brought against gentlemen sitting in this House for giving birth to sedition in America. The freedom with which they have spoken their sentiments against this unhappy Act is imputed to them as a crime. The imputation shall not discourage *me*. I rejoice that America has resisted. Three millions of people so dead to all the principles of liberty as voluntarily to submit to be slaves, would have been fit instruments to make slaves of all the rest."

Pitt's eloquence made a great impression upon the country; perhaps a still greater was effected by the appearance and examination of Benjamin Franklin at the bar of the House. "Poor Richard," with all his maxims on the tip of his tongue, ready for service against any and all authority that would take his money out of his pocket without his consent, answered all the questions put to him with the fluency and decision of a man who thoroughly understood and felt what he was talking about. When asked if he thought the Americans would submit to a modification of the Stamp Act, he replied : " No! never! unless compelled by force of arms !"   To a more friendly question put to him by a member who agreed with Mr Pitt, as to what was the feeling towards Great Britain entertained in the Colonies before the Stamp Act was proposed, he replied: " The best in the world.   The Americans submitted willingly to the Government of the Crown, and paid obedience to all the Acts of Parliament.   Numerous as the colonists were, they cost England nothing in forts, citadels, garrisons, or armies to keep them in sub-

jection. They were garrisoned at the sole expense
of a little pen, ink, and paper. They were led by
a thread. They had not only a respect but an
affection for Great Britain—for its laws, its customs,
and its manners. The natives of Great Britain
were always treated with particular regard in
America. To be an 'Old England man' was of
itself a character of respect, and gave a kind of
rank among us." "And what is the feeling now?"
asked the same friendly voice. "Oh, very much
altered." "If the Act be not repealed, what do
you think will be the consequence?" "A total
loss of the respect and affection of the people of
America, and of all the commerce that depends
on that respect and affection."

The result of the discussion was, that General
Conway brought in a bill for the total repeal of
the Stamp Act, which was carried by a large
majority—although the Ministry, with a view of
saving the dignity of the Crown and Parliament,
insisted on inserting a saving clause, to the effect
"that the Parliament had, and of right ought to
have, power to bind the Colonies in all cases whatsoever." This proviso was alike ungracious and
unnecessary; and the Americans, with a feeling
similar to that which might be indulged by a

hungry dog who had received a smart blow on the head for the bone that its master had given it to pick, growled at the substantial benefit, on account of the insult that accompanied it. Washington, who had taken no public part in opposition to the British Government, was exceedingly glad of the repeal of the Act. "Had the Parliament," he said in a contemporary letter, "resolved upon enforcing it, the consequences, I conceive, would have been more direful than is generally apprehended, both to the mother-country and the Colonies. All, there-fore, who were instrumental in procuring the repeal, are entitled to the thanks of every British subject, and have mine cordially."

The satisfaction of Mr Washington was premature. The *arrière pensée* that lay in the unlucky assertion of the absolute right of Great Britain to legislate for her Colonies, was destined at no distant time to reassertion in a manner quite as displeasing to the Americans as the Stamp Act. The Administration which succeeded that of Lord Rockingham, and of which Mr Pitt, now Lord Chatham, was a member, looking to the form rather than to the spirit, and erroneously thinking—even though Lord Chatham knew, and might have taught his colleagues better —that it was against the particular Stamp Act, rather than against taxation generally, that the Americans objected, endeavoured to raise a revenue from America by indirect rather than by direct means. The attempt was unfortunate. There were mischief, discontent, and latent rebellion in the spirit with which the Americans received it.

The new Ministry was described by Burke as " a diversified mosaic," and " a piece of tesselated pavement without cement." It included, as its Chancellor of the Exchequer, Mr Charles Townsend, who had been a vigorous supporter of Mr Grenville's Stamp Act. Under the auspices of this unwise financier, goaded to action by the continual taunts of Grenville, who asserted that nothing but " unworthy cowardice" prevented the British Parliament from taxing America, a Bill was introduced for imposing a duty upon all tea imported into the Colonies, together with smaller duties upon paints, paper, glass, and lead, all articles of British produce. The avowed object of the measure was to provide a fund for the payment of the British troops stationed in America, and for the salaries of the colonial governors, so as to render these functionaries independent of the local Assemblies. How Lord Chatham could have remained a member of an Administration that pro-

posed a measure so antagonistic to all his recorded
sentiments and convictions, was a mystery at the
time, and most of all to the Americans. The
passing of the Act attracted little notice at home.
In America it excited the greatest discontent. All
the writers and speakers who had been conspicuous
for their opposition to the Stamp Act, were loud
in the expression of their disapproval; and for the
first time in American history, the cry of " Independence " was raised, and received with favour.

One of the first results of the measure was
the proposal by Massachusetts of a General Congress of all the Colonies, to consider the state of
their relations with the mother-country. This proceeding was looked upon with great displeasure,
if not alarm, by the English Ministry. In view of
the probability that the Board of Revenue Commissioners instituted at Boston would be unable
to collect the duties under the new Act, two British
regiments were added to two which were already
stationed in the city. A town-meeting was immediately summoned, to protest against the presence
of this military force; and subsequently a Convention, to which more than a hundred towns and
villages in Massachusetts sent delegates, was held
in Fanueil Hall. Though the Governor, Mr Ber-

nard, denounced the Convention as treasonable, it continued its deliberations for several weeks, and did not separate until it had passed resolutions condemnatory of a standing army in the Colonies, and of the attempt of the Parliament of Great Britain—a body in which they were not represented—to tax the people of America.

Shortly after the opening of Parliament, the papers connected with these proceedings in Boston were laid before both Houses, and excited lively discussions. The House of Lords was particularly indignant, declared that the Boston Convention was an insult to his Majesty's authority and a usurpation of the powers of Government, and suggested that the Governor of Massachusetts should be directed to procure the fullest information touching all acts of treason, or misprision of treason, committed in the Colonies since the passing of the late Act in 1767, and to transmit the ringleaders to England for trial. The House of Commons was less vindictive, though there was a majority hostile to the pretensions of the Americans, by whom resolutions, somewhat modified from those of the Lords, were passed, and embodied in an address to the King. The Legislature of Virginia, of which Washington was a member, was in session when the news of these debates arrived; and, making common cause with Massachusetts, passed a series of resolutions in denial of the right of England to levy taxes upon the people of America—whether directly, as by the late Stamp Act, or indirectly, as by the levying of import duties upon tea or any other commodities. The Speaker was directed to forward these resolutions for concurrence to the Legislatures of all the other colonies. The Governor of Virginia, Lord Botetourt, acted in a very high-handed manner on this occasion. Without previous notice of his intentions, he appeared in the House of Burgesses, and, addressing the Speaker, said: "Mr Speaker, and Gentlemen of the House of Burgesses,—I have heard of your resolves, and augur ill of their effects. You have made it my duty to dissolve you, and you are dissolved accordingly!"

It was now that Washington first manifested sympathy with his countrymen. His somewhat sluggish nature was quickened, not so much by the events as by the opinions of the time. No man, unless his genius be of the very highest, or perhaps it may be said of the very coldest order, can escape the contagion of contemporary passion. Few even can escape the contagion of prejudice. Washington was not a man of genius, but a plain, rational country gentleman, with an excellent capacity for improving his personal fortunes and pushing his way in the world. It was not for him to move too soon or take the initiative in any matter that savoured of disaffection to the mother-country, to whose supremacy he was sincerely attached; but even he, cautious and slow as he was, found himself unable to resist the strong current that had set against English taxation in America. After the dissolution of the House of Burgesses, the members adjourned to a private house, elected a moderator, and proceeded to consider the state of affairs. The result was, that Washington brought forward Articles of Association, which had been drawn up jointly between himself and Mr George Mason, pledging all who signed them neither to import, consume, nor use any goods, merchandise, or articles of manufacture, on the importation of which into the American colonies duties, great or small, had been levied by the British Parliament. Massachusetts and other Northern colonies had previously adopted similar resolutions; and the example was imitated not alone by Virginia, but by the Carolinas and the other Southern colonies. It seemed for a while as if the Americans would rest satisfied with this passive resistance, and as if the British

Parliament, enlightened as to the true state of feeling in the Colonies, would repeal the obnoxious Acts. Neither of these expectations was realised. The American motto was "thorough"; the British policy was "half-measures." And, as usual with men and nations, "thorough" was successful.

Early in 1770 the Duke of Grafton resigned, and Lord North assumed the reins of office. His first public act as regards the Colonies was a blunder, which the Americans interpreted into an insult. Under Ministerial auspices, an Act was passed repealing all the import duties levied upon British and foreign goods in America by the Act of 1767, with the exception of the duty on tea. This duty was retained, not for the sake of any revenue which might be expected from it (for no tea was drunk in America, except an imitation called "hyperion," made of dried raspberry - leaves of indigenous growth, which it was considered both fashionable and patriotic to consume), but solely with the aggravating purpose of maintaining the right of Parliament to tax America. With the view of making the assertion of the right less unpalatable to the Americans, a discrimination was made between the duty levied on tea imported into England and that imported into the Colonies. The

English duty was a shilling per lb., the American duty was only threepence. But the Americans were not to be conciliated or blinded by a compromise, however seemingly favourable. It was the principle itself to which they objected, and not the amount to which they were made liable. "The properest time to exert our right of taxation," said Lord North, speaking the sentiments of George III. rather than his own, "is when the right is denied. To temporise is to yield; and the authority of the mother - country, if it be not now asserted, will have to be relinquished for ever. A total repeal cannot be thought of till America is prostrate at our feet."

For three years the Americans continued to use "hyperion"—only using tea itself when it could be procured from the smuggler; all the while encouraging in one another a spirit of hostility to the home Government. At last, in 1773, Lord North bethought himself of another half-measure, which, like most half-measures, did more harm than good. The non - consumption of tea in the Colonies operated unfavourably to the interests of that great mercantile monopoly, the East India Company. Having powerful friends and representatives in Parliament, the Company, which had a large stock of tea on hand in their warehouses in London, had influence enough to induce the Minister to carry through Parliament a Bill to enable the Company to re-export their teas without payment of export duty. As the Company could thus offer their teas at a very low rate in America, it was thought by the too clever Minister that the colonists would be tempted, by the cheapness of the article, to forget their principle—or their prejudice—and to make large purchases, thus yielding the point at issue between them and Great Britain. But the Americans, to use their own word, were too 'cute to betray themselves, or yield a cheap victory to the English Minister.

A little fleet of tea-ships having been despatched to America, the ports of New York and Philadelphia refused to receive the cargoes, and the ships returned unladen to Europe. The authorities of Charleston allowed the tea to be landed—to be placed in warehouses; but no one purchased even so much as a pennyworth, and the tea rotted in the stores. In Boston the people were more aggressive, and committed an act which expedited the final catastrophe, which the foremost minds in America had long foreseen. When the first tea-ship arrived in the harbour, a public meeting of the citizens was held in Fanueil Hall, which passed a resolution forbidding the captain at his peril to unload or attempt to land his cargo. A similar meeting was held on the morrow, which the Governor declared to be illegal, and ordered it to disperse. The meeting refused, and the militia declined to act against their fellow - citizens. The consignees promised, if the tea were landed, they would keep it in their cellars without attempting to put it upon the market, until they could receive orders for its return from England. This was not satisfactory to the people, who insisted that the ships should set sail immediately without unloading. Two other ships arrived while this dispute was pending, and samples of the commodity were sent on shore to the merchants; but all refused to buy. The captains, after a few days, resolved to return to England, but could not obtain a clearance at the custom-house, or a passport from the Governor to clear the port. The Bostonese interpreted this conduct of the Governor and his officials as an attempt to force the tea upon an unwilling people; though by what process of reasoning they came to such a conclusion, it is difficult to discover.

To cut short the matter, and dare British authority to do its worst, it was resolved to attempt a *coup-de-main*. It was generally expected that on the 17th of December the commanders of the British ships of war in the harbour had determined that the merchant captains should send their tea ashore under cover of the artillery. The ships were moored off Griffin's wharf. It was clear moonlight, when suddenly there appeared in the streets several persons—all known to be leading citizens of Boston—disguised as Indians, with painted faces and feathered caps and leggings, and brandishing tomahawks, shouting and yelling. One of them exclaimed, "Boston harbour for a teapot to-night!" and being joined by several others, until their numbers amounted to five - and - twenty, proceeded to the wharf, boarded the ships, overpowered the surprised captains, and in less than three hours, supported by the townspeople, deliberately broke open all the tea-chests in the three vessels, and threw the contents into the sea. The authorities took no steps to prevent the outrage; the ships of war were silent; and Admiral Montague, chief in command of the naval force, who was sitting on shore at the house of a friend, opened the windows as the daring masqueraders returned from their exploit, and said jeeringly, "Well, my boys, you've had a fine night for your Indian caper! but remember you'll have to pay the piper."

For some time previously to this occurrence,

Washington had been absent on his old battle-ground, the Indian frontier, to settle some land claims, which had arisen for services rendered in the Indian and French wars, on the part of officers and others under his command. On his return to Williamsburg he waited upon the Earl of Dunmore, who had been appointed Governor of Virginia on the death of Lord Botetourt, and learned from that nobleman, as well as from his political friends and colleagues in the House of Burgesses, the threatening turn which affairs had taken. Much curiosity, if not anxiety, was felt to know how the news of the Boston outrage would be received "at home." At last it was announced that the British Government was not only greatly offended with America generally, but disposed to be particularly vindictive against Boston. An Act was rapidly passed, called "The Boston Port Bill," by which all loading and unloading of goods, wares, and merchandise were to be prohibited in the town and harbour, and the establishment of the customs to be transferred to Salem.

This was shortly followed by a second Act, taking the appointment of judges, magistrates, and councillors from the hands of the people of Massachusetts, and vesting it in the Crown, such nominees to hold office only during the Royal pleasure. A third Act was even more outrageous to the feelings of the Americans — not in Massachusetts alone, but in all the other colonies— which provided that any person indicted for treason, murder, or other offence, might at the discretion of the Governor be sent to some other colony for trial, or even to England. The House of Burgesses of Virginia was in session when official notification of these measures arrived. All ordinary business was immediately postponed; a protest against the three Acts was entered upon the journals of the House, signed by Washington among other members; and a resolution adopted, setting apart the first day of June then ensuing as a day of fasting, humiliation, and prayer to Almighty God to avert from the American people the threatened deprivation of their rights and liberties, and the evils of civil war.

On the day following, when the Burgesses were still discussing the ominous state of the Colonies, they were summoned to attend Lord Dunmore in the council-chamber. As curt and decided as his predecessor had been on a similar but less urgent occasion, his lordship told them in few words that their resolution reflected so improperly upon the King and the Parliament of Great

Britain, that he had no alternative but to dissolve the House, and that it was dissolved accordingly. The members immediately dispersed, but met as private citizens in the evening in the large room of the principal tavern, where they passed a series of resolutions still more emphatic than those of the previous day—declaring that the cause of one colony was the cause of all, and urging the expediency and necessity of appointing delegates from each, to meet annually in General Congress to deliberate on the united interests of America. A resolution to the same effect was simultaneously, and without concert with Virginia, passed by Massachusetts; and meeting everywhere with general concurrence, the first Congress was summoned to meet at Philadelphia on the 5th of September next ensuing.

Lord Fairfax and his cousins — Washington's most intimate friends—though they did not wholly approve of the severe proceedings of the British Parliament, by no means approved of the Boston outrage, or of the manner in which it was condoned or applauded by the Americans. Washington had presided as moderator or chairman of a meeting of the inhabitants of Fairfax County, at which considerable indignation had been displayed by various speakers against the conduct of Great Britain; and

Bryan Fairfax, younger brother of George William, then absent in England, wrote him a letter, urging a respectful petition to the throne for the redress of grievances. Washington, in reply, said he would cheerfully sign a dutiful petition to the King, provided he saw the most distant chance of success—which he confessed he did not. Ultimately, however, a committee, appointed for the purpose by the public meeting, of which, as well as of the committee, Washington was chairman, resolved that the Congress about to assemble should be requested to petition the King, inasmuch as petitions to both Houses of Parliament had hitherto proved unavailing. This resolution was drawn up by Washington, and is remarkable not only as proceeding from his pen, but as giving the first hint that the Americans might be goaded to take up arms in defence of their liberties. The petition asserted the constitutional rights and privileges of the colonists; lamented the necessity of taking measures that might be displeasing; declared attachment to the King's person, family, and Government; desired to continue in dependence upon Great Britain; entreated him not to reduce his faithful subjects in America to desperation, and to reflect that *from the King there could be but one appeal!*

Washington was chosen as one of the seven delegates of Virginia to the General Congress; and a few days before the time appointed for its meeting, set out on horseback to Philadelphia with two of his colleagues, Patrick Henry and Edward Pendleton. There were fifty - one delegates in all— Georgia being the only colony unrepresented. They met punctually on Monday the 5th of September. A question arose as to the mode of voting,—whether by colonies or by individual delegates. Patrick Henry entered a protest against sectionalism. "All America," he said, "is fused into one mass. Where are your landmarks and boundaries of colonies? They are all thrown down. The distinctions between Virginians, Pennsylvanians, New Yorkers, and New Englanders exist no more. I am not a Virginian, but an American!"

The Congress, however, did not share his Celtic enthusiasm, but with Saxon stolidity declined to move quite so fast, and decided that each colony should have but one vote, whatever might be the numbers of its delegates — that they should deliberate with closed doors, and publish nothing but the resolutions which they might pass, unless by order of the majority. The Congress sat for fifty-one days. "It was such an assembly," says John

Adams, who was afterwards President, "as never before came together on a sudden in any part of the world. It discussed every subject that came before it with a moderation, an acuteness, and a minuteness equal to that of Queen Elizabeth's Privy Council." Lord Chatham in England was more eloquent in its praise: "When your lordships look at the papers transmitted to us from America — when you consider their clearness, firmness, and wisdom—you cannot but respect their cause, and wish to make it your own. For myself, I must declare and avow that, in the master States of the world, I know not the people or senate who, in such a complication of difficult circumstances, can stand before the delegates of America assembled in General Congress in Philadelphia."

It is known only by tradition what speeches were made; nor does it appear that Washington took any prominent part in the discussions. Nor is it likely that he did ; for he was a poor speaker, and, like some other soldiers, would rather hear the thunder of artillery than the sound of his own voice in a set oration. Whatever the speeches may have been, the business transacted was of the highest importance. The first was to issue a manifesto, declaratory of the determination of Congress to resist any force that might attempt to carry into execution the recent Acts of Parliament, in violation of the rights of the American people. The second was a series of resolutions drawn up by a committee of two members from each colony, which were adopted and promulgated by Congress as a declaration of colonial rights. This document was clear and straightforward, and had those greatest of all merits in argumentative literature—precision, concision, and decision. It set forth the natural right of the Americans to the enjoyment of life, liberty, and property. As distance and other circumstances prevented them from direct representation in the British Parliament, they claimed the power to legislate on their local affairs in their colonial assemblies. They consented to be subject to the legislation of the Imperial Parliament in all matters relating to the unity and safety of the kingdom and the general purposes of trade, exclusive of the right of the said Parliament to levy taxes, direct or indirect, external or internal, for raising a revenue in America. They declared the maintenance of a standing army in time of peace in any of the colonies, without the consent of the Legislature of each colony, to be contrary to law; and that the exercise of any legislative powers in

the Colonies by a council appointed by the Crown
was unconstitutional, and destructive to American
freedom.   They concluded by specifying and enum-
erating the various Acts passed by the British
Parliament in violation of these rights and principles, adding that to such grievous measures
America would not submit; and that, in hopes
their fellow-subjects in Great Britain would on
revision restore them to the state in which, before
the passing of these Acts, both countries found
happiness and prosperity, they had resolved upon
three peaceable measures: *first*, to enter into a
non-importation, non-consumption, and non-exporta-
tion agreement or association, binding all the
colonies; *second*, to prepare an address to the
people of Great Britain, and a memorial to all the
inhabitants of British America; and *third*, to prepare a loyal address to the King.

These State papers were duly prepared and forwarded to all the colonies and to the British Government.   The hand of Washington did not appear
in any of them, nor did he take a very active part
in supporting or proposing them.   Patrick Henry,
on returning to Virginia, having been asked whom
he considered the greatest man in Congress, replied
that, for eloquence, Mr Rutledge, of South Carolina,

was foremost; but that, for solid information and sound judgment, Colonel Washington was unquestionably the greatest man in the Assembly.

At this time the future independence of the Colonies was but a dream of the over-zealous and the imaginative. Washington, at all events, had not yet learned to look forward to it as the only possible solution of the difficulty. " I am well satisfied," he wrote to a friend, after the adjournment of Congress, " that no such thing is desired by any thinking man in all North America. On the contrary, I think it is the ardent wish of the warmest advocates for liberty, that peace and tranquillity upon constitutional grounds may be restored, and the horrors of civil discord prevented." But events, though marching slowly, were marching surely to the end that Washington deprecated; and when Congress reassembled for its second annual session in 1775, the military situation was so alarming, and the preparations for hostile acts against the British troops in other colonies so extensive, as to lead the thoughtful politicians, of whom Washington was one, to foretell an approaching catastrophe, if the British Government continued to be as obstinate as it had hitherto shown itself. One of the first acts of Congress this year was to appoint a sub-committee on military affairs—of which Washington, marked out for the post by his frontier experience, was elected chairman. This was his first decided step on the road that led to revolution.

Congress, although it adopted a second "humble and dutiful" petition to the King, did not wait to receive an answer before proceeding to measures which did not wear even the semblance of loyalty. Though John Adams declared the petition to be "imbecile," it had the effect of propitiating the timid, besides giving the bolder spirits an opportunity of predicting its failure. Georgia, which had hitherto stood aloof, cast in her fortunes with the other colonies; upon which Congress proceeded to form a Federal Union of the thirteen—leaving to each the right to regulate its own internal affairs, but vesting in Congress, which represented them all, the power of making peace or war, of entering into treaties and alliances, and of regulating external commerce. The Executive power was vested in a Council of twelve. These decisive measures—all clearly acts of rebellion—rendered it necessary for Congress, if it would not be overwhelmed by the power of the mother-country, to adopt means not alone of defence, but of possible aggression.

It ordered the enlistment of troops, the construction of forts, the provision of arms, ammunition, and military stores; and to provide money as well as men, authorised the emission of a paper currency to the extent of three millions of dollars, or £600,000 sterling. Each note bore the inscription of "The United Colonies," and the credit of the whole Confederacy was pledged for their redemption.

A British force held possession of Boston—which, however, was kept in check by a New England army, under the command of General Artemus Ward. This force was without clothing or pay, and but badly armed and provisioned. Had its true condition been known to General Gage, the British commander, it might possibly have been very summarily dealt with. Congress not only resolved to augment the Continental Army, as it now began to be called, but to provide means for clothing, feeding, and disciplining it. For this latter purpose, a man in whom Congress, the army, and the public had full confidence, was required to assume the responsible position of commander-in-chief. There was but one such man in America, and that was Colonel Washington, chairman of the Military Committee. His name was no sooner mentioned than it received general adhesion from the public, though not from Congress. For even at this early period of American history the little rivulet of jealousy between North and South, which in after-times broadened and deepened into a mighty river, and broke out into a torrent of Civil War in 1861, had begun to display itself. The Southern members objected to the command of the continental army being continued in General Artemus Ward, a New Englander or "Yankee"; while the Northern members, though not greatly objecting to Washington, would have preferred him more cordially if he had not been a Southerner. But the more the question was discussed, the more settled became the conviction that Washington was the best man for the emergency.

Washington made no sign. It was not for him to court the post of danger, but to be courted; and perhaps, with his characteristic prudence, he was not anxious to assume a post of such responsibility, with means so inadequate to the great end that he would be expected to accomplish. There were but three persons who had any chance of obtaining the appointment, — General Artemus Ward, who was already in command of an army sufficiently strong to coop up the British forces in Boston; John Hancock of Boston, a good militia officer, but inexperienced in actual warfare, and at that time President of Congress; and George Washington. John Adams, the second President of the United States, records in his Diary the scene that occurred in Congress when he took it upon himself to propose Washington for the perilous honour. After describing the military situation, with all its exigencies, he went on to state: " I had no hesitation to declare that I had but one gentleman in my mind for the important command, and that was a gentleman from Virginia, who was among us, and very well known to us all—a gentleman whose skill and experience as an officer, whose independent fortune, great talents, and excellent universal character, would command the approbation of all America, and unite the cordial exertions of all the colonies better than any other person in the Union. Mr Washington, who sat near the door, as soon as he heard me allude to him, from his usual modesty darted into the library. Mr Hancock was our President, which gave me an opportunity to observe his countenance. While I was speaking on the state of the Colonies, the army, and the enemy, he heard me with visible pleasure. But when I came to describe Washington for the commandership, I never remarked a more sudden and striking change of countenance. Mortification and resentment were expressed as forcibly as his face could exhibit them."

Congress had been only five weeks in session, when the question was brought to a decision. Though Congress was divided in opinion, the country was all but unanimous; and for ten days before the vote was taken, vigorous efforts were made by Washington's friends to induce the dissentient members to forego opposition, and start Washington on his career with all the advantage and prestige to be derived from unanimity of choice. These efforts were finally successful; and on the 15th of June 1775, Congress voted by ballot for the appointment. Washington was elected without a single dissentient, and was officially informed of the fact on the following day on his taking his seat, and that his pay had been fixed at five hundred dollars a-month (£100). He returned thanks very briefly—accepted the honour, not without misgiving. "Lest," he added, "some unlucky event should happen unfavourable to my reputation, I beg it may be remembered by every gentleman in the room, that I this day declare, with the utmost sincerity, that I do not think myself equal to the command I am honoured with."

He also added that he refused the salary—assuring Congress that as no pecuniary consideration could have tempted him to forego his domestic ease and happiness to accept so arduous an employment, he was firmly resolved not to make any profit by it. He expected, however, that his actual expenses would be paid, and of these he promised to keep an exact account.

On the 20th of June he received his commission, and on the 21st departed for the army. "He was now," as he himself wrote to his half-brother, John Augustine, "embarked on a wide ocean, boundless in its prospect, and in which perhaps no safe harbour is to be found." The ocean was indeed wide, but not boundless; and though he ultimately found a harbour, it was not until after he had been sorely buffeted by storms, and exposed to countless dangers, privations, discouragements, reverses, and calamities—in none of which did he ever wholly lose heart and hope, though he often lost faith in his countrymen. He saw the worst and the best of human nature; and learned in sorrow and suffering, as all must learn who attain to such high position, that it is no light thing to be an unprofessional patriot and the would-be saviour of a country.

WASHINGTON.

PART II.

It was not in the passive, intellectual nature of Washington to excite enthusiasm, but he had the faculty of inspiring confidence. He was pre-eminently truthful, and a man of business, slow to make up his mind; but when convinced of the right course to be taken, inflexible in working out his purpose. He knew how perilous it was to defy the might of such a country as Great Britain; but he was not appalled by the immensity of the effort, nor afraid of the consequences of failure to his life, his fortune, or his fame. He rightly considered that if the difficulties of the Colonies were great, the difficulties of the mother-country were great also. The Colonies were struggling to vindicate the principle that there should be no taxation without representation—a principle which the English

at home had successfully established at the cost
of revolution, of civil war, of the execution of a
king, and the deposition of a dynasty. A powerful
party in the British Parliament and throughout the
country were the upholders of this principle in its
application to the Colonies, and gave the Americans
their votes as well as their sympathy. It is true
that the party in power, backed by all the personal
influence and authority of the King, was obstinately
opposed to the claim put forward by the colonists;
but under a constitutional Government and a parliamentary *régime*, it was possible that at some
future election this party and the King might find
themselves in the minority. The longer the Americans resisted, the more likely they were to make
converts and friends among the English people. In
addition to this, the transport of armies across the
ocean was costly, tedious, and uncertain. The
British fleet could but blockade the coasts and
bombard the seaport towns of the Colonies; but
the vast interior lay behind, and was not only rich
enough to supply all the material wants of the
people, but was virtually impregnable. Besides,
England was just out of war with France, and
might probably be soon involved in another, either
with that or some other Continental power; and,

however willing to do so, was not able to put
forth her whole strength against her discontented
children.   It seemed to Washington that the true
policy of the Colonies was to worry and weary the
mother-country; or, as Mr Lincoln phrased it in
more unhappy circumstances nearly ninety years
afterwards, to "Keep pegging away." Upon this
policy he acted—combining it with that of Fabius,
until he became a greater even than Fabius himself in the tactics which the world has agreed to
call by the name of that ancient general.   It
was a long struggle.   Washington commenced it
in the prime and maturity of his days.   He was
an elderly man when it was brought to a conclusion, not so much by his own valour and prudence,
as by the help of an unexpected and welcome ally,
on whom he had no original right to calculate.

When he accepted the commandership-in-chief, a
battle had been fought, of which he was ignorant,
and of which the news first reached him between
Philadelphia and New York on his way to join the
army.   The British General, Gage, shut up in
Boston, with five thousand troops, by the ragged,
undisciplined levies under General Artemus Ward
of Massachusetts, and his coadjutors, General Put-
man of Connecticut and General Greene of Rhode

Island, had been reinforced on the 25th of May by the arrival in Boston Harbour of several ships of war and transports, with between 5000 and 6000 men, under the command of Generals Howe, Burgoyne, and Clinton. It came to the knowledge of General Ward that Gage, chafing under the state of siege to which he had been subjected, now intended to assume the offensive. To prevent this, the Americans resolved to fortify Breed's Hill and Bunker's Hill, two heights commanding the town from the suburb of Charlestown, separated from Boston by the Charles River. They worked at night secretly, and with such goodwill and success, in spite of a few shots fired at them at early dawn from the British ships of war in the harbour, the look-out in which had discovered their operations, that by sunrise, or soon after, they had completed the works and mounted their guns. The firing from the ships aroused Boston; and General Gage, reconnoitring through a glass, beheld the fortifications that had sprung up in a few hours upon the heights, bristling with armed men. At a council of war, immediately summoned, it was resolved to dislodge the Americans from a position which gave them the power to lay Boston in ashes. The expedition for this purpose, under the command of

Major-General Howe, crossed over the Charles in eighteen barges about noon, and landed a little to the north of Breed's Hill. Here General Howe discovered, to his great mortification, that by some inexplicable blundering his cannon-balls did not fit his cannon, and sent over in all haste to General Gage for a proper supply.

Meanwhile the Americans were receiving reinforcements and strengthening their position. The right cannon-balls having arrived, the British prepared for a general assault, and were received with a vigour which they little expected. They were thrice repulsed by the Americans—the two forces fighting all the while amid the blazing ruins of the wooden town of Charlestown, that had been shelled by the ships of war in the harbour. Ultimately the British gained the ground of Bunker's Hill, for which the main struggle was waged, but at a terrible loss, inflicted by troops whom they had been accustomed to despise as "a rabble-rout" of rustics and clod-hoppers. It was the first battle of the long and weary war; and though the dear-bought victory remained with the British, the Americans boasted of it then, as they boast of it now, as equivalent to a defeat. The British loss was 1054, of whom an unusually large proportion were officers. The

American loss was about 450. "To the Americans," says Mr Washington Irving, "this defeat had the effect of a triumph. It gave them confidence in themselves, and consequence in the eyes of their enemies. They had proved to themselves and to others that they could measure weapons with the disciplined soldiers of Europe, and inflict the most harm in the conflict."

Washington, accompanied by Major-Generals Lee and Schuyler, all on horseback, had started for Philadelphia on the 21st of June, and had proceeded for about twenty miles on the road to New York, when the party was met by a mounted courier, spurring on in all haste with despatches to Congress. Asking his news, they were told of the battle of Bunker's Hill. Washington eagerly inquired how the militia had fought. When told that they had stood their ground bravely, reserved their fire until at close quarters with the enemy, and then delivered it with deadly effect, he quickly ejaculated, "Thank God! The liberties of America are safe." On his arrival in New York, he was received by Mr Livingston, President of the Assembly of the colony, who delivered a congratulatory address. Mr Livingston, and those for whom he spoke, had not yet travelled so far on the road

to revolution as to entertain the idea of throwing
off the yoke of Great Britain. " Confiding in you,
sir," he said, " and in the generals under your command, we have the most flattering hopes of success
in the glorious struggle for American liberty, and
the fullest assurance that whenever this important
contest shall be decided by *that fondest wish of
every American soul, an accommodation with the
mother-country*, you will cheerfully resign the deposit
committed into your hands, and reassume the
character of our worthiest citizen." Washington's
reply was guarded, as became a man who looked
both before and after, and never committed himself
to the unforeseen. Speaking for himself and his
brother generals, he said : " When we assumed the
soldier, we did not lay aside the citizen ; and we
shall most assuredly rejoice with you in that happy
hour, when the establishment of American liberty
on the most firm and solid foundations shall enable
us to return to our private stations." There was not
a word of independence, not a word of the mother-
country, in this short and sensible speech.

Washington remained but one day at New York,
and proceeded forthwith to Cambridge, near Boston,
where he established his headquarters, and devoted
all his time and his best energies to the organisation

and discipline of the forces under his command. He ascertained that the continental or American army amounted to about 12,000 men — ill fed, ill clad, and incohesive; and the British army to 11,000 — well disciplined, armed, and provisioned. Behind the one army was a population of three millions, widely scattered over a country more than half of which was a wilderness, and still containing a lingering remnant of affection for the old country; behind the other, a population of sixteen millions, with immense wealth, an ancient prestige, and the theoretical right upon their side, but not wholly united as to either the justice or the expediency of using force against the Americans. In addition to these advantages, the old country possessed the command of the ocean. The odds were fearful; but Washington and the Americans having laid their hands to the work, thought it wiser to persevere, and take their chance of fortune, than to acknowledge error, or prove false to the principle which they had made the guiding-star of their conduct. His first great duty—as it impressed itself upon his mind—was to elevate the continental army, as regarded discipline and all soldierly qualities, to the same efficiency as the British,—a herculean labour, but one that did not daunt his courage, though it some-times taxed his patience and his temper, and some-times drew out of him ebullitions of wrath, and oaths that were fearful to listen to.

Of the 12,000 men under Washington, nearly 9000 were from Massachusetts. The other 3000 were from Connecticut, Vermont, New Hampshire, and Rhode Island, with a few from New York, New Jersey, Pennsylvania, Maryland, and Virginia. They were encamped in separate bodies, each with its own regulations and officers. Some had tents; some slept under trees, or in such barns and other buildings as were contiguous to the camp; and all, as Washington complained, "were strong-ly imbued with a spirit of insubordination, which they mistook for independence." Having, by official intercourse with the various generals and colonels of this motley host, ascertained its true value as a military force, he wrote to the President of Congress—the same John Hancock who had once aspired to fill the post of com-mander-in-chief — representing its manifold de-ficiencies, and urging the immediate appointment of a commissary-general and other officers. Above all things, he requested a supply of money, as already he felt the greatest inconveniences for want of a military chest. But his chief annoyance arose from the rebellious and discontented spirit of his officers and men. In another letter to Congress, written after he had been four months in command, he complained that half of the officers of the rank of captain were inclined to retire, and that their example operated injuriously upon the men. Volunteers would not take service unless they were personally acquainted with and approved of the character, appearance, and sobriety of the colonel, the lieutenant-colonel, and the captain. Connecticut men would not act under Massachusetts officers, or Rhode Islanders under any but a Rhode Island commander. Three weeks after, the disgusted General wrote a still more emphatic letter to Congress. "I am sorry," he said, "to be necessitated to mention to you the egregious want of public spirit which prevails here. Instead of pressing to be engaged in the service of their country, which I vainly flattered myself would be the case, I find we are likely to be deserted in a most critical time. Our situation is truly alarming; and of this General Howe is well aware. No doubt, when he is reinforced, he will avail himself of the information."

Writing to his friend Joseph Reed, who had for a short time acted as his private secretary,

he described his difficulties with greater bitterness of heart. "Such dearth of public spirit,"
he said, "and such want of virtue—such jobbing
and fertility in all the low arts to obtain advantage
of one kind or another, in this great change of
military arrangement—I never saw before, and I
pray God's mercy that I may never be witness to
again. What will be the end of these manœuvres
is beyond my scan. I tremble at the prospect.
We have been till this time (November 28th) enlisting about 3500 men. To engage these, I have
been obliged to allow furlough as far as fifty men
to a regiment; and the officers, I am persuaded,
indulge many more. The Connecticut troops will
not be prevailed upon to stay longer than their
term, saving those who have enlisted for the next
campaign, and are mostly on furlough. Such a
mercenary spirit pervades the whole, that I should
not be surprised at any disaster that may happen.
Could I have foreseen what I have experienced, and
am likely to experience, no consideration on earth
should have induced me to accept this command."

Washington, it has been alleged, had a prejudice against the New Englanders—or "Yankees,"
as they then were and still are called by the inhabitants of the Southern and Western States—and

neither understood nor admired their character. "The common people here," wrote his friend and admirer, General Greene, who was proud to serve under him, "are exceedingly avaricious. Their genius is commercial, from their long intercourse with trade. The sentiment of honour, the true characteristic of a soldier, has not yet got the better of self-interest. His Excellency (General Washington) has been taught to believe them a superior race of mortals, but finding them of the same temper and disposition, passions and prejudices, virtues and vices, as the common people of other countries, they sank in his esteem." There was one Yankee, however, in addition to General Greene, for whom Washington had the highest respect— Jonathan Trumbull, Governor of Connecticut, whom he was accustomed to call " Brother Jonathan," and to whose advice and opinion he was always inclined to defer. Trumbull was a Puritan of the Donald Cargill and Balfour of Burley type—a wielder of " the sword of the Lord and of Gideon "—a political and religious fanatic, who would strike hard for the glory of God, on the principle of " Smite, and spare not," but who, on all ordinary occasions when his religious passions and prejudices were not excited, was a pious, humane, and sensible man. Writing to Washington to encourage him in his perilous career, Mr Trumbull said—" Congress has with one united voice appointed you to the high position you fill. The Supreme Director of all events hath caused a wonderful union of hearts and counsels to exist among us. Now, therefore, be you strong, and very courageous. May the God of the armies of Israel shower down the blessings of His divine providence upon you; give you wisdom and fortitude; cover your head in the day of battle and danger; add success; convince our enemies of their mistaken measures, and that all their attempts to deprive these colonies of their inestimable constitutional rights and liberties are injurious and vain." Washington's familiar epithet for this sturdy Covenanter has become national; and " Brother Jonathan " stands for America, as " John Bull " does for England.

The year 1775 produced no great change in the military situation. It came to Washington's knowledge, towards its close, that General Howe, whom he was anxious to attack and drive out of Boston, was secretly fitting out a combined naval and military expedition for some distant port. Washington having reason to believe that the object of the expedition was New York, despatched General Lee to place that city in a state of defence. After many delays, and much opposition from his councils of war, Washington, on the 4th of March 1776, took possession of Dorchester Heights, which the army had long been engaged in fortifying; and as the position commanded Boston, the British, after thirteen days, evacuated the place. This was Washington's first real triumph—a triumph, however, which was followed by many serious reverses and humiliations. As soon as the British fleet, with the army under General Howe, had put out to sea, Washington marched to New York, with the object of preventing the enemy's landing. But New York was by no means as zealous in the revolutionary cause as New England, and Washington did not meet the popular support on which he had calculated; and when the British took easy possession of Long Island and Staten Island on the 27th of August, he deemed it prudent to evacuate New York, march through New Jersey, and take up a position behind the Delaware.

Meanwhile a great event, in which Washington had no share, had fixed upon America the attention of the world. On the 2d of July—a day for ever memorable in the history of America, and of Europe also, in which the act that was then consummated was destined to play the part of leaven in the lump,

F

and cause a fermentation to the old system of government that has not even yet worked itself out—the American Congress, sitting with closed doors, decreed by unanimous vote that "the United Colonies were, and of right ought to be, free and independent States." The people of Philadelphia—though the discussions of Congress were kept secret—knew the solemn nature of its deliberations, and gathered in large but quiet crowds around the State House, to await the tolling of a bell in the steeple that was to announce to the city that the independence of the United States had been finally asserted. The bell had been imported from England twenty-three years previously, when no thought of disaffection had entered the American mind, and bore the significant, and, as it now appeared, prophetic inscription from Holy Writ, "Proclaim liberty throughout all the land, and unto all the inhabitants thereof." The inscription was held to be of good omen, and when the circumstance was made known throughout the Colonies, excited among the religious population a feeling of pious satisfaction and of cheerful hope. On the 4th of July the Declaration was solemnly read to the people from the steps of the State House, since called "Independence Hall," and publicly proclaimed amid the shouts and acclamations of the multitude.

" I believe that this day," wrote Mr Adams, " will be celebrated by succeeding generations as their great anniversary festival. It ought to be commemorated, as the day of deliverance, by solemn acts of devotion to Almighty God. It ought to be solemnised with pomp and parade, with shows, games, sports, guns, bells, bonfires, and illuminations, from one end of the continent to the other, from this time forth for evermore." It needed no such prompting to set aside the day for remembrance in America; and even if the time should ever arrive when civilised men shall cease to express their joy at public events by the barbarous noise of guns or the letting off of fireworks, the 4th of July will not remain uncelebrated.

When the news of this decisive act arrived at New York, and when bells had been rung and guns fired in honour of the occasion, a mob of several hundred people, chiefly boys and street blackguards, such as in all countries and in all times are ready for any work of destruction, gathered around a leaden statue of King George III. that stood in the centre of the " Bowling Green," and in view of the batteries of the fort (now known as Governor's Island), suddenly bethought themselves that as monarchical rule had been abolished in America, there was no reason why the statue of a king should affront the gaze of a Republican people. Just as after the surrender of Napoleon III. at Sedan, when the Paris mob vented its spite against its monarch by breaking his bust in pieces, the crowd of New York rushed upon and clomb up the statue of George III., and, with savage joy in their work, levelled it with the ground. It was afterwards molten down and converted into bullets for the use of the continental army.

Washington received in camp the official notification of the Declaration of Independence, and on the 9th of July caused the proclamation to be read at six o'clock in the evening at the head of each brigade of the army. "The General hopes," he said in his published order to the troops, "that this important event will serve as a fresh incentive to every officer and soldier to act with fidelity and courage, as knowing that now the peace and safety of the country depend, under God, solely on the success of our arms; and that he is now in the service of a State possessed of sufficient power to reward his merit, and advance him to the highest honours of a free country."

The Declaration of Independence was originally drawn up by Thomas Jefferson, a young Virginian lawyer of great promise, which his after-years did not belie. It was much modified in Committee as regarded its phraseology, but not greatly as regarded its spirit. The document merits all the praise that has been bestowed upon it, for clear exposition, logical argument, and noble assertion,—though it contained, unsuspected at the time, two sentences pregnant with calamity and war. " We hold that *all men* are created equal ; that they are endowed by their Creator with certain *inalienable* rights ; that among them are life, *liberty*, and the pursuit of happiness." To sow this formula was to sow dragon's teeth ; and the armed men who sprang from them, crimsoned with their blood the battle-fields of the great Civil War. The second formula —that to · secure their rights, Governments are instituted amongst men, *deriving their just powers from the consent of the governed*—justified the South-ern Secession, put the North into a logical dilemma, and led to the commission of a wrong which its after-success condoned but did not justify. Rebels themselves in 1776, Jefferson and his countrymen did not foresee that what had happened as against Great Britain, might hereafter happen as against themselves, and that in 1861 the Secession of the Southern States might be as fairly justified by their own arguments as the secession of the Colonies from the mother-country. Washington's position as Commander-in-Chief, which had rendered necessary the resignation of his seat in Congress, deprived him of the honour of signing the great historical document.

Before abandoning New York, which was rendered untenable by the British occupation of Long Island and Staten Island, and the presence of the main body of the British fleet under Admiral Lord Howe in the beautiful bay, Washington wrote a doleful letter to Congress, in which he suggested that it might be better to burn down the city than to leave it standing for the winter-quarters of the enemy. "Our situation," he said, under date of September 3d, "is truly distressing. The check our detachment sustained on the 27th has dispirited too great a proportion of our troops, and filled their minds with apprehension and despair. The militia are dismayed, intractable, and impatient to return. Great numbers have gone off—in some instances almost by whole regiments. With the deepest concern I am obliged to confess my want of confidence in the generality of the troops. Our number of men fit for duty is under 20,000. Till of late I had no doubt in my own mind of defending this place, nor would I have yet, if the men would do their duty,—but this I despair of."

Washington afterwards thought better of the matter. New York was evacuated, and not burned; and the General, anxious, perplexed, sad at heart, but not despairing of ultimate success, resolved to make the best of his faint-hearted troops, to get rid of the worst of them, and to supply the places of the inefficient and cowardly by new and better men. Before his retrograde movement was completely effected, an encounter of a detachment of his forces with the British near Bloomingdale, on Manhattan Island, a few miles above New York, ended so disgracefully, that the usually calm and phlegmatic man lost all command over himself. At the first sound of the cannonade opened by the British on his detachment, Washington rode from Harlem Heights to see what was the matter. He was met by a brigade of Connecticut men flying from their posts in panic without firing a shot. There were but sixty or seventy British and Hessians, but their fears magnified them into as many hundreds; and they fled, says Washington Irving, in "headlong terror. Losing all self-command at the sight of such dastardly conduct, Washington dashed his hat upon the ground in a transport of rage, and exclaimed, 'And these are the men with whom I am to defend America!' In a paroxysm of passion"—

and the historian adds, despair, which never even in the darkest moments entered this strong man's mind—"he snapped his pistols at some of them, threatened others with his sword, and was so heedless of his own danger that he might have fallen into the hands of the enemy, who were not eight yards distant, had not an aide-de-camp seized the bridle of his horse and absolutely hurried him away." The incident led to no important result; and retiring to Dobb's Ferry, twenty-two miles up the Hudson River, he set himself to the work of reorganisation. And a difficult work he found it. The Connecticut militia dwindled down from 6000 to 2000 men; the volunteers from Delaware and Pennsylvania departed homewards, to the great disgust of Washington and of his young friend and adjutant-general, Joseph Reed. "When I look around," wrote the latter to his wife, "and see how few of the number who talked so loudly of death and honour are around me, I am lost in wonder and surprise. Some of our Philadelphia gentlemen, who came over on visits, on the first cannon-shot went off in a most violent hurry. Your noisy sons of liberty, I find, are ever the quietest on the field."

Washington never had much faith in volunteers

who enlisted for a short period; and every day that passed over his head, diminished his confidence in and respect for such soldiers. He finally resolved to urge upon Congress the imperative duty of enlisting troops for the whole duration of the war, however long it might be; and wrote a letter to the President, setting forth the total inefficiency and probable disastrous failure of the existing military system—the discontent, insubordination, and waste that prevailed in all ranks of the service, and the harassing duties, too often unavailing, that it imposed upon officers who were really willing to fight and die for their country. This letter produced its effect; and Congress passed an Act for the raising of eighty-eight battalions, to be furnished by the several States of the Confederacy, according to their population and ability. The pay of the officers was augmented. Each volunteer who engaged to serve until the conclusion of the war was to receive a bounty of twenty dollars and a grant of a hundred acres of land. Those who enlisted for three years only, were to receive the money without the land. The States were authorised to send commissioners to the army; to arrange with the Commander-in-Chief the appointment of officers in their quotas; and, in default of the action of the States within a pre-

scribed period, Washington was empowered to fill
up the vacancies. These measures produced the
good effect anticipated. But their operation was
slow. The end to be attained was yet far distant.
The road to be travelled was dark and stormy,
and encumbered by perils that, could they have
been foreseen, might have broken even the proud
spirit of Washington. The jealousy of subordinate
generals was not among the least of the troubles
before him, nor the meanest among the many
lions in his path. But he held on, always on the
point of throwing up his commission in disgust, but
never carrying into effect a purpose for which a
smaller-minded man would have found abundant
justification.

Abandoning the line of the Hudson, and the
State of New Jersey, sometimes called "the Jerseys,"
Washington fell back behind the Delaware—not
without incurring the reprobation of General Lee, a
subordinate in whose sagacity and energy he reposed
great confidence, who accused him in a letter to
Joseph Reed, which in Reed's absence was opened
by Washington, of fatal indecision, which the writer
held to be a greater disqualification for high command in great emergencies than stupidity, or even
the want of personal courage. Washington was

pained, but held his peace. He found means, however, to silence Lee and other cavillers for a while by a second movement across the Delaware to Trenton, where he surprised and thoroughly defeated a considerable force of Hessian auxiliaries under Colonel Rahl. This done, he again crossed the river to his old quarters, unwilling to try conclusions with the powerful force under Lord Cornwallis that was hastening forward to meet him.

But his victory, though it raised his own spirits and those of his officers, did not reconcile the volunteers to renewed service. The battle was fought in the last week of December, and the term of enlistment of some of his best and hardiest troops expired with the year. It was with difficulty, and chiefly by the promise of a new bounty of ten dollars per man, that a considerable proportion of these weary patriots were induced to serve for six weeks longer. But there was not sufficient money in the military chest to pay the mercenary soldiers, who were not ashamed to haggle with their country for cash in the day of its peril. Washington in this emergency sent a special messenger post-haste to his friend Robert Morris, a banker at Philadelphia, setting forth the circumstances, and adding, " If you could possibly collect a sum, if it were but one hundred, or one hundred and fifty pounds, it would be of service." Such were the difficulties that early beset and nearly proved fatal to the cause of American Independence.

Yet if his men were but of poor material, Washington found consolation in the confidence of Congress, and the hope that a better disciplined, less mercenary, and more patriotic army might be ultimately got together. On the 27th of December, immediately after the defeat of Rahl, and perhaps to some extent consequent upon that episode of brighter fortunes, Congress invested him with all but dictatorial power in military affairs, accompanying the formal resolutions which it had passed with a complimentary letter, which must have been as pleasant as a gleam of sunshine after long-continued storm. " Happy is it for this country," wrote the Committee, " that the General of its forces can safely be intrusted with the most unlimited power, and that neither personal security, liberty, nor property will be in the least degree endangered." Washington's reply was dignified and statesmanlike. After thanking Congress for the honour conferred upon and the responsibilities intrusted to his keeping, he said, " that instead of thinking himself freed from civil obligations by this mark of confidence, he should constantly bear in mind that, as the sword was the last resource for the preservation of their liberties, so it should be the first thing to be laid aside when those liberties were established."

General Howe was puzzled at the defeat of his Hessian auxiliaries; and expressed his amazement that these old-established regiments of a people who made war their profession, should lay down their arms to a ragged and undisciplined militia. Fate, and Washington's extreme caution, had more amazement of the same kind in store for the British commander—though at that particular moment it was possible that Washington was as much amazed as himself. But Washington at that time, and to the close of his military career, was the tool of circumstances; and, as Napoleon said of the English at Waterloo, never knew when he was beaten. He never planned rebellion; he threw off his allegiance to his sovereign with regret; he never exactly knew what he was doing; was in constant imminency of failure and collapse; and finally won the cause of America, less by his own prowess, and that of his sullen and uncertain army, than by the aid of France; and last, and very certainly not least, the loss of patience of the British Government, and its slowly formed but fully matured conviction, that the allegiance of the American provinces was not worth purchasing at the cost which it entailed.

To narrate all the incidents of Washington's military operations, until success finally crowned his efforts, is not within the purpose of this book. It must suffice to state briefly that the campaign of 1777 did not commence until the early summer, and that it was but partially favourable to the American cause. General Gates, a rival of Washington, who secretly intrigued to supplant him in the chief command, was at the head of an army of upwards of 10,000 men, and gained a victory over General Burgoyne, whom he forced to capitulate. Burgoyne's army had been reduced by capture, death, and the desertion of Canadian and loyalist American auxiliaries, to less than half the force opposed to him. By this capitulation—by the terms of which the British were allowed to retire with the honours of war, and on the sole condition of not again serving against the provinces—the Americans gained a serviceable train of artillery, 7000 stand of arms, and a large quantity of clothing, tents, and military stores. Washington, at the head of the main army, was less fortunate. He was twice defeated—once at Brandywine, and the second time at Germantown. The latter misfortune led to the occupation of the city of Philadelphia by the British, and to the retreat of Washington to Valley Forge.

Here he entrenched himself and established his winter-quarters, under circumstances the reverse of cheerful. He had, it is true, the support of a majority in Congress, which stood loyally by him; and the aid, countenance, and friendship of General Lafayette, at the head of a French contingent. But the country was losing heart; his soldiers, though of better stuff than the Yankee militia, on whom he had so long and so reluctantly been compelled to place his main reliance, were inadequately supplied not only with blankets to protect them from the severe winter of America, but with ordinary clothes, and sometimes even with rations, though these when distributed were of the coarsest kind. And for surplusage of unfavourable fortune, a powerful cabal was formed against him by three of his principal subordinates, including the victorious General Gates, with the view of having him removed from the command. But Congress had faith in the Commander-in-Chief, and sent a commission to the camp to hear all complaints, and to investigate all Washington's plans for the entire remodelling of the army. The commission remained at Valley

Forge for three months; and finding, as all generals and all nations, if not all commissions, have at all times discovered, that money is the main sinew of war, it prevailed upon Congress to increase the pay and the allowances of the officers, and to grant a gratuity of eighty dollars to every non-commissioned officer and soldier who should serve until the conclusion of the war.

At the same time, Baron Steuben, a Prussian officer who had learned his business under the Great Frederick, undertook the difficult task of disciplining the rough American army on the Prussian model. But as the Baron spoke little or no English, his progress for a while was not rapid; and his commands to the men had to be conveyed through his aide-de-camp, Major Walker, who acted as interpreter. On one occasion, the raw militiamen having exhibited unusual stupidity or obstinacy, and the Baron having exhausted all his copious stock of German and French oaths in swearing at them, suddenly broke out with the polyglot objurgation—"Viens, mon ami Walker! Sacre! God dam! Dummer Eseln and Pumpernickelen! I can curse no more—les sacrés badauds et gauches! God dam!" By degrees, however, the army got into better training. The increased

bounty had an admirable effect; while the ratification of a defensive treaty with France, which arrived
in camp early in the spring, not only greatly gratified the men, but still more greatly tended to inspire
a bold determination on the part of the public to
prosecute the war with unflagging vigour.

The campaign of 1778 opened far more favourably for the Americans than that of the preceding
year. An unaccountable dilatoriness and remissness
paralysed the operations of the British commander,
in consequence of which Washington found himself
able to abandon the line of the Delaware, and to
march upon that of the Hudson. Though in this,
as in other movements, he seemed scarcely to gain
ground, yet he never really lost any; but with
that constant and perpetual dripping which wears
away the stone, he was exhausting the resources
and almost the hopes of the enemy. Lord Carlisle,
one of the commissioners deputed by the British
Government, after the surrender of Burgoyne, to
visit America with the view of arranging a compromise, was far more impressed with the blunders
of his own countrymen than with the genius or
the success of the Americans. It was said by
General Gates, and repeated by the smaller fry of
Washington's detractors, that heaven had evidently

foreordained the triumph of the American cause,
or it never could have held up its head so long as
it had done in face of the incompetency and indecision of Washington.   Lord Carlisle, writing
home to his friend George Selwyn, formed an equally
unfavourable estimate of the conduct of the English.   " Everything," he said, " is upon a great scale
on this continent.   The rivers are immense; the
climate violent in heat and cold; the prospects
magnificent; the thunder and lightning tremendous.
*We have nothing on a great scale with us but our
blunders, our misconduct, our losses, and our disgraces.*"

On the 13th of July, Washington received a de-
spatch from Congress informing him of the arrival
of a French fleet on the coast, instructing him to
concert measures with Admiral the Count D'Estaing
for offensive operations against the British by sea
and land, and empowering him to call on the
Northern States, from New Hampshire to New
Jersey, both inclusive, for quotas of militia.   The
French fleet was composed of twelve ships of the
line and six frigates, with a land force of 4000
men.   The intention of the Admiral was to enter
the Bay of New York by Sandy Hook and the
Narrows, and to attack the British fleet under Lord
Howe—a force much inferior to his own; and in

case of success, to bombard New York from the sea, while Washington co-operated from the land. This enterprise, however, was abandoned, as was a subsequently proposed attack upon Rhode Island. In the meanwhile, the British fleet had been largely reinforced by a squadron under Admiral Byron, and the strength of the two navies was nearly equalised. The French fleet, however, did nothing; it suffered from violent storms, as well as from the indecision of its commander. Its arrival had excited American hopes to so high a pitch, that its inactivity and failure created a mingled feeling of despondency and anger. The winter of 1778 found Washington engaged in the occupation and defence of the New England States; while the British, farther south, occupied New Jersey. Washington retired into winter quarters in December, and protected the line of the Hudson.

The year 1779 was unfruitful of military events. The English and the Americans during all that time accomplished little beyond keeping a watch upon each other's movements. In 1780 a new French naval and military armament was despatched to America, and arrived off Newport in Rhode Island in July, under Admiral De Grasse and General the Count De Rochambeau; but the superiority of the

British at sea was so great as to prevent the execution of the plans of the combined French and
American forces.   The year was unmarked by military events of any supreme importance,—though
rendered memorable in American annals by the
defection or treason of "Benedict Arnold," a man
whose name to this day is never pronounced in the
United States without execration, and as the syn-
onym of all that is base, unpatriotic, and treacherous; and by the hanging as a spy of the brave
British officer, Major André—a deed of questionable
severity, that remains as great a blot upon the
otherwise fair fame of Washington as the execution
of the Duc d'Enghien remains upon that of the
first Napoleon.   Had the American commander
been chivalrous enough to have acceded to the
request of the doomed man, that he might meet the
fate of a soldier and not that of a felon, the stain
would have been less conspicuous, and impartial
history might have recorded of Washington that he
was not only a man with a brain to think and a
hand to execute, but with a heart not altogether
incapable of mercy and kind feeling.

The war continued to drag on its weary length,
with the usual episodes of disaffection and insubordination among Washington's too scanty armies,

until July 1781, when he was joined at Dobb's Ferry, on the Hudson, by the French army under Rochambeau. The French Government not only sent men, but, what was equally valuable to the mercenary and discouraged militia of the States, money to the extent of six millions of livres, or £240,000 sterling, with a promise of further subsidies in case of need.

An unsuccessful attempt against New York, which was still held by the British and protected by the British fleet, decided Washington to transfer the seat of war farther south, and trust to the co-operation of the French fleet under Admiral De Grasse to effect a landing on the shores of the Chesapeake. The result of these continued manœuvres was almost the only gleam of real success that had cheered the mind of Washington since the commencement of the war. On the 14th of September, along with Rochambeau and his faithful Lafayette, and aided by 3000 French put ashore by the Count De Grasse, he established his headquarters at Williamsburg, in Virginia. Lord Cornwallis, with a British force of greatly inferior numbers, advanced to Yorktown, and took possession of it unopposed. The move was fatal to the British arms, and decisive of the campaign. On the 30th

of September, Washington, fully informed of the
numerical weakness of Cornwallis, advanced with
his French allies, and completely invested the place.
With a French fleet in the York River in front
of the town, and with the American and French
armies on all other sides, the position of Cornwallis
was desperate, unless he could be relieved. No
relief was at hand.   On the 6th of October
the first parallel of the siege was opened at a
distance of only 600 yards from the enemy.   On
the afternoon of the 9th, all being ready, Washington himself put the match to the first gun, and
a furious cannonade immediately followed, which
was maintained for several days, and but feebly
responded to by the British.   To surrender to the
despised "continental rabble," even though they
were aided by trained French soldiers, was galling
to the pride of Cornwallis.   Seeing the impossibility
of effectual resistance without help from New York,
the British commander devised a plan of escape by
the river; but it was defeated by an unexpected
storm of wind and rain.   His fortifications were
tumbling in ruins; the incessant cannonade had
half destroyed the town; his men suffered from
sickness and want of food; and on the 17th he
proposed a cessation of hostilities for twenty-four

hours, that two officers of each army might meet to settle terms for the surrender of Yorktown. Cornwallis demanded conditions much more favourable than Washington felt himself at liberty to grant.

Ultimately, on the 19th, no succour being probable, Cornwallis surrendered with his whole force as prisoners of war. The officers were allowed to retain their side-arms—both officers and soldiers their private property. The men were to be retained in Virginia, Maryland, and Pennsylvania, and to receive the same rations as American soldiers. The officers were to be allowed to return to Europe on parole, or to retire to Canada and other British possessions in America. The whole force that surrendered amounted to 7073 men. Lord Cornwallis was sad at heart; still sadder he was when he learned in due time that on the very day of his capitulation Sir Henry Clinton, the British Governor of New York, had sailed to his relief with twenty-five ships of the line, fifty-two gun-ships, and eight frigates, and a military force of 7000 of his best troops. Sir Henry arrived off the capes of Virginia five days after all was over with Cornwallis. After hovering about the entrance of the Chesapeake for another five days, during which he learned all the unhappy particulars of the British discomfiture, he returned to New York.

The British power in America never made any real head against this calamity. Congress, and indeed the whole American people of the thirteen States, were exuberant in the expression of their delight. Thanks were unanimously voted to Washington, De Rochambeau, and De Grasse; and it was decreed that a marble column, commemorative of the alliance between France and the United States, and the victory achieved by their associated arms, should be erected in Yorktown. And after the fashion of the King of Prussia at Sedan, the Almighty was solemnly praised for the signal discomfiture of Great Britain. The Liberal party in England received the news with mingled feelings of joy and regret, in which, however, the joy predominated, because it was thought the American victory prefigured the speedy close of a war which was fast becoming distasteful to all parties. The British Premier, Lord North, was greatly troubled. When the news was announced to him in Downing Street, he is reported to have stretched forth his arms wildly, and exclaimed, as he paced up and down the official apartment, " Oh God ! it is all over ! "

And it *was* all over in effect, though the war still

continued with the languid force of a ball that was wellnigh spent. Washington remained on the defensive, resorting to the offensive whenever he found or could make a fair opportunity to strike a blow with advantage. But the details of his small defeats and small successes between the surrender of Cornwallis and the conclusion of peace with Great Britain, may safely be left to the voluminous histories of the United States, wherein they are duly recorded. Negotiations for peace were commenced in 1782; the French forces were withdrawn; active hostilities almost entirely ceased; and Washington, towards the close of the year, withdrew into winter quarters at Newburgh, on the Hudson. On the 20th of January 1783 a general treaty of peace was signed at Paris; but the news did not arrive in America until the 23d of March, when it was received simultaneously by Congress and by General Washington in welcome letters from the Marquis De Lafayette. A few days afterwards, Sir Guy Carleton, who had succeeded to the chief command of the British force in America, officially notified that he was ordered to proclaim a cessation of hostilities by sea and land.

Great were the rejoicings of the Americans—except among that large and influential party who were sometimes called Tories, but who called themselves Loyalists and United Empire Loyalists. Many of these resolved to return "home," as they fondly called England; but the greater number departed with Sir Guy Carleton's army on the evacuation of New York, and betook themselves to Canada, or the other faithful British provinces, where their descendants still remain, and glory in the old title that their grandfathers assumed.

On the 8th of June, preparatory to laying down his commission, Washington addressed a letter to each of the governors of the thirteen States on the subject of the dissolution of the army, and the future policy of a Union that was now as independent in fact as it had long been in theory. "The great object," he said, "for which I had the honour to hold an appointment in the service of my country being accomplished, I am now preparing to return to that domestic retirement which, it is well known, I left with the greatest reluctance, —a retirement for which I never ceased to sigh through a long and painful absence, and in which, remote from the noise and trouble of the world, I meditate to pass the remainder of my life." He had a presentiment that the success of America in the great struggle against the mother-country might produce dangers to liberty and prosperity as great, though of a different kind, as those which might have followed upon failure; and he did not hesitate, in eloquent language, to warn his countrymen. Describing the condition of the people of America as that of "sole lords and proprietors of a vast tract of continent, comprehending all the various soils and climates of the world, and abounding with all the necessaries and conveniences of life," and congratulating them as the acknowledged possessors of absolute freedom and independence, he added— "This is the time of their political probation; this is the moment when the eyes of the whole world are turned upon them; this is the moment to establish or ruin their national character for ever."

Lest they should allow the mutual jealousies and fancied conflicting interests of thirteen sovereign States to prevent a complete union, or allow the interference of any European Powers among them for the subservience of European objects, he specially recommended four things to their earnest consideration. The first was the establishment of an "indissoluble union," and the perfect obedience of the several States to the constitutionally elected Federal heads; second, a sacred regard to public justice in the payment of all debts contracted for the pro-

secution of the war; third, the establishment of a
national militia, as the palladium of their security,
and the first effectual resort in case of hostility;
and fourth, a disposition among the people of the
United States to forget local prejudices and policies,
to make mutual concessions, and to sacrifice individual advantages to the interests of the community.
He made no mention of or allusion to negro
slavery, which few Americans at that time—and in
which few Washington was not included—thought
to be other than a healthful and advantageous
institution for all parties.   But before the close of
his life and his official career, this unconsidered
seed of evil had cropped above the soil, though it
gave but few indications of the upas-tree into
which it was destined to expand.

At noon on the 23d of December, in presence
of a brilliant assemblage of spectators, Washington
formally resigned his military command, and yielded
up his commission to Congress.   He was no orator,
but he spoke on this occasion with much dignity
and feeling.   "I consider it," he said, "an indis-
pensable duty to close this last solemn act of my
official life by commending the interests of our
dearest country to the protection of Almighty God,
and those who have the superintendence of them

to His holy keeping. Having finished the task assigned to me, I retire from the great field of action; and bidding an affectionate farewell to this august body, under whose orders I have long acted, I here offer my commission, and take my leave of all the employments of public life." The President, on receiving the commission, bore testimony to Washington's arduous, patient, and unselfish services. " You retire," he said, " with the blessings of your fellow-citizens; but the glory of your virtues will not terminate with your military command—it will continue to animate remotest ages." Many of the ladies present at this great historical scene were affected to tears, and some among the sterner sex were not ashamed to betray the like honourable emotions.

Next morning Washington took his departure for his estate at Mount Vernon—feeling, as he himself wrote to his friend De Witt Clinton, eased of a load of care, and hoping " to spend the remainder of his days in cultivating the affections of good men, and in the practice of the domestic virtues." He was once again a farmer and a country gentleman —having nothing to occupy his mind but his crops, his negroes (he had no tenantry), his sports on land and water, the exercise of a liberal hospitality, and the re-establishment of a fortune that had been sensibly impaired by his unpaid devotion to public affairs during all the best years of his life. His aged mother was still alive to glory in the greatness and the virtues of her son; but the friend of his youth, his first patron and employer, Lord Fairfax, was no longer in the land of the living. The old lord was stanch throughout the war in his allegiance to Great Britain, and deplored the conduct of the Americans, and of their general, whose character, nevertheless, he did not cease to respect. He was in his ninety-second year when the news arrived of the surrender of Lord Cornwallis, and the consequent downfall of British power. The blow was too much for his failing strength to bear. He sat silent for a while, and then called for the negro slave who acted as his valet. "Carry me to bed, Ire," said the old lord—"carry me to bed! It is high time that I should die!" These were the last articulate words of the good old Cavalier, who died a few day afterwards, sincerely mourned by Washington and all the inhabitants of Virginia, who respected his sturdy loyalty, although they did not share it.

During the next six years Washington's time was wholly employed in congenial and quiet pursuits.

He was visited by his friend Lafayette; he made tours of business to his old surveying-grounds on the Ohio and Kanawaha rivers; he kept open house when at home at Mount Vernon, for the most eminent of his American friends, and for distinguished foreigners who sought his acquaintance; took special interest in the political and internal affairs of his own State of Virginia; devoted attention to the encouragement of popular education, and for the civilisation of the Indians; and accepted the office of delegate to the National Convention which was charged with the duty of drawing up the first constitution of the United States. He was not without great and grave anxiety for the stability of the Union which he had been so main an instrument in establishing; and the correspondence which he maintained on the subject with the statesmen whom he ranked among his friends, betrays in every page his alarm lest his countrymen should not be fitted for the quiet enjoyment of republican but constitutional liberty. The " Sovereign " States, as they called themselves, were each jealous of the creation of a Federal or Central power, which Washington held to be essential if the Union was to guard itself effectually against foreign attack—especially against England. It is true that George

III. had sensibly, as well as magnanimously declared, that "as he had been the last man in his dominions to acknowledge the independence of the United States, so he would be the last man to raise a finger against it." But the King was not the Government, and the King might soon die; and there was a general feeling in America that the Old Country might at some time or other be engaged in hostilities against the New.

In a letter, dated 1785, to James Warren of Massachusetts, Washington expressed his doubts and fears. "The Confederation," he said, "appears to me to be little more than a shadow without the substance, and Congress a nugatory body—their ordinances being little attended to. To me it is a solecism in politics, indeed it is one of the most extraordinary things in nature, that we should confederate as a nation, and yet be afraid to give the rulers of that nation (who are creatures of our own making, appointed for a limited and short duration, and who are amenable for every action, and may be recalled at any moment, and are subject to all the evils which they may be instrumental in producing) sufficient powers to order and direct the affairs of the same. By such policy as this, the wheels of Government are clogged, and our brightest prospects, and that high expectation which was entertained of us by the wondering world, are turned into astonishment; and from the high ground on which we stood, we are descending into the vale of confusion and darkness."

In another letter of the same year, to John Jay, at that time Secretary for Foreign Affairs, he was even more despondent as to the fitness of the Americans for a republican form of government. "We have probably," he wrote, "had too good an opinion of human nature in forming our Confederation. Experience has taught us that men will not adopt and carry into execution measures the best calculated for their own good, without the intervention of coercive power. I do not conceive we can exist long as a nation without lodging somewhere a power which will pervade the whole Union in as energetic a manner as the authority of the State Governments extends over their several States. To be fearful of investing Congress, constituted as that body is, with ample authority for national purposes, appears to me the very climax of popular absurdity and madness."

But while thus dubious of the people, he did not share the opinions of those who believed that the establishment of a monarchy would be a cure for the evil. "I am told," he continued in the same letter to Mr Jay, "that even respectable characters speak of a monarchical form of government without horror. From thinking proceeds speaking, thence acting is often but a single step. But how irrevocable and tremendous! What a triumph for our enemies to verify their predictions! What a triumph for the advocates of despotism to find that we are incapable of governing ourselves, and that systems, founded on the basis of equal liberty, are merely ideal and fallacious! Would to God that wise measures may be taken in time to avert the consequences we have but too much reason to apprehend!"

An insurrection in the now orderly and conservative, but then very riotous and troublesome, State of Massachusetts lent force and poignancy to all Washington's misgivings. The discontent grew out of mercantile distress, the pressure of newly imposed taxation, and the disorders incident to large issues of paper money, which had been necessary during the progress of the War of Independence. The principles of the insurgents were summed up in one sentence by General Knox, the Secretary at War: "They are determined to annihilate all debts, public and private, and to issue an unlimited supply of unfunded paper money, which shall be legal tender in all cases whatever." Riotous and armed assemblages, brought together for the purpose of overawing the State Government, had been so frequent, and, as time wore on, so formidable, that it had been found necessary to call out the militia, fully armed, to keep order. In view of these circumstances, Washington wrote to Colonel Humphreys of Newhaven, in Connecticut: " What, gracious God! is man, that there should be such inconsistency and perfidiousness in his conduct? It was but the other day that we were shedding our blood to obtain the constitutions under which we now live—constitutions of our own choice and making; and now we are unsheathing the sword to overturn them! The thing is so unaccountable that I hardly know how to realise it, or to persuade myself that I am not under the illusion of a dream."

It was under the influence of fears and feelings like these that Washington took part in the deliberations of the Convention, which sat with closed doors for a period of nearly four months. The result was a Constitution such as Washington desired and approved, but which was far from giving satisfaction to the country, and more especially to that large party whose shibboleth was

"State Rights," as opposed to "Federalism," or
the concentration of too much power in the hands
of the general Government. Only three of the
thirteen States to which it was submitted for
ratification accepted it unanimously; five others by
a bare majority, and with an expressed proviso
of amendments which they specified; while two
States, North Carolina and Rhode Island, rejected
and refused to abide by it. Even the Federalists
were not wholly satisfied, thinking that the powers
confided to the Central Government were not adequate to preserve order, and prevent civil strife or
disunion; while the adherents of State sovereignty
and State rights saw in the document the preparation for and the seed of a nascent despotism. The
ratification of the instrument by nine States out of
the thirteen was necessary to its validity; and as
the separate Conventions assembled at different
times, a year elapsed before the final decision.

During all this period an active correspondence
was carried on between Washington and his political friends, in which, though nothing was overtly
said, much was covertly thought on the subject
of the Presidency. Washington, with all his
unaffected modesty, could not but feel that his
military services, and the universal respect enter-

tained for his character and abilities, pointed him out to his countrymen as one who might command a nomination for the Presidency, if he would consent to fill the office. He had, it is true, declared that his retirement from public life was final; but everybody knew that such decisions were not irrevocable, and that their true meaning might resemble that concealed under a young lady's negative, which only required a proper amount of importunity to be converted into an affirmative. The possibility, and indeed the probability, that such pressure would be applied at the appointed time, must have been constantly present to his mind, though he seems to have taken especial care, while the Constitution remained under discussion, not to betray to the public that his thoughts wandered in that direction.

The necessary ratification of the Constitution was received by Congress in September 1788, and an Act was immediately passed appointing the first Wednesday in January 1789 to elect the electors, who, in their turn, were to elect the President and Vice-President. Washington's name was almost simultaneously brought forward in every State of the Union; and as in these circumstances reticence to his friends and correspondents was not necessary, he unburthened his mind freely to all whom he admitted to his esteem. In answer to Colonel Henry Lee, he wrote: "Notwithstanding that my advanced period of life" (he was only in his fifty-seventh year), "my increasing fondness for agricultural amusements, and my growing love of retirement, augment and confirm my decided predilection for the character of a private citizen, yet it would be no one of these motives, nor the hazard to which my former reputation might be exposed, nor the terror of encountering new fatigues and troubles, that would deter me from an acceptance, but a belief that some other person who had less pretension, and less inclination to be excused, could execute all the duties fully as satisfactorily as myself." To Alexander Hamilton he wrote: "If I should receive the appointment, and if I should be prevailed upon to accept it, the acceptance would be attended with more difficulty and reluctance than ever I experienced in my life." To his old friend and comrade-in-arms, General Lafayette, he wrote: "If I know my own heart, nothing short of a conviction of duty will induce me again to take an active part in public affairs. And in that case, if I can form a plan for my own conduct, my endeavours shall be unremittingly exerted, even at the hazard of former fame or present popularity, to extricate my country from the embarrassments in which it is entangled through want of credit; and to establish a general system of policy, which, if pursued, will ensure permanent felicity to the Commonwealth. I think I see a path clear and direct as a ray of light, which leads to the attainment of that object. Nothing but harmony, honesty, industry, and frugality are necessary to make us a great and happy people. Happily the present posture of affairs, and the prevailing disposition of my countrymen, promise to co-operate in establishing those four great and essential pillars of public felicity."

Whatever his other correspondents may have thought of the matter, Lafayette could have no doubt of Washington's acceptance, after the receipt of a letter such as this. There were no other candidates who had even the shadow of success against him; and on the 4th of March, Washington, who had been unanimously elected—the first and the last time that ever such an extraordinary compliment was paid to the public spirit and private worth of an American—"the Father of his country," as he now began to be called, became unofficially aware of the honour that had been conferred upon him. It was not until fifty days afterwards—on the 14th of April—that Congress was in a position to notify the fact officially to Washington himself, and to John Adams, formerly Minister of the United States in Paris, who had been elected to the honorary and all but nominal office of Vice-President. On the 16th of April the new President—leaving Mrs Washington to follow shortly afterwards—departed from his farm at Mount Vernon for New York, which was at that time the seat of the Federal Government. An entry in his diary recorded the fact: "About ten o'clock this day (April 16th) I bade adieu to Mount Vernon, to private life, and to domestic felicity; and with a mind oppressed with more anxious and painful sensations than I have words to express, set out for New York with the best disposition to render service to my country in obedience to its call, but with less hope of answering its expectations." His progress all the way was what is commonly called an "ovation." Guns were fired; bells rang merry chimes; flags were displayed from steeple, tower, and house-top; triumphal arches were erected; girls robed in white garments strewed flowers upon his way; the people shouted and cheered, and fussy civic dignitaries presented congratulatory addresses at every town and city through which he passed. On his arrival at Elizabethtown

Point, whence he was to proceed through the Kill van Kull to New York, a committee of both Houses of Congress was in waiting to receive him. He and his cortege, which like a snowball had gained volume in rolling, embarked on board of a state barge specially constructed for the occasion, manned by thirteen pilots, one for each State in the Union, and all arrayed in white uniform. Several other gaily decorated barges of less imposing construction, crowded with civic and other officials, accompanied by their wives and daughters, followed, and flashed along the smooth waters of the Kill and the beautiful bay of New York, to the sound of instrumental bands, playing "Yankee Doodle" and other excellent airs, to the appointed landing-place near the Battery. New York was then a small city, but it poured forth almost its whole population to welcome the chief magistrate. He was received on landing by the Governor of the State, and by the municipality of the city, and escorted on foot to the rendezvous prepared for his reception. Washington was of too cold and too wise a temperament to be unduly elated on this or on any other occasion. He wrote in his diary the same evening: "The display of boats which attended and joined us on this occasion, some with vocal and some with instrumental music on board, the decoration of the ships, the roar of cannon, and the loud acclamations of the people which rent the skies as I passed along the wharves, filled my mind with sensations as painful (considering the reverse of this scene, which may be the case after all my labours to do good) as they are pleasing."

It had been a matter of anxious and sometimes of acrid debate among American politicians to discover a proper title for the President, and a proper ceremonial to be observed, so that his high station should receive befitting honour. John Adams, the Vice-President, who had been accustomed to official etiquette by his long residence at the most aristocratic and splendid Court in Europe—that of the Tuileries—was of opinion that the President should be addressed as his " Highness," and that the ceremonial of his Court, and of all his official life, should be as nearly regal as it was possible to make it. Thomas Jefferson—who was an ultra-Republican in practice and in theory, and would have abolished the silly title of Esquire, and the more sensible of " Mr," if the innovation had been possible—was for calling the President the " President," and nothing more, and for depriving the office of any factitious dignity, and of all form and ceremonial whatsoever, except such as would be employed in the family of the humblest citizen towards the head and father of the household. Washington, who was an aristocrat by nature, by education, and by the habit of military command, inclined more towards the views of Adams in this not very important matter than to those of Jefferson. A compromise between the two extremes was soon effected. The President became " His Excellency " instead of " His Highness " ; and a not very stringent code of etiquette was adopted, of which the principal proviso was, that the President might invite, but was never to be invited—and that his invitations to dinners or balls, whenever he chose proper to issue them, should be looked upon as " commands," as such missives are usually considered when issued by European sovereigns.

His inauguration, and the administration of the oath of office, took place on the 30th of April, amid rejoicings similar to those which had greeted his arrival ten days previously. Washington, in private communion with himself in his regularly kept diary, bore steadily in mind the great truth that all popularity, however deeply rooted it may appear, is fickle and precarious. " I greatly fear," he wrote, " that my countrymen will expect too much from me. I fear, if the issues of public measures should not correspond with their sanguine expectations, that they will turn the extravagant, and I might almost say undue praises, which they are heaping upon me at this moment, into equally extravagant, though I will fondly hope unmerited praises." It may be remarked that even to himself Washington would not admit that the praises were wholly undue—a good opinion of himself which was as useful to him during his term of office as it was certainly well founded.

Washington as a statesman had almost as many difficulties to contend with as those which he had confronted as a soldier; and these difficulties sprang from the same source, and were more largely due to the temper of his own people than to any foreign enemies or opponents. The measures that chiefly occupied his time and that of Congress during the four years of his first term of office, were those necessary for the common defence of the States against possible foreign aggression,—for the naturalisation of immigrants,—for the establishment of a uniform system of currency, weights, and measures,—for the encouragement of agriculture, manufactures, and commerce,—for the promotion of science and literature,—and for the support of public credit. The last topic was the one which involved the most acrimonious discussion, and envenomed to the greatest degree the animosity of rival factions. The question of the funding of the debt and the establishment of a National Bank, that appears so simple and elementary, nearly split the new Union asunder before it was finally cemented, and created controversies and antagonisms that lasted long after Washington had been gathered to his fathers, and far into the lifetime of the succeeding generation. The ultra-Democrats and Republicans, with Jefferson at their head, considered a National Bank to be not only an aristocratic and *quasi* feudal institution, but one of which the establishment would act with fatal effect upon the liberties of the country.

Alexander Hamilton, one of the most remarkable men—perhaps, next to Washington himself, the most remarkable man—which the American revolution had produced, took the opposite side. He was at the head of the " Federal," as Jefferson was at that of the " Union " party ; and the war upon the subject waged furiously both in and out of the Cabinet, Washington himself inclining strongly towards the views of Hamilton. The National Bank was ultimately established, with a capital of ten millions of dollars, or two millions sterling, of which eight millions were to be held by individuals, and two millions by the Government. The discussions on this as on other topics that proved almost equally irritating, lasted into the fourth year of Washington's Presidency. He had not given universal satisfaction, and had never expected to do so; but as his term drew near to its natural close, a very general feeling of anxiety was felt and expressed in all the States of the Union as to the choice of a successor. Even those who considered themselves powerful, able, and popular enough to aspire to the office—Jefferson and Hamilton among the number—thought it their duty to abstain from pushing their claims, and to urge upon Washington the propriety, the expediency, and, in short, the paramount duty, of consenting to be put in nomination a second time. Washington was coy as before, and with greater reason. Power and its exercise, which had necessarily brought him into collision with parties in whose opinions he could not agree, and whose schemes he could not advance, had impaired his pristine popularity. In addition to this, he had assumed a certain amount of pomp and ceremonial, such as driving about in a carriage-and-four, and sometimes in a carriage-and-six; and in enshrouding himself from the intrusion on his privacy of the unauthorised and unknown vulgar, who, on the plea of political, wished to establish a social equality, against which his cold and exclusive nature revolted.

Taking advantage of these circumstances, his enemies—and no man, however pure-minded and virtuous, can attain power without creating them —represented that he was not at heart a Republican; that his tastes and manners were aristocratic; and that he not only had leanings towards the establishment of a monarchy, but would gladly have placed upon his own brow the royal crown of America. Nothing could be falser than the last of these allegations, however much of truth there might be in the charge of aristocratic hauteur, and of a splendour of outward show in his official life, distasteful to the austere school of Republicans. Washington was goaded out of his usual meekness at the charge of royal ambition. "I," he said, "who would rather live quietly at my farm of Mount Vernon than be emperor of the world, to be accused of wanting to make myself a king!" It was too disgusting, too much for his philosophy to bear; and he relieved his mind by more than one oath, in the most emphatic vernacular. But, secure in conscious rectitude, he learned to treat the accusation with contempt, and consented to be nominated for a second term of office. All moderate and sensible men rallied around him, and he was duly re-elected.

His second term was stormier than the first, no less in the domestic than in the foreign policy of the Union. He had scarcely been reinstalled a month, when the Revolution in France, which owed much of its early impetus, if not its origin, to the successful revolution and example of America, reached an unexpected crisis. Not only Washington, but the ultra-Democratic Jefferson, his Secretary of State or Foreign Minister, was scandalised at the excesses of the French Jacobins, justly fearing that their follies and crimes would discredit republicanism all over the world. The news that more particularly disquieted Washington, and conjured before his mind a vision of troubles for the Union, and for himself as its chief magistrate, was the declaration of war against Great Britain by the French Republic, which arrived in New York in April 1793. The American people were greatly excited. They had not forgiven the King and Government of Great Britain for the protracted opposition to the Independence of the United States; and as the war was between a monarchy which had been their foe, and a republic which was their friend and imitator, the public feeling was strong in favour of France. The unreasoning and impulsive mob, not content with barren sympathy, were for an immediate declaration of an alliance with France; and desperate speculators and adventurers began to fit out privateers in all the great seaports of the Union, to prey upon British commerce. Washington was alarmed and indignant. He sympathised with France; but he would not plunge his country into an unjust war with Great Britain. He hastened from Mount Vernon, where he was enjoying a few days of repose, and summoned a Cabinet Council to meet at Philadelphia. It was unanimously resolved that the President should issue a proclamation of neutrality, forbidding the citizens of the United States to take part in any hostilities on the seas, or to carry to either of the belligerents any articles deemed contraband of war by the usages of civilised nations.

This wise and necessary measure created much dissatisfaction, and did more to diminish the already waning popularity of the President than any previous or future act of his official life. The proclamation was declared to be a royal edict, a daring assumption of monarchical power, and a shameless

I

manifestation of hostility to France and partiality for England. In the midst of the ferment of opinion thus excited, a pert, conceited, and silly young man, named Genet—the "Citizen Genet," as he called himself—arrived in America, as ambassador from the French Republic. He landed at Charleston, in South Carolina, where, instead of proceeding at once to present his credentials to the President, he remained for several days engaged in efforts, by no means unsuccessful, to induce the leading merchants and shipowners to fit out privateers against Great Britain. Mr Jefferson, the Secretary of State, had previously received and communicated to the President information from the American Minister at Paris, that Genet had been furnished by his Government with 300 blank commissions for privateers, to be given clandestinely to such Americans as might be inclined to accept them. He found the people of Charleston well inclined to the adventure—the contiguity of that port to the West Indies having familiarised them with the profitable extent of the British trade with those islands. When at last he had accomplished what he could at Charleston, he left that city and proceeded by land to Philadelphia. His progress all the way was a triumphal one. He was everywhere received with addresses of welcome, and escorted in and out of the towns and cities by public and civic processions. The head of this young ambassador, who was described by Hamilton as " a busy man rather than a man of business," was wellnigh turned by these manifestations of popularity before he arrived at Philadelphia. In this city the climax of his preposterous welcome was attained, to the sore annoyance of the President, who saw in the excited state of public feeling a possibility of entanglement in the wars of Europe, with which he conscientiously believed the United States had, and ought to have, nothing to do.

The capture of a British ship, the Grange, in American waters, by one of Genet's privateers, and of several others on the ocean by the same agencies, brought matters to a crisis. The British Minister demanded a restitution of the prizes. Washington and his Cabinet were unanimously of opinion that restitution should be made of the Grange; but with regard to the vessels captured on the high seas, there was a difference of opinion, and the case was reserved for the decision of the Courts of Justice.

Genet, who had the worst of all faults possible in an ambassador—impulsiveness and a deplorable

excess of zeal—was indignant, and wrote a series
of injudicious and insulting letters to the Secretary
of State, and in other ways kept up an agitation
which was mischievous in the extreme, and as
likely by its consequences to embroil the United
States with France as with Great Britain.   Washington did not endure the nuisance of Citizen
Genet in a kindly or patient spirit, and fretted
over the worry so much as to affect his health.

"The President is not well," wrote Jefferson to
his friend Madison in June.   "He is extremely
hurt at the attacks made upon him in the public
papers.   I think he feels these things more than
any other person I ever met with.   I am extremely
sorry to see it."   But the annoyances caused by the
fussy Genet were more serious than those caused by
the press.   Another British ship, the Little Sarah,
was captured by a French privateer, and brought
into Philadelphia, where she was manned with a
crew of 120 men—of whom nine - tenths were
Americans—and fitted out and armed as a privateer,
under the name of the Little Democrat.   The Government, on deliberation, resolved to prevent the
departure of this vessel.   Citizen Genet was furious.
He appealed to the Government to reverse its decision.   He met with a courteous but firm refusal.

He then threatened to appeal to the people of the United States against their Government, and made use of other improper menaces.

Washington at last lost temper with this jackanapes, and unburdened his mind to Jefferson on the subject. "Is the Minister of the French Republic to set the acts of this Government at defiance *with impunity?* and to threaten the Executive with an appeal to the people? What must the world think of such conduct? and of the Government of the United States in submitting to it?" The Little Democrat ultimately managed to put to sea and escape, no doubt with the connivance of the subordinate authorities charged with the duty of preventing her, but greatly to the anger of the President. The result was, that Washington determined to get rid of the Citizen Genet, once and for ever; and instructions were sent to the American Minister at Paris, courteously asking the French Government to recall M. Genet, and appoint some more acceptable person in his place. The request was agreed to, but not before Washington and his Cabinet had resolved, in case of refusal, to supersede Genet's functions, to deprive him of his privileges, arrest his person, and ship him off to his native country. Luckily his supersedure by his own

Government was received just in time to prevent recourse to this extreme measure.

Nor was the Federal Government much happier in its relations with Great Britain than with France. It is always the fortune of great Powers who are neutral in great wars to offend both belligerents, and to be accused of an injurious want of sympathy, if no more flagrant offence can be surmised or invented against them. Washington was too wise and prudent a man to willingly give Great Britain the slightest cause of just complaint; and though the privateer question, and the energy with which the British Government made captures of the privateers under French colours that were fitted out from American ports, brought matters to the extreme of irritation throughout the United States, Washington defied unpopularity in his attempt, happily successful, to do right—alike to France, the old ally, and to Great Britain, the ancient opponent, of the United States. Though his military and political character were both attacked—and it was declared that he was neither a soldier nor a statesman—he held on the even tenor of his way, supported by his Cabinet,—not unpained by the gross ingratitude of his countrymen, but allowing no signs of his anger and disappointment to publicly escape him.

The domestic matter that troubled his administration almost as much as Citizen Genet's insolence and the difficulties with Great Britain, was a popular insurrection in Pennsylvania that was known as "The Whisky Rebellion," and at one time assumed very formidable dimensions. It was said of the English by Lord Castlereagh, that they had an ignorant impatience of taxation; and the same charge might have been brought with equal truth against the Americans in the earlier stages of their national independence. An excise duty upon alcoholic liquors which had been rendered necessary for the maintenance of public credit, was highly obnoxious to the people, both for its novelty and its directness, and excited such particular animosity in the west of the great State of Pennsylvania, that it was found impossible to collect the revenue. The Excise officers were opposed in the execution of their duty by bands of armed men. The militia called out to oppose these predatory gangs were overpowered by superior force, and the agitation rose to such a height that the Whisky rebels at last found themselves to be 7000 strong.

Washington was annoyed and indignant. "If the laws," he said, "are thus to be trampled upon with impunity, and a minority (and a small

one too) is to dictate to the majority, there is
an end put at one stroke to Republican Governments." On the 7th of August 1794 he issued
a proclamation warning the insurgents to disperse,
and declaring that if tranquillity were not restored
within three weeks next ensuing, an adequate military force would be employed to compel submis-
sion to the law. And to prove that he meant no
idle threats, he made requisitions on the governors
of the four contumacious States to provide an
army of 12,000—afterwards augmented to 15,000
—men, for the restoration of order. The insurgents
were slow to be convinced; and ultimately, in October, Washington took the command of the army, and
marched into Western Pennsylvania.

. The leaders of the insurrection had possibly
failed to convince themselves that Washington was
in earnest. At last convinced of their mistake, they
surrendered without striking a blow, and craved the
clemency of the Government. After due time and
the imprisonment of some of the chief instigators
—who, however, were not subjected to any severer
punishment—the troops were withdrawn; and the
Whisky Rebellion, that at one time threatened to
spread to other parts of the Union, became a thing
of the past and a portion of American history.

It was happily suppressed without effusion of blood, which it might not have been had the President been less prompt, less vigorous, and less determined to perform his duty, however unpopular.

As Washington's second term drew towards its close, a desire for his re-election was again expressed. But it met with little support, as it was well known to Washington's friends that his resolution to retire into private life was final, imperative, and irrevocable. He had often said, with evident truth and fervency, that he had had but one regret in having allowed himself to be put in nomination a second time, and that that regret had endured during the whole four years, and would last him to the end of his life. Under these circumstances, other candidates were selected, and the ultimate choice fell upon John Adams for President, and Thomas Jefferson for Vice-President.

Washington employed such scanty leisure as the cares of State and the superior attractions of his farm allowed him, in drawing up an elaborate Farewell to his countrymen,—a legacy of wisdom to succeeding ages. He warned the people of the danger of disunion, of the impolicy of mingling in the disputes of Europe, and pointed out for their avoidance the growth of sectional

jealousy and animosity among them, as if, though he
mentioned no word of slavery, the sunset of life
had given him the " mystical lore " to see the coming event which, sixty-six years afterwards, deluged
his native Virginia in blood.   The whole document
is pervaded by a melancholy spirit, as if he all but
despaired of the successful establishment of a
Republican Government; but it sank deep into the
hearts of the succeeding generations, and did the
good service to the nation which it was intended
to perform.

Such a man as Washington could not be allowed
to retire from public life without proper manifestations of grateful respect and good wishes from both
Houses of Congress, and from all the public bodies
of the Union.   " May your own virtue," said the
address of the House of Representatives, " and a
nation's prayers obtain the happiest sunshine for the
decline of your days, and the choicest of future
blessings.   For our country's sake, and for the sake
of republican liberty, it is our earnest wish that
your example may be the pride of your successors,
and thus, after being the ornament and safeguard
of the present age, become the patrimony of our
descendants."   There was but one dissentient—a
Mr Giles from Virginia, who declared that he did

not regret the President's retirement; that he could not conscientiously eulogise either his wisdom or his firmness, inasmuch as, in his opinion, the President's want of both of these qualities had conducted the foreign affairs of the nation to a calamitous crisis, not yet at an end. Mr Giles had his say to himself, though there were not wanting newspapers, both in the North and the South, which re-echoed and approved his sentiments.

Washington did not live long to enjoy his well-earned repose. For nearly two years he was as happy as he desired, and in his own way. He superintended his farm and estates, planned and executed improvements, superintended his domestic affairs, and looked after the interest and career of Mrs Washington's children and grandchildren—he had no family of his own—and of his numerous nephews and nieces. He was even called upon to leave his retirement to take the nominal command of the army of the United States, in view of an approaching rupture with Great Britain, which was happily averted.

On the 12th of December 1799, he unfortunately caught cold in a storm of mingled snow, rain, and hail, to which he was exposed when riding around his farm. He refused on his return home to change his clothes, treating the exposure as a thing of no account, against which he had been well protected by his greatcoat. He was seized with bronchitis during the night, and on the following morning, by his own desire, before the doctor who had been summoned had arrived, he was bled in the arm by the overseer of his estate. Three physicians were called in, and more bleeding was resorted to ; and the result of the ill-advised phlebotomy was the death of the patient on the third day, not from his malady, but from his doctors. His last words were, " 'Tis well !"

The grief of the nation was great and sincere. The voice of cavil and detraction was hushed upon his grave ; and the United States, for the first time, and possibly for the last, were of one mind as regards the merits and services of a great American citizen.

By his will Washington gave freedom to his slaves. As a statesman and a philosopher, and to some extent a philanthropist, he had long been of opinion that slavery was wrong. He wrote in 1786, thirteen years before his death, to his friend Mr J. F. Mercer, that he never would purchase another slave,—" it being among my first wishes," he said, " to see some plan adopted by which slavery may be abolished by law." In 1797 he wrote to his nephew : " I wish from my soul that the Legislature of this State [Virginia] could see the policy of a gradual abolition of slavery. It might prevent much future mischief." The words were prophetic, though it will not fail to be remarked by all impartial students of American history, especially of that tremendous chapter of it which records the great Civil War under President Lincoln, that Washington never admitted or hinted that any right to deal with the difficult question was inherent in the Federal Government. It was for Virginia, as for any other State, to deal with it at its pleasure. The United States had no control or jurisdiction.

The world has done ample justice to the character of Washington. His own countrymen, after death had put its solemn seal upon his career and services, did him more than justice, and all but idolised his memory. He was not great in the highest sense of the word. He was not brilliant. He was not even successful, except by aids which he could not have anticipated, and which it would have been better for the self-love of his country if he had never accepted. He wore out evil fortune mainly by the incapability, which he shared with the English, from whom he sprang, of never knowing when he was beaten, and by the dogged pertinacity and perseverance which are characteristics of the race. He was essentially a good man; and though subject to occasional fits of violence, was cautious, prudent, just, honourable, unwearied in the pursuit of the right, and inflexible in his adherence to it when discovered. He was a man of his age—a little in advance of it, perhaps, but never so much in advance of it as to incur the reproach of being rash, impracticable, or utopian. Living, he attracted but little love—as little as Aristides the Just; but dead, he commanded the admiration of Europe and the affectionate veneration of America, as one " who was first in war, first in peace, and first in the hearts of his countrymen."

JOHN ADAMS.

JOHN ADAMS, when elected to the Vice-Presidency in 1788, was past the prime of life; and eight years afterwards, when the suffrages of his countrymen placed him in the chair of Washington, he had almost completed the mystic multiple of seven times nine, the "grand climacteric." His career was very different from that of his predecessor. It was the fortune of the one to win his laurels at home, under the eyes of his countrymen; that of the other, to establish his reputation by diplomatic services abroad. The one was a man of the sword, the other of the pen. The talents of Washington were not brilliantly developed until his later manhood. The genius of Adams shone forth in his early youth. When Washington, at twenty-three, was a subordinate in the service of Great Britain—never dreaming that the time could possibly come when he should rebel against his sovereign — Adams, at twenty, when there was no ill-feeling between the Colonies and the mother-country, and no grievance large enough to form the subject of complaint, was looking far into the future, and beholding events invisible to other eyes.   In a letter, still preserved, addressed to his friend Nathan Webb, written when he was at college, he predicted that the French would be expelled from the American continent; that the Colonies would assert their independence; that they would become a great naval Power, able to contest the supremacy of the seas; that the force of all Europe combined could not prevail against them; and that in less than a century the population would exceed that of Great Britain.   The prophecy would have been remarkable if uttered by a grey-headed philosopher who had passed a long life in the study of men and history; but coming sharp and well-defined from the brain of a boy, it was little short of marvellous.

John Adams was a descendant of one of the early Puritans who first colonised New England, and was born at Quincy, in the township of Braintree, in Massachusetts, on the 19th of October 1735.   His father was a man in good circumstances; and the boy exhibiting at a very early age a strong love of reading, and a readiness for the acquisition of knowledge, it was determined to give him the best education which America could afford. It was evident to all who watched his early years that he was quite able to educate himself, even had there been none to usher him through the gates of the great temple of knowledge.

He received his first instruction in the rudiments of classical literature from Mr Marsh, of Braintree, a gentleman who, in an after-time, had the good fortune to train the early years of two of the most distinguished statesmen whom the United States ever produced,—Daniel Webster, the most eloquent of Americans ; and the late Josiah Quincy of Boston.

John Adams was admitted a student of Harvard College in 1755, and graduated with distinction four years afterwards. It was then, as it is now, the practice of the young men of America who aspire to take part in political life, to choose the law as their profession. John Adams, like others, saw that the law was the great avenue to distinction, and was admitted to the Bar in 1758. He immediately commenced practice in Braintree, and early secured a fair share of business. But Braintree was too narrow a field for his ambition ; and after playing the part of rural attorney and advocate for

K

eight years, he removed into Boston——at that time
the principal port of the Colonies.

The change was for his advantage : business
flowed in upon him; and he rapidly became, by
all but universal consent, the leading man in his
profession. During his first year's residence, he
published anonymously in the 'Boston Gazette'
a series of papers, in which he exposed the
oppressive character of the canon and feudal
laws. These papers were afterwards republished
in London — a rare compliment, at the time, to
an American author. In the same year, when
the smouldering discontent of the colonists first
broke out into a blaze, under the operation of
the obnoxious Stamp Act, Adams, as was to have
been expected from a man who had so early foreseen the future independence of the Colonies, did
not hesitate to throw himself, heart and soul, into
the movement. He soon became conspicuous among
his people for the vigour with which, by voice and
pen, he denounced the conduct of the British
Ministry in its attempt to tax the Americans without their consent. "The proper time," said Lord
North in England, "to exert our right of taxation,
is when the right is denied. To temporise is to
yield; and the authority of the mother - country,

if it is now unsupported, will have to be relinquished for ever. A total repeal [of the Stamp Act] cannot be thought of until America is prostrate at our feet."

On the very day in which the ill-judged measure thus ominously supported was passed by the British Parliament, a fatal riot took place in Boston, of which the results very greatly exasperated the pre-existent ill-feeling. The populace of the city insulted a portion of the British garrison while under arms in the streets; the soldiers resented; and a general scene of confusion ensued. The first rioters were put to flight, pursued by the military; the alarm-bell was rung; a large crowd gathered around the Custom-House, threatening to burn it to the ground, and pelted with stones and brickbats the troops employed to protect it. Before the tumult could be quelled, the soldiers had found it necessary for their own protection to fire into the crowd. Four persons were killed and several wounded. This unfortunate occurrence received the magniloquent name of the Boston Massacre, and excited much unreasonable and unjust indignation against the military, who had not only acted in self-defence under circumstances of cruel provocation, but in strict execution of their duty. The public anger, however, was so great, that in order to allay the excitement, or turn it into a safer channel, the authorities of Massachusetts directed the prosecution for wilful murder of the officers in command of the British troops.

Looking around for the highest legal talent in the colony to undertake their defence, the inculpated gentlemen fixed at once upon Mr Adams. The lawyer and the politician had different interests in the question, and Mr Adams took time to consider. The lawyer triumphed, and, at the obvious risk of his popularity, he undertook the defence. His zeal, his eloquence, his abilities, and his learning were not able to procure the acquittal of his clients; but he succeeded in persuading the jury that the offence was of no deeper dye than manslaughter. This verdict, though it fell short of expectation, had the anticipated effect. It allayed the public excitement, which gradually cooled down, or fed itself upon the other aliments which were only too abundant at the time. The legal profession justified the conduct of Mr Adams; and his fellow-citizens speedily forgot the circumstances, or only remembered them to approve the courage of an advocate who would not permit his political convictions to interfere with his professional honour.

In the year 1773 he was nominated by the House of Assembly as a member of the Council of State for the colony; but the British Governor, Mr Hutchinson, put his veto upon the appointment. He was again nominated in 1774, with the like result, from the adverse action of the new Governor, General Gage. But a higher office, over which British Governors had no authority, was conferred upon him by his fellow-citizens. He was one of five gentlemen selected by Massachusetts to represent its interests and wishes at the General Congress of the thirteen colonies, which met at Philadelphia on the 26th of October. The assembling of this great historical body was the virtual commencement of the revolution that established, after long struggles, the independence of America. Mr Adams played a prominent part in all its deliberations, and became conspicuous for the audacity with which he braved all the power of the British Government to coerce the Americans.

In 1775, when in his fortieth year, and in full and lucrative practice at the Bar, he was offered the Chief-Justiceship of his native colony. This office he felt bound to decline, chiefly, if not solely, upon the ground that the proper execution of its duties would have rendered necessary his withdrawal from political life—a sacrifice which he did not feel himself strong enough to incur. In this Congress Mr Adams made the acquaintance and friendship of many eminent men, struggling, like himself, in the great cause which he had at heart, and who, like himself, in after-years became Presidents of the Republic. The proceedings of this Congress excited marked attention in England; and the great Lord Chatham, to whose eloquent support and sympathy American liberty owed more than the Americans have ever yet acknowledged, declared that, although he had studied and admired the history of the free States of antiquity,—the master States of the world, —yet he had never seen surpassed the solidity of reasoning, the force of sagacity, and the wisdom of conclusion displayed by this illustrious body.

In 1776 matters had reached such a crisis that the Colonies convinced themselves that the time had come for the declaration of their independence. It fell to the lot of the second Congress, of which, as of the first, Mr Adams was a distinguished member, to take this irrevocable step. To Mr Lee, of Virginia, was assigned the honour of proposing, and to Mr Adams, of Massachusetts, of seconding, this momentous resolution. To five members—Mr John Adams, Dr Benjamin Franklin, Mr Roger Sherman,

Mr R. R. Livingston, and lastly, Mr Thomas Jefferson, a greater in peace than Washington was in war—was confided the task of drawing up the document which was to declare to Americans, to Europe, to the world, and to present and all future time, the reasons which had induced the Colonies to throw off their allegiance, to sever the ties of consanguinity and friendship, and to take their place as free and independent States in the great comity of Christendom. Some of the merit of suggestion in this memorable State paper is doubtless due to Adams, Franklin, and other members of the Committee; but it was essentially, when it appeared before the world, the work of the master-mind of Thomas Jefferson. His impress and superscription were visibly upon it; his purpose and phraseology pervaded it; and it received from his hands the most minute, careful, and anxious revision in its every word and sentence. The debates in Congress on this great subject were secret and unreported; but the fact is recorded, on the authority of Jefferson, who never bestowed unmerited praise, that Adams was "the Colossus of the debates.

Adams himself, in after-life, was neither so generous nor so just as Jefferson in appreciation of the merits of a great fellow-labourer. He declared that there was not a single new or unhackneyed idea in the Declaration of Independence; that the substance of it was contained in the Declaration of Rights and in the Journals of Congress of the year 1774; and that the essence of the whole document was contained in a pamphlet by James Otis of Boston, and printed at the expense of that city, before the Congress assembled.

Against this charge the good-natured Jefferson defended himself without bitterness — denied that he had ever seen Otis's pamphlet, and admitting the want of novelty in the arguments, many of which were to be found in Locke's Essay on Government, and were as old as Greece and Rome, declared that he had considered it no part of his duty to invent new ideas, and to bring forward no sentiment or argument which had ever been used before. But the charge of Adams was an after-thought; for while the document was under the consideration of Congress, where it met with very formidable opposition from an able and compact minority, he was constantly on his feet, warding off attacks, disposing contemptuously of unimportant criticisms, defending the document as a whole and in all its parts, and doing battle for it, as was said at the time, like a wild animal fighting for its young. He originally made an objection himself to the word "tyranny," as applied to the conduct of George III., contending that this was to make the King personally responsible for the acts of his Ministry; but he waived it in deference to the opinion of Jefferson, and the obnoxious charge was not only retained, but several times reiterated. Jefferson, in defending himself against an imputation which sprang from the ill temper rather than from the convictions of Adams, made no greater accusation against his crotchety friend than that of deficient memory, adding, "This, however, I will say for Mr Adams, that he supported the Declaration with zeal and ability, fighting fearlessly for every word of it."

Though his speeches have not been preserved, the tradition of Congress was, that he spoke fearlessly and well, and fully merited the magnanimous praise of Jefferson. His most celebrated speech was one delivered on the last day of the discussions on the Declaration of Independence, of which the heads and the principal passages were preserved, and has come down to posterity, perhaps not exactly as he spoke it, but as it emerged in an after-time from the alembic of the mind of Daniel Webster, just as the speeches of the early days of parliamentary reporting in England emerged from the mind of the great Dr Johnson.

"Sink or swim, live or die, survive or perish," he said, "I give my hand and my heart to this vote. It is true, indeed, that in the beginning we aimed not at independence. But there's a Divinity which shapes our ends. The injustice of England has driven us to arms; and, blinded to her own interest for our good, she has obstinately persisted, till independence is now within our grasp. We have but to reach forth to it, and it is ours. Why, then, should we defer the Declaration? Is any man so weak as now to hope for a reconciliation with England, which shall leave either safety to the country and its liberties, or safety to his own life and his own honour? Are not you, sir, who sit in that chair—is not he, our venerable colleague near you,—are you not both already the proscribed and predestined objects of punishment and of vengeance? Cut off from all hope of royal clemency, what are you, what can you be, while the power of England remains, but outlaws? If we postpone independence, do we mean to carry on or to give up the war? Do we mean to submit to the measures of Parliament, Boston Port Bill and all? Do we mean to submit and consent that we ourselves shall be ground to powder, and our country and its rights trodden down in the dust? I know we do not mean to submit. We never shall submit. Do we intend to violate that most solemn obligation ever entered into by men—that plighting, before God, of our sacred honour to Washington, when, putting him forth to incur the dangers of war, as well as the political hazards of the time, we promised to adhere to him, in every extremity, with our fortunes and our lives?

"I know there is not a man here who would not rather see a general conflagration sweep over the land, or an earthquake sink it, than allow one jot or tittle of that plighted faith to fall to the ground. For myself, having, twelve months ago, in this place, moved that George Washington be appointed commander of the forces raised, or to be raised, for defence of American liberty, may my right hand forget her cunning, and my tongue cleave to the roof of my mouth, if I hesitate or waver in the support I give him. The war, then, must go on. We must fight it through. And if the war must go on, why put off longer the Declaration of Independence? That measure will strengthen us. It will give us character abroad. The nations will then treat with us, which they can never do while we acknowledge ourselves subjects in arms against our sovereign. Nay, I maintain that England herself will sooner treat for peace with us on the footing of independence, than consent, by repealing her Acts, to acknowledge that her whole conduct towards us has been a course of injustice and oppression."

The uncertain temper and dictatorial moods of Adams, added to the fact that he was a "Yankee" and Puritan, rendered him unpopular in Congress among the delegates from the Southern States. He admits in his Autobiography that he was regarded with suspicion by the wealthy and conservative classes, both in and out of Congress—though he had not sufficient self-knowledge to be aware, or sufficient candour to admit, that his self-assertion was too aggressive, and his propensity to quarrel about trifles too strong, to render him a beloved friend, a comfortable colleague, or even an agreeable companion. But he was a born orator, and spoke the sentiments of the great bulk of his countrymen; and as such, he naturally became a power in the new State, and acquired the respect, if not the admiration, of his contemporaries.

Within three months after the Declaration of Independence, Congress appointed foreign commissioners to several of the European States. Benjamin Franklin, Thomas Jefferson, and Giles Deane were nominated as commissioners to France, to negotiate treaties of alliance and commerce. Jefferson declined the mission.

The practice of Adams at the Boston Bar had somewhat diminished in consequence of the great amount of time which he had devoted to public business; and when, in 1777, he was offered the post of commissioner to Paris which Jefferson had refused, he willingly accepted the offer and its emoluments. He had been married for about twelve years to a lady of the Scriptural name of Abigail—a strong-minded person of puritanical stock, and of considerable literary ability. His eldest son, John Quincy, who lived to be President of the United States, and who was at this time in his eleventh year, accompanied him to Paris. They remained until June 1779, when they returned to America. Mr Adams was shortly afterwards appointed Minister Plenipotentiary to Great Britain—though it was very doubtful if the British Government would consent to receive him — to negotiate, if possible, a treaty of peace and commerce. He once more set out for Paris in a French frigate, accompanied by his wife and young John Quincy. No satisfactory progress having been made on the long and weary road which was to lead at last to the recognition of American independence by Great Britain, and finding in consequence nothing to do in France, and no probability of being listened to by, or even tolerated in, England, Adams applied for another mission, and was accordingly accredited to the Hague, where he arrived in July 1780.

Here he remained for upwards of two years, acting as financial agent of the United States for the whole of Europe, having a general authority from Congress to borrow on American credit whatever sums might be requisite for the support of his own and other missions, and for all ordinary and necessary expenses, as well as for the payment of interest due in Europe on the public debt. Towards the end of 1782 he was ordered to proceed to Paris, to co-operate with Dr Franklin and the other commissioners in the negotiations for peace with the mother - country. The weariness of the British people with the war, the growing strength of the Opposition in Parliament, and finally, the surrender of Cornwallis at Yorktown, all betokened that the end so long pursued in America was close at hand. A treaty of peace between France and Great Britain was signed at Paris, and the independence of the

United States was formally acknowledged in 1783. John Adams, glad of the opportunity to visit the home of his ancestors, passed over into England, where he remained for several months, a careful student of the public and private life of the people. He held at this time no official appointment in England, for he was still nominally Minister to the Netherlands.

On the 7th of May Congress resolved that a Minister Plenipotentiary should be appointed to act in conjunction with Mr Adams at the Hague, and Dr Franklin in Paris, in negotiating treaties of commerce with foreign nations. The appointment was offered to Mr Jefferson, and accepted; and the two friends—for such they had remained, lukewarmly perhaps on the side of Adams, as befitted his temperament and training; cordially on that of Jefferson, as befitted his more genial nature—were destined to meet after a long separation, and to renew their early intimacy. Immediately on arrival at Paris, the new Minister called upon Dr Franklin; and the colleagues despatched a joint note to Mr Adams, to summon him to their deliberations. Their stay in the French capital was more agreeable to Jefferson than to Adams: the former was French in his ideas and sympathies; while Adams, with his puritanic notions, and with the general bent of his mind, felt himself more at home among the English.

The progress of the negotiations was slow. The Count de Vergennes, on the part of France, thought it advisable to leave the matter to the course of legislative action in both countries. The King of Prussia was more willing, and agreed to the basis of a treaty, which was in due time concluded; while Denmark and the Netherlands listened favourably to the proposals. In the meanwhile Dr Franklin, who had grown old and infirm, obtained the long-sought permission to return home, and Mr Jefferson was appointed sole Minister in his place. In February 1785, Mr Adams received a similar commission to the Court of St James's, and left France in May to enter upon the fulfilment of new and more congenial duties. On the 2d of June he was presented to King George III. He appears to have been well satisfied with his reception, for he wrote home to Mr Jay, the Secretary of State, that " the King, in his opinion, was the most accomplished courtier in his dominions, and possessed all the affability of Charles II., with all the domestic virtues of Charles I." But this was when the novelty was most novel, and before its first fresh gloss had been worn off by usage and familiarity;

for at a later period of the same year, and after he had been six months in London, he again wrote to Mr Jay : "So much of the King's time is consumed in small-talk, that he is in all the affairs of society and government as weak, as far as I can judge, as we always understood him to be in America. He is also as obstinate as [the devil]. He has a pleasure in his own will and way, without which he would be miserable. He has an habitual contempt of patriots and patriotism, and takes a delight in mortifying all who have any reputation for such qualities." Perhaps the King agreed with the great lexicographer Dr Johnson, that "patriotism was the last resource of a scoundrel."

Jefferson was not so favourably impressed by the King as Adams had been on his first visit. Having settled with his colleague on a summary form of a commercial treaty to be offered to Great Britain, he came over from Paris to London for the purpose of presenting it to the Marquis of Carmarthen, the then Foreign Secretary. Both Ministers attended the royal levee, and were presented to the King and Queen. Jefferson has left upon record that nothing could be more ungracious than their notice of Mr Adams and himself, and that the King turned his back upon both of them. The Marquis

L

of Carmarthen was equally cold and distant, and confirmed Jefferson in the belief that the King and the Government looked upon them and their mission with equal aversion. Adams, whose vanity was at times wholly irrepressible, went still further, and entered in his diary, *apropos* of a great ball at the French ambassador's, at which he met many political and fashionable celebrities, his conviction that he was wholly out of place among them. The Marquis of Lansdowne and the Earl of Harcourt entered into affable conversation with him; but as regards the rest, there was an awkward timidity, which he accounted for in a manner very gratifying to his sense of his own importance. "*These people*," he wrote, "*cannot look me in the face. There is conscious guilt and shame in their countenances when they look at me. They feel that they have behaved ill, and that I am sensible of it.*" Mr Adams is represented at this time as a fat, podgy man, about the medium height, with a bald head, and a fussy, consequential manner; and it is just possible that the expression on the faces of the English lords and ladies, which he interpreted into a sense of shame, was nothing but a sense of the ludicrous, or a painful struggle to avoid laughing.

While Mr Jefferson was in England, he and Mr

Adams visited Stratford-upon-Avon and other places
of note. At Stratford-upon-Avon, each of the two
Ministers " cut a chip, *according to custom*, from
Shakespeare's chair "; and Adams entered in his
diary the not very brilliant idea that " Painting and
Sculpture would be thrown away upon Shakespeare's
fame." At Worcester he turned aside to visit the
famous battle-field, and became unusually excited
by standing on such " holy ground." The people
in the neighbourhood appeared so " ignorant and
careless," that he was provoked to make a set
speech to them of the purest " buncombe." " Do
Englishmen," he asked, indignantly, " so soon forget
the ground where liberty was fought for ? Tell
your neighbours and your children that this is holy
ground,—much holier than that on which your
churches stand. All England should come on a
pilgrimage to this hill once a-year." Adams
thought his speech a very appropriate one, and
records that " the rustics " were much pleased with
it. Possibly they were much amused—as Jefferson,
who was present, cannot but have been, though, like
a wise man, he said nothing.

The diplomatic duties of his various foreign
missions were not very onerous, and made no large
demands upon the time and attention of the

Minister. To occupy a leisure that to a man of his literary tastes would have been intolerable, he wrote an elaborate ' Defence of the Constitution and Government of the United States,' which was published in three volumes in 1787. During his residence in England he remodelled this work, which, with many additions, omissions, and emendations, was republished in 1794, under the title of 'A History of the Principal Republics of the World.' This work was designed to prove, by ample induction from ancient and modern history, that the great safety of the American Republic lay in strict adherence to Federalism and centralisation of power, as opposed to the decentralising action of State rights. In these opinions he was diametrically opposed to Jefferson, and laid himself open to, and speedily incurred, the charge of monarchism.

When it was known in America that General Washington was willing to serve his country in peace as well as in war, and that he would not only accept the office of President if elected, but that his election would in all probability be unanimous, there was, though so early in the history of the United States, so much jealousy between North and South, that it was thought advisable to associate a Northern Vice-President with a Southern President.

The idea recommended itself to all moderate men; and although the South chafed somewhat at the compulsion of conferring office upon a "Yankee," the name of Mr Adams grew into favour, and he was ultimately adopted as the national candidate. Thirteen years earlier, when the revolt of the Colonies was at fever-heat, this sectional antagonism had not betrayed itself; and the fervent orator, Patrick Henry of Virginia, declared that all America was thrown into one mass, and that the distinction between Virginians, Pennsylvanians, New Yorkers, and New Englanders had ceased to exist. "I," he exclaimed, "am not a Virginian, but an American!" But this feeling was not permanent, and in the year of the Declaration of Independence, in view of the violent passions excited by the discordant interests, real or supposed, of the two great divisions of the Confederacy, Mr Adams declared that "it required more serenity of temper, a deeper understanding, and more courage than fell to the lot of Marlborough, to ride on the whirlwind."

In 1787, when the Constitutional Convention assembled, the growing spirit of sectionalism had been largely developed, and the Southern jealousy of New England found frequent, and often violent, expression. "If the government is to be lasting,"

said Colonel Main of Virginia, " it must be founded
in the confidence and affection of the people, and
must be so constructed as to obtain these.   The
majority will be governed by their interests.   The
Southern States are in the minority in both Houses.
Is it to be expected that they will deliver themselves bound hand and foot to the Eastern [New
England] States, and enable them to exclaim, in the
words of Cromwell on a certain occasion, ' The Lord
hath delivered them into our hands ' ? "

Whatever jealousy of a similar kind might have
existed in the North and East, was suppressed out
of deference to General Washington, and the South
accepted the nomination of Mr Adams almost as
cordially as the North accepted that of Washington.
Adams was at his post in London when first informed
of the honour intended for him—an honour which
neither at that time, nor during the eight years that
he enjoyed it, he very highly appreciated.   He considered the position alike beneath his talents and
his services.   " My country," he wrote, " has in its
wisdom conferred upon me the most insignificant
office that ever the invention of man contrived or
his imagination conceived."   It had, however, one
chance of promotion and power — the succession
to the Presidency, should the President die during

his incumbency. This chance occurred thrice in American history, but never offered itself to John Adams.

But if he thought little of the Vice-Presidency, he thought much of the dignity of the Presidency, and would, if he could have had his own way, have surrounded it with much of the regal splendour to which he had been accustomed in England and France. In this respect the sympathies and prejudices of his countrymen did not go along with him, as was abundantly proved during the eight years' administration of Washington, when the comparatively modest state which he assumed drew down upon him the imputation of aristocratic, if not monarchical, display.

Mr Adams never reconciled his mind to the station that he consented to occupy — though he tolerated it in the anticipation, fully realised in due time, that it would serve as a stepping-stone to the higher office to which his ambition had always pointed. To occupy a mind naturally active, and to while away the tedium of a position in which, as he complained, he could neither do good nor evil, he commenced a second literary work, and wrote a series of " Discourses on Davila," which he published in Fenno's 'Gazette

of the United States.'   The work was an analysis
of Davila's History of the Civil Wars of France in
the sixteenth century, and its object was to warn
his countrymen by French example of the dangers
to be apprehended from powerful factions contending against each other in an ill-balanced form of
government.   The work was not a success.   Its
object was wholly mistaken ; and he was a second
time charged, principally in the South, with advocating monarchy, or labouring to prepare the way
for the establishment of an hereditary Presidency.
To counteract the anticipated evil effect of this
publication, Mr Jefferson and his friends, strong
for State rights as opposed to Federalism, republished Paine's 'Rights of Man,' and disseminated
it broadcast over the country.

The French Revolution of 1789 filled Jefferson
with delight, and Adams with dismay.   And when
events culminated in the execution of Louis XVI.
and Marie Antoinette, Adams wrote from Philadelphia to his wife Abigail at Braintree : " The
Queen of France is no more !   When will these
savages be satisfied with blood ?   No prospect of
peace in Europe ; therefore, none of internal harmony in America."   In the same letter he wrote
of Washington.   " His position," he said, " is highly

responsible and very distressing. The anti-Federalists and the Frenchified zealots have nothing now to do, that I can conceive of, but to ruin his character, destroy his peace, and injure his health. He supports all their attacks with firmness, and his health appears to be very good." It is evident, however, notwithstanding all the drawbacks to the comforts of, and all the annoyances which Washington experienced in, the Presidential chair, that Mr Adams would have been very well pleased to sit in it.

Though Washington, as President, took little interest in the two related questions of the slave-trade and of domestic slavery; and though Mr Adams, as Vice-President, could have had but little influence on either subject, even if disposed to exercise it,—these great matters, partially obscured by the superior importance of foreign politics, and the fiscal hardships resulting from the pressure of the public debts, were by no means left in abeyance. The Northern and Eastern States had the greatest objection and aversion to the African slave-trade, and a weaker objection to the existence of negro slavery in the South, but had a political far more than a philanthropic or Christian repugnance to either. The two questions were fully debated

in the Convention of 1787, and foreshadowed—
though none foresaw or could have imagined it
at the time—the disruption of seventy-four years
later. From the period of the adoption of the
amended Constitution until the outbreak of the
great Civil War, there was continual antagonism,
more or less violent, between the South and the
North,—not upon the slave-trade, for that was
abolished after a certain time by mutual and almost
unanimous consent, but upon the question of State
rights as opposed to Federalism or centralisation,
and upon that of negro slavery as opposed to the
rights of man. In these disputes the New England
States were for the most part the aggressors; and
both sections, whenever either felt itself damaged
or aggrieved by the pretensions of the other, raised
the cry of secession and disruption of the Union.

It became generally known in the autumn of
1796 that General Washington imperatively refused
to be put a third time in nomination. Mr Adams,
who had long made his calculations and perfected
his preparations for bringing his own claims before
his countrymen, began to work with all the vigour
demanded by the circumstances. The South was
in favour of Jefferson, New England was in favour
of Adams, and a large party in New York and the

Middle States inclined in the same direction, less from love of Adams than from a feeling, to use a common colloquialism, that "turn and turn about was fair-play," and that a Southern President having been in office for eight years, it was just as well and expedient that a Northern man should supply his place. The question at issue was not only between South and North, but between State rights and Federalism. Parties were too evenly balanced to give either of them a strong assurance of victory; but as there were many candidates in the field, there was the possibility of a party preponderating at the last moment, by the wasting or "scattering" of votes upon those who had no chances.

The Federalists or Northern party nominated John Adams for President, and Thomas Pinckney for Vice-President. The Republicans, as they were then called—or Democrats, as they are called now—nominated Thomas Jefferson and Aaron Burr. The other candidates were Samuel Adams, Oliver Ellsworth, John Jay, and George Clinton, and five others of less note. On the final declaration, the votes in the Electoral College stood,—for Mr Adams, 71; for Mr Jefferson, 60; for Mr Pinckney, 59; for Mr Burr, 30. Mr Adams received the entire vote of New England, as well as of New York, New

Jersey, and Delaware; one from Pennsylvania, seven from Maryland, and one each from Virginia and North Carolina. Mr Jefferson received the entire votes of South Carolina and Georgia, and of the two new States of Kentucky and Tennessee, that since the conclusion of the war had been admitted into the Union; fourteen from Pennsylvania, twenty from Virginia, four from Maryland, and eleven from South Carolina.

In consequence of these numbers, which no one had anticipated to fall as they had fallen, the two highest on the list were severally declared President and Vice-President. The demarcation between Northern and Southern politics was clearly defined. Though both were represented in the new Government, Federalism and the North were triumphant in the person of the President, and Republicanism and the South virtually defeated in the person of the Vice-President, who, though nominally the second person in the State, had no more power or influence over the policy of his superior than he could have exercised in his private capacity—and in all probability, not half as much.

Adams was exultant, Jefferson resigned. "As regards this office" (the Vice-Presidency), Jefferson wrote to his friend Madison, "it is the only one in the world about which I am unable to decide whether I would rather have it or not have it. . . . I can have no feelings which would revolt at a secondary position to Mr Adams. I am his junior in life, I was his junior in Congress, his junior in the diplomatic line, his junior lately in our civil government. . . . I agree with the Romans, that the general of to-day should be the soldier of to-morrow if necessary." Jefferson knew his own strength, made no complaints, and on this, as on every other occasion, resolved to bide his time.

On the 8th February 1797, the votes for President and Vice-President having been officially opened and declared in the presence of both Houses of Congress, it became the duty of the Vice-President, who *ex officio* acts as president or chairman of the Senate, to proclaim that John Adams (himself) and Thomas Jefferson had been duly elected President and Vice-President. The joy of Adams broke out irregularly in the form of a prayer that formed no portion of the official programme: "And may the Sovereign of the universe, the Ordainer of civil government on earth for the preservation of liberty, peace, and justice among men, enable them both to discharge the duties of those offices with conscientious diligence, punctuality, and perseverance."

On the 4th of March the new President and Vice-President took the oaths of office, in presence of the Senate and of the retiring President, who was under no obligation to attend the ceremony. In his inaugural address he eulogised the Constitution, and declared that when he first saw it in a foreign land, he approved of it as "better adapted to the genius, character, situation, and relations of this nation and country than any which had ever been proposed or suggested; that it was not then, nor had been since, any objection to it in his mind, that the Executive and Senate were not more permanent;" that he never had a thought of "promoting any alteration in it but such as the people themselves, in the course of their experience, should see and feel to be necessary or expedient." He asked, "What other form of government could so well deserve the esteem and love of the people?" What that was "essential, any more than mere ornament and decoration, could be added to this by robes and diamonds?" or whether "authority could be more amiable and respectable when it descended from accidents, or institutions established in remote antiquity, than when it sprang fresh from the hearts and judgments of an honest and enlightened people?"

He paid a warm tribute to the public services of his illustrious predecessor. He declared himself in favour of peace and a rigid neutrality between the belligerent powers of Europe, and expressed his "personal esteem for the French nation, formed in a residence of seven years chiefly among them, and a sincere desire to preserve the friendship which had been so much for the honour and interest of both nations."

This inaugural did not give unqualified satisfaction to the Federalists, by whom it was stigmatised as temporising, as a playing of fast and loose, and as a lure to catch the favour of his opponents. But Adams himself, on the day of its delivery, whatever might have been his feelings in an after-time, was delighted with it, and at the effect it produced, or seemed to have produced, on the assemblage. His mind was radiant with satisfaction, and with the sweet fulfilment of hopes that had been long deferred. "The leave-taking of Washington on this memorable occasion was affecting. There was," he wrote to his wife, " scarcely a dry eye but Washington's; and all agreed that, taken all together, it was the sublimest thing ever seen in America."

The popularity of Jefferson, so superior to his

own, was displeasing to Adams. Like a king, he desired to have no rival near his throne, and his first thought seems to have been how best to remove Jefferson from a too close intimacy with his councils. The relations between the United States and the French Republic were, and had for some time previously been, so unsatisfactory as to justify the prominent mention which had been made of them in the new President's inaugural address. Adams disliked the French, and hated their Revolution; Jefferson admired the people, and entirely approved the great events of 1789, and all which had sprung from them. Would it not be well that Mr Jefferson should accept a mission to Paris, in order, if possible, to bring about a better understanding between the two Republics? Mr Adams has left on record his own account of the transaction:—

"I sought and obtained an interview with Mr Jefferson. With this gentleman I had lived on terms of intimate friendship for five-and-twenty years, had acted with him in dangerous times and arduous conflicts, and always found him assiduous, laborious, and, as far as I could judge, upright and faithful. Though by this time I differed with him in opinion concerning the practicability and success of the French Revolution and some other points,

I had no reason to think that he differed materially from me with regard to our national Constitution. I did not think that the rumbling noise of party calumny ought to discourage me from consulting men whom I knew to be attached to the interest of the nation, and whose experience, genius, learning, and travels had eminently qualified them to give advice. I asked Mr Jefferson what he thought of another trip to Paris, and whether he thought the Constitution and the people would be willing to spare him for a short time.

" ' Are you determined to send to France ? '

" ' Yes.'

" ' That is right,' said Mr Jefferson ; ' but without considering whether the Constitution will allow it or not, I am so sick of residing in Europe that I believe I shall never go there again ! '

" I replied, ' I own I have strong doubts whether it would be legal to appoint you ; but I believe no man could do the business so well.' "

Jefferson has also left a record of this remarkable proposal :—

" The President found me alone in my room, and shutting the door himself, he said he was glad to find me alone, for that he wished a free conversation with me. He entered immediately on an

M

explanation of the situation of our affairs with
France, and the danger of rupture with that nation
—a rupture which would convulse the attachments
of this country; that he was impressed with the
necessity of an immediate mission to the Directory;
that it would have been the first wish of his heart
to have got me to go there, but that he supposed
it was out of the question, as it did not seem justi-
fiable for him to send away the person destined to
take his place in case of accident to himself, nor
decent to remove from competition one who was a
rival in the public favour."

Mr Adams had evidently his doubts, and would
as evidently have been highly gratified if it had
been in Mr Jefferson's power to remove them.   But
Mr Jefferson was too strict in his adherence, both
to the letter and spirit of the Constitution, even
had his personal feelings inclined him to the acceptance of the mission, to be lured from the line of
duty by the tempting offer.   Mr Adams no sooner
saw that his " friend " was inflexible, and that he
was right, than he, too, came round to Mr Jefferson's opinion, and found abundant reasons against
the appointment, which had so lately seemed good
in his eyes.   He had grand ideas of his own power
and dignity—ideas which he was very slow to

abandon. In his own mind he was a king *de facto*, though temporarily, and thought that the nomination of the second person in his realm as ambassador to a foreign nation would be much too great a compliment to bestow. He was the sun; and the moon (Jefferson) shone with a light which, though but the reflection of his own, was a light superior to any other in the Presidential heavens.

" If we wish not to be degraded in the eyes of foreign nations," he wrote to General Knox, " we must not degrade ourselves. What would have been thought in France if the King had sent Monsieur his eldest brother as an envoy ? What of the King of England, if he had sent the Prince of Wales ? Mr Jefferson is in essence in the same condition. He is the first prince in the country, and the heir-apparent to the sovereign authority *quoad hoc.*"

In a subsequent letter to Mr Gerry, he continued to harp upon the same magnificent string, glorifying the Vice-President through his superior luminary, the President. " I expected," he wrote, " that Mr Jefferson would refuse the mission. Indeed I made a great stretch, in proposing it, to accommodate the feelings, views, and prejudices of a party. I would not do it again, because, upon more mature reflection,

I am decidedly convinced of the impropriety of it.
. . . We cannot make foreign nations respect our
nation or its government if we place before their
eyes the persons, answering to the first princes of
the Government, in the low and subordinate character of a Foreign Minister. It must be a piti-
ful country, indeed, in which the second man of the
nation will accept of a place upon the footing with
the *corps diplomatique*, especially Envoy ' Such a one,'
Ambassador ' Such a one,' and Plenipotentiary ' Such
a one.' The nation must hold itself very cheap
that can choose a man one day to hold its second
office, and the next send him to Europe to dance
attendance at levees and drawing-rooms, among the
common major-generals, simple bishops, earls, and
barons, but especially among the common trash of
envoys, ambassadors, and ministers plenipotentiary!"

The vain man's head was turned by the fulness
of his new-blown majesty. When he was playing
second to the great Washington, he was a discontented nobody—not a prince at all, but the humble
occupant of the most insignificant office that the
wit of man ever devised. Circumstances were
altered. He who had been elected as second to the
great John Adams was like the heir-apparent of a
throne, and not to be confounded with such common

people as the aristocracy of Europe or the trash of the diplomatic service.

With these *quasi* regal notions influencing his conduct, it was not surprising that Mr Adams should endeavour to act a kingly part between contending parties in his realm. Forgetting that he was the elected President of a party, and that the party expected his allegiance, and the bestowal of office on his political friends, he attempted to be impartial, as a king should be, and to bestow his favours equally upon his friends and his opponents. The experiment was unsafe, and proved fatal to his reputation and his usefulness. Washington, like himself, was a Federalist; and though Washington's Cabinet was composed of somewhat incongruous materials, only kept in working harmony by their respect for Washington himself, Adams retained that Cabinet without possessing any portion of the power over the members which Washington had wielded. The result was foreseen, and the elements of disintegration in his councils soon manifested themselves. But foreign rather than domestic affairs were for the first few months of his Presidency sufficient to tax the utmost powers of his statesmanship. The war between Great Britain and France—at least that portion of it which was waged upon the ocean—was highly injurious to American commerce; and the United States, in endeavouring to carry out a policy of strict neutrality between the combatants, suffered the usual fate of neutrals in great wars, and displeased both parties. John Adams knew the power of Great Britain too well, and was at heart too sincere an admirer of the people and of their institutions, not to look upon another war with that country as the greatest of calamities, and not to desire its avoidance by every means consistent with honour. At the same time, he knew equally well that it would be a sore blow to the prestige of Republicanism if the two Republics, so recently established in the Old World and the New, were to be entangled in a war which a little patience and good feeling on both sides might prevent.

The difficulties with France had first arisen under Washington's administration. In November 1796, M. Adet, the French Minister, had addressed a letter to the American Secretary of State recapitulating various complaints against the Government of the United States, denouncing the *insidious* proclamation of neutrality and the wrongs growing out of it. He had, moreover, sent this letter to the newspapers, with the object, as Washington sup-

posed, of producing an effect on the approaching
Presidential election, and of favouring the candidature
of Mr Jefferson. Washington was never
ungrateful to the French Monarchy for the aid it
had given to American independence, but he owed
no gratitude to the French Republic, and was not
the man to yield to any insolent or unjust demands
which France or any other country might put forward.
"I have always," he said, "given it as my
decided opinion, that no nation had a right to intermeddle
in the internal concerns of any other; and
that if this country could, consistently with its
engagements, maintain a strict neutrality, and
thereby preserve peace, it was bound to do so, by
motives of policy, interest, and every other consideration
that ought to actuate a people situated as
we are, already deeply in debt, and in a convalescent
state from the struggle we have been engaged
in ourselves."

As Mr Munroe, the United States Minister, was
supposed to have misunderstood or failed to act
up to his instructions, he was recalled, and Mr
Pinckney appointed as his successor. Washington,
by this time, was out of office, and Mr Adams,
who inherited and approved his foreign policy,
learned that the French Directory had refused

to receive the new Minister, and ordered him to leave the country. The excitement in America was great, and rendered much more violent than it might have been by the systematic efforts of an anti-British and pro-Gallican party to provoke a war between what they called their "natural enemy" and the United States.

Under the circumstances, Mr Adams convened a special session of Congress. He addressed to the Senate on its assembling a very spirited speech, in which he designated the address of M. Barras, the President of the French Directory, as more offensive than the refusal to receive the American Minister, and studiously marked with indignities towards the Government of the United States. He complained of the French Directory for evincing an evident desire to separate the American people from their Government, to persuade them that they had different interests and affections. Such attempts, he said, ought to be repelled with a decision sufficient to convince France and the world that the Americans were not a degraded people, humiliated under "a colonial spirit of fear and sense of inferiority, and regardless of national honour and character." Though France was thus aggressive, he relied upon negotiations to prevent further evil; and in the meanwhile, in case of accident, he strongly recommended Congress to provide effectual means of defence, and for the vindication of the national honour. Washington, in his retirement at Mount Vernon, fully approved of the President's policy, and consented at a somewhat later time, as already recorded in our sketch of his life and career, to reassume, in view of the possible danger, the post of Commander-in-Chief—an acceptance which in itself, as Adams took pains to assure him, was worth the services of an additional army.

The storm blew over, and the United States avoided war both with France and Great Britain, —but not without leaving behind, in the excited passions of the pro-Gallican and the pro-Anglican parties, a feeling of bitterness against the well-meaning President, who had disappointed them both, and thought more of his country than of the factions that might have ruined it. The necessity of providing for a war that it might not have been possible to avert with honour, increased the domestic difficulties of the Administration. Fears of the creation of a standing army, and the powers that might be exercised by the President as its Commander-in-Chief, were everywhere excited; while the passage of Alien and Sedition Laws, and the prosecutions instituted under them, added fuel to the flame of discontent—which faction, as is its wont, took care to fan. It was chiefly, however, in the South, where Mr Adams had never been popular, and where the opposition to centralism was keenest, that these discontents were most general. Two eminent men did their best to turn the agitation to their own account, and had their reward on a future day by election to the Presidency.

In the Legislature of Virginia a series of resolutions were introduced declaratory of State rights, and condemnatory of the alien and sedition laws, as having the tendency and the intention of changing the character of the Government from a confederation of Free States into a unity of States and a national Government. These resolutions were drawn up by Mr Madison. In Kentucky similar resolutions were carried, and though not actually drawn up, were sketched and inspired by Mr Jefferson. These resolutions affirmed, far more distinctly than those of the Virginian Legislature had done, the separate rights of the States. They declared, " that whensoever the general Government assumes and delegates powers not expressly conferred upon it by the terms of the Union, its acts are unauthoritative, void, and of no force; that each

State acceded as a State, and is an integral party, its co-States forming as to itself the other party; that the Government created by this compact was not made the exclusive and final judge of the extent of the power delegated to it, since that would have made its discretion, and not the Constitution, the measure of its powers; that, as in all other cases of a compact among parties having no common judge, each party has an equal right to judge for itself, as well of the infractions as of the mode and measure of redress."

In these pregnant sentences lay the whole doctrine that was, in after-years, brought forward to vindicate the secession of the Southern States, and to justify those States in resisting by force of arms the attempt of the Northern and Western States to compel their return to a Union that had become repugnant, and which they judged to be disadvantageous.

The doctrine was not novel. It was warmly and pertinaciously asserted in all the debates on the Federal Constitution so early as 1787, before the first President had been elected, and was never abandoned, either in the South or the North, though suffered at times to rest unmentioned. Whenever a dispute more than usually violent arose between the sections, the weaker section threatened secession. The threat was always the proof that the party which had recourse to it was losing ground, and was always held as a rod *in terrorem* over the head of the dominant faction, to warn it not to push its advantages too far. During seventy-five years it was like the cry of "wolf" raised by the shepherd-boy in the fable, — a cry often reiterated, with the result that quiet people refused to believe in it. But the wolf came, nevertheless, and played more havoc in the fold, from 1861 to 1865, than the worst alarmists ever imagined to be possible.

Mr Ellsworth, in the debates on the Constitution, expressed the whole Southern idea when he said: " Under a national Government we should participate in the national security, but that was all. What he wanted was domestic happiness in his own States. The national Government could not descend to the local objects on which this depended. It could only embrace objects of a general nature. He turned his eyes, therefore, for the preservation of his rights to the State Government." So anxious was he that there should be no mistake on a subject that appeared so vital, that he moved the omission of the obnoxious word " national " from the Federal

Constitution; and it was struck out accordingly by unanimous consent.

It is in the nature of the puritanic mind to be aggressive—to be despotic—to sink or to swim! The old formula that the earth belongs to the saints; that we are the saints, and that therefore we must rule the earth,—was no idle doctrine in the hearts of the men who came over in the Mayflower to colonise New England. Neither did its force greatly diminish in the minds of their descendants, as Washington often painfully discovered during the long and weary years in which he fought the all but hopeless fight of Independence. The elation of the Federalists in having elected Mr Adams —a President, if not of their own stamp entirely, at least of their party and section—often betrayed itself in a manner that was highly disagreeable to the South.

In 1798, in the second year of Mr Adams's incumbency, Mr Jefferson complained, in a letter to John Taylor of Virginia, that the South "was completely under the saddle of Massachusetts and Connecticut, who rode it very hard, cruelly insulting its feelings, as well as exhausting its strength and substance. Their natural friends, the three other Eastern States, join them from a sort of family pride, and they have the art to divide certain other parts of the Union, so as to make use of them to govern the whole." Still the grievances were not so serious as to drive Mr Jefferson to approve, although he thought of secession as a remedy. His correspondent had hinted that Virginia and North Carolina might form a Confederacy of their own, and enjoy a separate existence. " Seeing," wrote Jefferson, " that we must have somebody to quarrel with, I would rather keep our New England associates for that purpose than see our bickerings transferred to others. They are circumstanced within such narrow limits, and their population is so full, that they will soon be in the minority; and they are marked, like the Jews, with such perversity of character, as to constitute, from this circumstance, the natural division of our parties."

Mr Adams was quite aware of the ill feeling. Speaking of the second Congress, he wrote: " I have found this Congress like the last. There is a strong jealousy of New England, and of Massachusetts in particular;" and in the life of Gouverneur Morris it is stated, " that during the administration of Mr Adams, Virginia was almost in open revolt against the national authority, merely because a Yankee, and not a Virginian, was President."

The objections of Jefferson and the great party which had made him Vice-President, and which hoped to make him President, were not wholly confined to the consolidation of power in the hands of the North, but to its consolidation in any hands whatever. " Our country," he wrote, at a time when the United States all lay on the Atlantic side of the Ohio, and did not cover a tithe of their present area, " is too large to have all its affairs directed by a single Government; and I verily believe that if the principle were to prevail of a common law being in force in the United States, it would become the most corrupt Government on the face of the earth. What an augmentation of the field for jobbing, speculating, plundering, office-building, and office-hunting would be produced by our assumption of all the State powers into the hands of the General Government!" Jefferson as well as Adams could look into the future. They were both political prophets, and the prophecies of both were abundantly fulfilled.

During the administration of Mr Adams, the seat of Government was at Philadelphia; but at a very early period after the adoption of the Constitution, it was resolved to transfer it to the new city, on the banks of the Potomac, which was named in honour of Washington.   This transfer was not effected without some difficulty and many intrigues; for New York, Baltimore, Annapolis, Philadelphia, and other cities, were candidates for the profitable honour of lodging the Executive and the Legislature.   There was a strong party in favour of Germantown, in Pennsylvania; and a bill fixing the seat of Government at that place was actually agreed upon by both Houses, but afterwards failed on account of an informal amendment, which proved fatal to it.   In June 1790, during the first Presidency of General Washington, an Act was finally passed for establishing the Federal capital on the river Potomac, at some place between the mouths of the eastern branch and the Connogocheaque.   The uncouth name of this little river excited much amusement, and the press of all the great cities teemed with jokes and squibs.   In one of them, a Philadelphian servant-girl represented her master's indignation at the proposed removal, and hopes that the representatives of the people

> " may die in a stall,
> If they leave us in debt for our Federal Hall ;
> In fact, he would rather saw timber or dig,
> Than see them removing to Connogocheaque,
> Where the houses and kitchens are yet to be framed,
> The trees to be felled, and the streets to be named."

Though Mr Adams took up his official residence in Washington,—that city of the grandest promise and, until lately, of the meanest performance,—and lived in it for a few months in woful discomfort, it was not until the last week of his Presidential tenure that Congress organised a Government, partly municipal, partly congressional, for the city and the neutral district of Columbia, half of which was ceded by the State of Maryland and half by that of Virginia, for the purpose. In the Federal capital the Federal law was supreme; and in this small territory, great in its pretensions and in its hopes of the future, the first real victory of nationalism against the co-operated Federalism of State Rights was first secured. Mrs Adams, who was a smart letter-writer, and fond of displaying her literary powers, wrote an account to her daughter in November 1800, a few months before her husband was reluctantly compelled to retire into private life, of her experiences in the embryo city, and the unfinished palace of the Presidents :—

" I arrived here on Sunday last, and without meeting any accident worth noticing, except losing ourselves when we left Baltimore, and going eight or nine miles on the Frederic Road, by which means we were obliged to go the other eight through the

N

woods, where we wandered two hours without finding a guide or the path.   Fortunately, a straggling
black came up with us, and we engaged him as a
guide to extricate us out of our difficulty; but woods
are all you see from Baltimore until you reach the
city, which is only so in name.   Here and there is
a small cot, without a glass window, interspersed
among the forests, through which you travel miles
without seeing any human being."

Her account of the President's official residence
is equally entertaining :—

"The house is upon a grand and superb scale,
requiring about thirty servants to attend and keep
the apartments in proper order, and perform the
ordinary business of the house and stables.   The
lighting the apartments, from the kitchen to parlours
and chambers, is a tax ; and the fires we are obliged
to keep, to secure us from daily agues, is another
cheering comfort !   If they will put me up some
bells (there is not one hung through the whole
house, and promises are all you can obtain !), and let
me have wood enough to keep fires, I design to be
pleased.   I could content myself almost anywhere
for three months; but, surrounded with forests, can
you believe that wood is not to be had, because
people cannot be found to cut and cart it ? . . ·

We have not the least fence, yard, or other convenience without; and the great unfinished audience-room I make a drying-room of, to hang up the clothes in."

Mr Adams, as became his superior dignity as a man and a philosopher, cared for none of these things. Provided he could but continue to be President, he would have been delighted with much inferior accommodation, or no accommodation at all.

During the last year of his administration, a young politician appeared in Kentucky, whose opinions for many years gave a bias to public affairs, and laid the basis of an agitation destined to convulse and almost to destroy the Union. This was Mr Henry Clay, who, in the Legislature of the new State, whence he had immigrated from his native Virginia, declared the deep hostility of a respectable minority to the institution of slavery, and his support of a proposition for its safe and gradual abolition. He did not propose to emancipate any living slaves, but to decree that all slaves born after a certain date should be free on arriving at a certain age, and that their masters in the interval should cause such education to be given to them as should fit them for the exercise of the duties of citizenship. Neither North nor South was quite ripe for the proposal; and the young statesman, destined to be great hereafter, incurred nothing but obloquy for his premature wisdom.

Mr Adams had always that high opinion of his own merits which justified him in his own mind for aspiring to re-election. But it was not to be. He met the fate of the impartial politician of whom the poet sang, who placed all his glory in moderation, and was consequently distrusted by both parties —accused of Toryism by the Whigs, and of Whiggism by the Tories. He was put in nomination at the usual time; and although the whole of the New England States condoned his offences and gave him their undivided vote, New York and nearly the whole South went against him, and the Democratic, anti-Federal, State Right, and Southern nominee, Mr Jefferson, was elected in his stead. Mr Adams did not take his defeat in good part; and his personal mortification was greatly increased by the public rejoicings that everywhere, except in New England, were the result of his opponent's triumph. It was not merely his own defeat — it was the crushing discomfiture of his party, and led to their exclusion from power, with but slight intervals, for more than half a century.

It was the leaning of Mr Adams towards Great

Britain, his aristocratic notions, and his supposed respect for monarchy as an institution, that impaired during his Presidency the popularity that he had won in his earlier years, when in the first Congress he had thundered in favour of the Declaration of Independence, and denounced the injustice of the mother-country. An unfortunate sentence in one of his public addresses, which stated that "he once had the honour of standing in the presence of the King of England," was made the most of by his enemies; and he never afterwards regained any large share of public favour beyond the bounds of his native State. Within those limits, however, he always maintained a high place in public estimation, and regained in retirement any portion of it which he may have lost when he was in power.

A recent biographer of Jefferson (Dr Randall) speaks of him as "glorious, delightful, honest John Adams! the American John Bull! the comic uncle of an exciting drama! Every playgoer knows well the fiery old gentleman who goes blustering about the stage, grasping his stick till it quivers, throwing the lovers into a terrible consternation, hurrying on the catastrophe which he is most solicitous to prevent, pluming himself most of all upon his sagacity, while he alone is blind to what is passing under his nose! Such is something like the impression left upon the minds of those familiar with the characters of this period, respecting the man who, as Franklin well said, was always honest, often great, and sometimes mad. Mr Adams, however," the same writer observes, "should not be wholly judged by his administration. None of the men of the Revolution came out of the storm and stress of that era quite unscathed. In the revolutionary period, this high-mettled game-cock appeared to glorious advantage, made a splendid show of fight, animated the patriotic heart, and gave irresistible impetus to the cause. But he was ludicrously unfitted to preside with dignity and success over a popular Government, which must do everything with an eye to its effect upon the people. His own Cabinet intrigued against him. They regarded Hamilton as their real chief; and Hamilton, far more than Adams, *was* the influencing mind of the Government. One who would understand and like John Adams must read his Diaries and Letters—which, of all the writings of that time, are the most human and entertaining."

Washington, who was not only desirous, but over-joyed, to retire from the fatigues and responsibilities of office, did his successor the honour to attend at his inauguration, and to be an actor in the pageant. Mr Adams was not magnanimous enough to forgive Mr Jefferson for his triumph. Still more, he was so uncourteous as to exhibit his displeasure and disappointment in the face of the world, by ostentatiously refusing to be present when his successor was sworn into office. He and Mrs Adams took leave of the White House and of the city in the early morning of the day of inauguration. So far from acting a part in the ceremony of his rival's exaltation, he would not even permit his eyes to behold it.

Mr Adams never returned to public life. He was in his sixty-sixth year; and if he could not be continued in the highest office, he would not, at that age, accept a lower position. He retired to his birthplace in Massachusetts; learned to forgive Mr Jefferson, with whom he renewed epistolary correspondence; and devoted his abundant leisure to the pursuits of literature, and mainly to the writing of his Autobiography—a book in which he did full justice to himself, and no injustice of any sensible amount to his coadjutors or his enemies. His life was prolonged far beyond the ordinary span; and for more than a quarter of a century after he had ceased to be President, he continued to be more or less of a power in the State, and one whose opinion and advice were sought by younger politicians. In the year 1813, when he was approaching his seventy-eighth year, Jefferson, who had reached threescore and ten, and had ceased to be President five years previously, wrote to his old predecessor to remind him that they were fast becoming the only survivors of the signers of the Declaration of Independence, and that " they, too, must go ere long." The friends—and to some extent foes during a transitory period—never again met; but their correspondence was both frequent and cordial on all the great political questions that every now and then surged up to trouble the thoughts of statesmen, and fill them with fears for the stability of the Union, on which so many hopes and such mighty interests were based.

The house of Mr Adams at Quincy was the resort of all the political and literary celebrities of New England, and sometimes of those of New York and Pennsylvania; but the Southern people seldom ventured so far North, and when they did venture, seldom found much congeniality of taste or sentiment among people whom they disliked as Puritans and " Yankees."

Mrs Adams took her full share, as became an

authoress of repute and a "strong-minded woman,"
in all the political and literary questions that interested her husband and his friends. One who
visited the couple in 1816, when Mr Adams was
eighty-two, has left a description of them. "Mr
Adams," he says, "shook as if palsied, but the mind
and the heart were evidently sound. His spirits
seemed as elastic as a boy's. He joked, laughed
heartily, and talked about everybody and everything with the most complete *abandon*. He seemed
to be a vast encyclopedia of written and unwritten
knowledge, which gushed out on every possible
topic, mingled with lively anecdotes and sallies of
wit."

The same visitor described Mrs Adams as "an
elderly and stately female. A cap of exquisite
lace surrounded features still exhibiting intellect
and energy, though they did not wear the appearance of ever having been beautiful. Her dress was
snowy white, and there was that immaculate neat-
ness in her appearance which gives to age almost
the sweetness of youth. With less warmth of
manner and sociableness than Mr Adams, she was
sufficiently gracious, and her occasional remarks
betrayed intellectual vigour and strong sense."

Mr Adams was accused during his Presidency of

wishing to render the office hereditary in his family. The charge had no other foundation than his admiration of constitutional liberty, with the power of Parliament at a maximum, and that of the sovereign at a minimum, as in Great Britain, which, more than the liberty of French or American republicanism, was the liberty of which his judgment approved. But though nothing which he did, or could have done, brought about the result which his enemies accused him of favouring, he lived to see his son elected to the Presidency, after the office had been filled with credit and efficiency by such great statesmen as Jefferson, Madison, and Monroe.

Mrs Adams died in 1818, and it was not until 1825 that this great honour devolved upon the family. Mr Adams was by this time close upon ninety, and no longer in the full possession of his bodily or mental faculties, so that the satisfaction wholly denied to the mother was partially denied to the father. He knew that his son had been elected to the Presidency; but his mind, as far as the world could discover, was not sufficiently clear to derive enjoyment from the new lustre thus shed upon the name.

The end was fast approaching. The 4th of July 1826 was the fiftieth anniversary of the Declaration of Independence. Adams and Jefferson were still alive—venerable but decrepit old men—the one in his ninety-first, the other in his eighty-third year. It had been resolved, some months previously, that the day should be celebrated all over the United States with more than ordinary rejoicings, and to this end it was determined that Mr Adams, Mr Jefferson, and all the other patriots then living who had signed the memorable document, should be invited by the Mayor of Washington to attend the celebration in the Federal city. Mr Jefferson was able, ten days before the great anniversary, to write a long and eloquent letter, expressive of his regret that the state of his health compelled him to decline the invitation. Mr Adams was all but unconscious—less from positive disease than from gradual decay—when the letter reached him.

The day was celebrated with all the noisy demonstrations of artillery and fireworks, all the shouts of the multitude, all the ringing of bells, all the flaunting of banners, all the declamation of frothy oratory, and all the soberer utterances of true patriotism, with which it always has been, and probably always will be, celebrated in America. But though none but the members of two families knew it at the time, it was celebrated in a manner which none could have anticipated—in a manner that was awful to the witnesses, and which, when afterwards made known to the public, sent a thrill of excitement through the country. On that day, amid the noise, the uproar, and the splendour of the jubilee, Adams and Jefferson both expired at their homes,—the one in Virginia, the other in Massachusetts.

Mr Adams in the morning was awakened from his usual comatose sleep by the merry peals of the bells. He had long been so unconscious of what passed around him, that he was asked, with but faint hopes of a coherent reply, if he knew what the bells were ringing for? A gleam of intelligence shot into his fading eyes as the question was repeated, and he answered faintly, "Oh yes! it is the 4th of July—the glorious Fourth!" He paused for a while, and added, "God bless it! God bless you all!" This was in the early morning, and he again sank into unconsciousness, until about noon, when he rallied and said, "It is a glorious day." There was again a pause, and he said, "Jefferson yet survives!" These were his last articulate words; and at six in the afternoon he calmly expired. At the time he spoke, Jefferson had gone

before him on the road appointed for all living, and
the old old man was the survivor by several hours
of his younger contemporary. Even in death it
seemed as if the old vanity, or self-appreciation,
whichever it may be most charitable to call it, had
gleamed through his mind : " Great will be the loss
when I depart ; but let my country be comforted,
—Jefferson still survives."

The city of Boston, proud of its distinguished
son, convened a public meeting in Faneuil Hall, on
the 2d of the following month, to commemorate the
services of the two departed patriots. The orator
of the day was Daniel Webster, who, being himself a native of Massachusetts, gave the palm of
precedence to the merits and virtues of his great
fellow-citizen. He rendered ample justice to Jefferson ; but as befitted the expectations of his
partial audience, he exalted Adams to still higher
rank among the great and good men whom his
country had produced. Death had thrown the
kindly veil of forgetfulness over the little foibles
and faults to which all who live are liable, and
had crowned his head with that aureole of saint-
ship which surrounds the virtues of the dead when
their virtues only survive in the popular memory,
and stand no more as impediments in the path of

the living. As far as the tribute to John Adams was involved, the oratory of Webster — greatest orator of his day—was not so much a commemoration as an apotheosis. "Alas!" he said, quoting his friend Josiah Quincy—who on the 4th of July delivered in the same hall the anniversary address—"when we were all hoping that the sound of a nation's joy rushing from our cities might yet break the silence of his aged ear, and that the rising blessings of grateful millions might yet visit with glad light his decaying vision, his vision was at that very moment closing for ever. Alas!" continued Mr Webster, "the silence which was then settling on that aged ear was an everlasting silence! For lo! in the very moment of our festivities, his freed spirit ascended to God who gave it. Human aid and human solace terminated at the grave, or we would gladly have borne him upwards on a nation's outspread hands, accompanied with the blessings and the prayers of millions."

Posterity—out of the boundaries of New England—has not wholly ratified the verdict, or placed the name and services of John Adams on the high pedestal where Mr Webster would have been content that they should remain for ever. All admit his abilities, his honesty, and his patriotism; but it is only Massachusetts that ranks him among the demi-gods. As a young man he was among the greatest, if he were not the very greatest, of his country. As a man of middle age he did not attain the high standard which his youth led his contemporaries to predict. He was a respectable, a useful, a zealous public servant, and an average diplomatist, with small opportunities of distinction, which he made the most of. In later life, and when he had attained the highest summit of his ambition, and wielded, as far as a President could wield, the destinies of his country, he offended the party by whose suffrages he was elected, and never conciliated in any appreciable degree the party that had opposed him. The adopted of Federalism, he threw back the cause of the Federalists for sixty years. "Whom the gods love, die young," said the ancients. Perhaps, and most probably, if John Adams had died immediately after the Declaration of Independence, his name, next to that of Washington, might have stood highest and brightest in the long muster-roll of American worthies.

THOMAS JEFFERSON.

THE name of Thomas Jefferson stands clear and bold on the page of American history: a man of strong convictions and unflinching courage; ever anxious to discover the right, and ever fearless to uphold it. The rebellion of the Colonies was essentially democratic in its origin, its progress, and its results; but no true democrat arose to shape the future Republic upon the broad principles of popular liberty, until Jefferson put the impress of his genius upon the Declaration of Independence. When Washington and the earlier patriots only sought for a redress of grievances, and never dreamed of severing the connection of the Colonies with the Crown, Jefferson saw that the only effectual remedy was independence, and the only possible form of Government in the New World Republicanism. He held this faith when he stood alone; he held it until all America agreed with him.

Washington lost heart at times—Jefferson never. The soldier, in the solitude of his tent on the field, foiled or impeded at every turn by the apathy, discontent, or incapacity of the men with whom he had to deal, more than once despaired of the fortunes of his country; the philosopher, in the silence and seclusion of his study, never allowed the possibility of failure to enter into his thought. The soldier was an aristocrat, and had small faith in the multitude; the philosopher, though born an aristocrat, was a man of the people, and never doubted either the justice of their cause or the certainty of its triumph.

Thomas Jefferson was born at Shadwell, in the county of Albemarle in Virginia, on the 2d of April 1743, the third child, but eldest son, of Peter Jefferson—a planter of fair estate—by his wife, Jane, a daughter of John Randolph, also a planter. The Jefferson family were among the earliest settlers in the Old Dominion, arriving from the foot of Snowdon in Wales, at a time when the whole population of Virginia, exclusive of the Indians, scarcely exceeded 600. They were proud of their descent from the ancient Britons, and no less proud of the Keltic element in their blood, which they strengthened by a Scottish intermarriage. Peter Jefferson is

o

described as having been a man of gigantic stature and herculean strength, rough in his manners and simple in his appearance, as a backwoodsman should be; but a scholar and a gentleman, well read in the contemporary English literature of Pope, Swift, and Addison, and still more familiar with Shakespeare and the early poets and dramatists. He was a "muscular Christian" when the phrase was uninvented, and thought that a man owed as much duty in this world to that divine structure the body, as to the diviner essence the soul. To maintain the strong mind in the strong body was his constant aim as regarded himself; and with his force of character it was not likely that he would pursue, or allow to be pursued, a different course in the education of his son.

Under his father's direction, and inspired by his example and companionship, the young Jefferson was taught to ride, to row, to swim, to hunt, and to shoot; and in the evenings, when the family assembled in the common room, he was instructed in arithmetic, mathematics, and music, and taught to keep accounts. He wrote a clear and beautiful hand, and acquired those habits of regularity and system for which the son afterwards became more noted than his father. The elder Jefferson, the strong good man, however, was not destined for length of days, and died in his forty-ninth year, leaving his son Thomas, then fourteen, to the care of his mother, who does not appear to have been a person well fitted for the responsibility. During his last illness, he repeatedly expressed the wish that his son should receive "a thorough classical education," and in his own old age Jefferson remarked to one of his grandsons that if he had to decide whether he had derived the greatest pleasure and advantage from the estate which his father had left him, or from the education which he had given and recommended, he should decide in favour of the education.

He remained at the boarding-school of the Rev. Mr Maury, within fourteen miles of Shadwell, for two years after his father's death. During this time he never forgot his father's precepts or example, either as to intellectual or to physical exercise. He made rapid progress in his studies, passed the leisure hours of the day in pedestrian excursions, and the leisure of his evenings in the study of the violin, on which instrument he soon became a proficient, and with which he solaced himself to the latest years of his life.

At the age of seventeen, in accordance with

his own wish, and without solicitation from his
mother, he entered the College of William and
Mary, at Williamsburg in Virginia. On his way
thither from the paternal plantation, he stopped at
Hanover to spend the Christmas holidays with his
father's friend, Colonel Dandridge, at whose hospi-
table house a large party was assembled. On this
occasion he made the acquaintance, speedily to
ripen into friendship, of a young man named Patrick Henry, seven years older than himself, who
was destined to be his associate and colleague in
the early events of the coming Revolution, and to
enrol his name among the most illustrious in American history. The young man had dissipated a
good estate by bad management and bad luck in
business, was uncouth in his manners and in his language, was without money, or a profession by which
to earn it; but full of life, vigour, genius, and confidence in his own mental resources.

Three months after Jefferson's arrival at College,
he received a visit from his new friend, who informed him that "in the meantime" he had studied
law, and had come to the capital to obtain licence
to practise. The preparation was short, but Henry
received his licence, and became not only one of
the most eminent statesmen and orators, but, strange

to say, one of the most successful lawyers in America. It is not chicanery that succeeds in a new country, but strong common-sense, and of that invaluable commodity the young aspirant had more than the usual allowance.

Jefferson, in a letter which he wrote in the last year of his presidency to a favourite grandson, described the life which he led at school and college as an example for the youth to follow. "When I recollect," he said, "that at fourteen years of age the whole care and direction of myself was thrown on myself, without a relation or friend qualified to advise or guide me," which says little for his mother, "and recollect the various sorts of bad company with which I associated from time to time, I am astonished I did not turn off with some of them, and become as worthless to society as they were. But I had the good fortune to become acquainted very early with some characters of high standing, and to feel the incessant wish that I could become what they were. Under temptations and difficulties, I asked myself what those great men would do in my situation ?—what course is it that would insure their approbation ? I am certain that this mode of deciding on my conduct tended more to correctness than any powers of reasoning which I possessed. . . . From the

circumstances of my position, I was often thrown
into the society of horse-racers, card-players, fox-
hunters, as well as of scientific and professional
men, and many a time have I asked myself in the
enthusiastic moment of the death of the fox, the
victory of the favourite horse, or the issues of a
great question eloquently argued at the bar, or in
the great council of the nation, which of these
kinds of reputation I should prefer? That of a
horse-jockey, a fox-hunter, an orator, or the honest
advocate of my country's rights?"

Among the great men whose names he cited to
his grandson as having influenced his early life, was
Dr Small, a Scotsman (and it is noted by his bio-
graphers that *all* his preceptors were of that nation),
professor of mathematics, and *ad interim* professor
of moral philosophy. Between teacher and pupil
a friendship, very rare under similar disparity of
age, was speedily formed, and Jefferson became the
chosen companion of the professor's leisure, and
gained from constant social intercourse with him and
his friends instruction more valuable than could be
imparted by public teachings. He never, during
the whole course of a long life, forgot the benefits
he derived from the worthy doctor, or spoke of him
but in terms of enthusiastic gratitude, as one who

had not only shaped his public career, but qualified him to pursue it with honour.

Jefferson had a love for mathematics, music, and the study of languages, which are often associated in minds of unusual intellectual power. In addition to a deep acquaintance with the Greek and Roman classics, he read with facility in French, German, Italian, and Spanish; and when Macpherson's Ossian was first published, he sent to Scotland for Gaelic grammars and dictionaries, in order that he might study the language, and read Ossian in the original. "He was not ashamed to own that he thought this rude bard of the North the greatest poet that had ever existed." It does not appear that his enthusiasm was long-lived; that he made any progress with the Gaelic; or that his admiration of Ossian was not mainly due to the promptings of the Scottish professor whom he so highly venerated. When he had attained his nineteenth year, and had finally made up his mind as to the choice of a profession, Dr Small gave up his appointment in the university and returned to his native land, having previously procured from his intimate friend, Mr George Wythe, the ablest and most successful lawyer in the Colony, the admission of his favourite pupil to that gentleman's office as

a law student.   Jefferson was of that class of men
who, whenever they find anything to do, do it
thoroughly, and was as exemplary in the dry study
of the law as he had been in the more attractive
study of the classics.

Always fonder of the society of his seniors than
of his juniors, he recorded with satisfaction in the
evening of his life that when a student in his teens,
he often made one of a *partie carrée* at dinner,
of which the other three were the English Governor Mr Fauquier, Mr Wythe, his future master
and partner, and Dr Small, his preceptor.   To the
conversation of these gentlemen, in their convivial
intercourse at the dinner-table, he admits that he
was greatly indebted for knowledge of the world.
During all his life, he was a good talker and listener.
He had the art of extracting from every one with
whom he conversed the special knowledge which
such person possessed—whether he were a politician, a lawyer, a soldier, a sailor, a mechanic,
a gardener, or an ostler, a white man or a negro;
and he had also the method as well as the industry to record in his note-book every fact which
he thus gleaned, so that if it wholly escaped his
memory it could be referred to in case of need.
Mr Fauquier, who was the darling of the Virginians

during his governorship, was in some respects a dangerous companion. He was an inveterate gambler—the only defect in an otherwise admirable character. But Jefferson was both too young and too prudent, and the Governor himself too much of a gentleman, to allow the one to be tempted or the other to be the tempter into vice or dissipation.

Unlike his friend Patrick Henry, who thought three months' study of the law sufficient, Jefferson devoted five years to it in Mr Wythe's office, and at the end of that time, being in his twenty-fourth year, was admitted to the Bar. He was not, however, so wholly engrossed with law as to neglect his music, his mathematics, his languages, or his long daily walks; or not, as is the nature of ardent young men, to fall, or fancy that he fell, in love. The baptismal name of the lady who enthralled his boyish heart was Rebecca, and he celebrated her charms, in songs and verses, under the more romantic appellation of Belinda. But nothing came of his verses or his wooing; and Rebecca Burwell married a more favoured suitor, somewhat abruptly to Jefferson's mind, though he was too wise a youth to break his heart at the disappointment.

His practice at the Bar was successful, and his

career would doubtless have been as brilliant as was possible in a young colony, if he had given his whole mind to so jealous and exacting a mistress. His fees were small, though his business was large, and as he always kept an accurate account of his incomings and outgoings, it is easy to trace how steady was his progress. In his first year of practice he was engaged in 68 causes; in his second, in 115; in his third, in 198; and so on, until his eighth year at the Bar, when his causes amounted to 337. His average annual income for his whole term of practice was 3000 dollars, or £600,—a sum about equivalent to £1000 in the present day. But his heart was not wholly in the law; he had his plantation and his negro slaves to attend to. More than all, the discontents that rapidly ripened into revolution, made such demands upon his time as to leave his business with but a partial hold upon his energies.

It was while he was yet a student in Mr Wythe's office, that the first rumble of the distant thunder-clouds of war was heard. In 1764, the year when he attained his majority, news arrived in Virginia that the British Parliament had passed an Act declaratory of its right to tax the Colonies. The Virginian Legislature, then in session, and of which Patrick Henry, the broken merchant who had mastered the mysteries of law in three months, was a member, addressed a remonstrance to the King and Parliament, denying the right, and earnestly though respectfully deprecating its enforcement. Parliament paid no heed to this or to any other remonstrances from the Colonies, and in point of fact had already passed the Stamp Act before many of the remonstrances had reached London. The younger generation of Virginians were indignant; and Patrick Henry, afterwards called by Burke "the Demosthenes of the Forest," took the lead among them.

It was the last day of the session of 1765, when the news arrived that the Stamp Act had received the royal signature. Patrick Henry was in his place; paper was not abundant, and tearing out a blank page from an old volume of Coke upon Lyttleton, over which he had been poring to supplement his scanty legal knowledge, and to while away the time while a drowsy speaker was holding forth upon a subject of no importance, he hastily drew up a series of resolutions, which he presented for the consideration of the House. They set forth the proposition that the colonists brought with them to America *all* the rights of British subjects; that the taxation of the people by themselves or their representatives in Parliament was the distinguishing characteristic of British freedom; that all power to levy taxes in the Colonies lay in the several legislative bodies of the said Colonies; and that any attempt to vest such power in any other persons or bodies whatsoever, had a manifest tendency to destroy British as well as American freedom.

Jefferson was present at the door of the lobby of the House of Burgesses, and heard the speech with which his friend prefaced his resolutions. He described it as a splendid display of oratory—the equal of which he never heard from any other man —"the speech of one who spoke as Homer wrote." The resolutions were carried by a majority of one only; but they had such an effect on Jefferson's mind, already predisposed, as to impel him to take his first great leap into the stormy ocean of political strife, from which he never again emerged. His admiration of Henry's oratory was possibly enhanced by the fact that he himself was unfitted by weakness of voice to excel as a public speaker. He addressed an audience in a speech seldom comprising more than a few sentences, and in a tone scarcely louder than that of ordinary conversation. His thoughts flowed more freely from his pen than from his tongue; and knowing where his strength as well as his weakness lay, he wisely refrained from emulating the oratorical fervour which he admired so highly.

In the year 1769, having been previously appointed a Justice of the Peace, he was elected a member of the House of Burgesses. The House, shortly after assembling, passed a series of resolutions—in which Patrick Henry's fine Roman hand was distinctly apparent—which were not considered respectful to the British Crown, in the matter of the obnoxious Stamp Act, and of a recommendation made in the British Parliament that persons accused of treason in the Colonies should be transported to England for trial. Lord Botetourt, the new Governor, was so highly displeased at the tone and temper of the resolutions, that he summarily dissolved the House. The indignant majority immediately adjourned to the " Apollo," the long room of the Raleigh Tavern in Williamsburg, where they forthwith formed themselves into an association, with power to add to their number, pledging themselves, during the continuance of the Act for raising a British revenue in America, not to import, purchase, or consume a variety of articles of British merchandise, which they enumerated. Among the signatures to this document were those of George Washington, Patrick Henry, and Thomas Jefferson.

Many members of the minority failed to be re-elected to the next Legislative Assembly; but no member of the anti-British majority was rejected by the constituencies.

Mr Jefferson, though so young a man, was prosperous enough in his profession and in the produce of his plantation to build himself a new and more commodious house than his father's, in which he had continued to reside at Shadwell, along with his mother, a brother, and two unmarried sisters. But before his new mansion at Monticello was completed, his old house was destroyed by fire in the absence of the family. In this calamity, his father's library—to which he had made many additions—his father's papers, and most of his own, were consumed. A negro slave was despatched to Williamsburg with the evil tidings. He knew his master's weaknesses, and kept his most consolatory news to the last. "De old house is burned to um ground, massa!" "But were none of my books saved?" inquired Jefferson. "Nary one," said the negro, grinning as only negroes can. "That's bad news, indeed!" "Not so bery bad, massa; *we saved um fiddle!*"

Two years afterwards, Monticello having been completed and furnished with a new and more extensive library than that destroyed, Mr Jefferson took into it that best of all adornments and treasures —a beautiful, accomplished, and affectionate wife. Being in his twenty-ninth year, he wooed and won Martha Skelton, six years younger than himself, daughter of John Wayles, a successful lawyer of good property, and widow of Bathurst Skelton, a planter. The lady was not only young and handsome, and unencumbered with a family, but she was an excellent manager and woman of business—a great attraction in the eyes of so methodical a man as Jefferson; but, better still, she loved music, sang well, played the spinet and the harpsichord, and admired and extolled her lover's performances on his favourite violin. The marriage was in all respects a happy one, and was blessed with a progeny of five daughters and one son. The son and two daughters died in their infancy, and only one daughter arrived at mature age.

Political events had long been hastening to a catastrophe, which Thomas Jefferson, John Adams, and Patrick Henry had long had the sagacity to foresee. The passage of the Boston Port Act, with the object of punishing that city for the transgression of the few citizens who had boarded the English tea-ships in the harbour, and thrown the obnoxious commodity into the sea, to prevent its being taxed by the British Government, was as much resented by Virginia as by Massachusetts. Jefferson, Henry, and three other members of the House of Burgesses, under conviction, as Jefferson relates in his Memoirs, of the necessity of arousing the Virginians from the comparative lethargy into which they had fallen, resolved that the appointment of a day of fasting, humiliation, and prayer, to avert from the Colonies the evils of civil war, and to turn the hearts of the British King and Parliament to moderation and justice, would be a certain mode of awakening all classes to the importance of the crisis. Such an observance in Virginia, so much in accordance with the puritanic notions of their suffering fellow-colonists in Massachusetts, would serve to unite both North and South in the one great object of resistance. So Jefferson and his colleagues thought; and they accordingly "cooked up" (the phrase is Jefferson's own) a resolution, somewhat modifying the puritanic formulas, and waited next morning upon one Mr Nicholas, "whose grave and religious character was more in unison than their own with the tone of the resolution," and asked him to propose it in the House of Burgesses. Mr Nicholas readily agreed,

and moved it on the very same day, when it passed
without a dissentient.   The Earl of Dunmore, who
had succeeded Lord Botetourt as Governor, imitated
the example set by his predecessor, and sent a curt
message of six lines to the House, summarily dissolving it, on the ground that the wording of its
resolution was an insult to the King and the Parliament of Great Britain.   As before, the members
adjourned to the "Apollo," entered into an association
of their whole number, in which they were joined
by several clergymen and eminent citizens, pledging
themselves never to purchase tea or any other
article taxed, or attempted to be taxed, by Great
Britain; declaring that in their opinion an attack
upon one colony was an attack upon all; and recommending a conference of the leading men of all the
colonies, to consider the propriety of holding an
annual Congress for the discussion of grievances.
The day of fasting, humiliation, and prayer was
duly observed throughout Virginia, and Jefferson
wrote that the effect "was like a shock of electricity, arousing every man, and placing him erect
and solidly on the centre."

A Convention of the colony having been resolved
upon, to organise and represent public opinion, Mr
Jefferson was elected as the delegate of his native

P

county of Albemarle. He was prevented from attending by a severe attack of dysentery, which confined him to his house. He had prepared an elaborate " draught of instructions " to be presented to that body, for the guidance of the delegates who were to be appointed to the General Congress, which afterwards met at Philadelphia. These instructions were written in great haste, with a number of blanks, and with some inaccuracies and uncertainties of historical facts, which he neglected at the time, knowing that they could be readily corrected at the meeting. When at the last moment he found himself unable to attend personally, he caused two copies to be made—one of which he sent to Mr Peyton Randolph, the President of the Convention, and the other to Patrick Henry. The fate of the document was remarkable. " Whether," says Mr Jefferson in his Memoirs, " Mr Henry disapproved the ground taken, or was too lazy to read it (for he was the laziest man in reading I ever knew), I never learned; but he communicated the paper to nobody." Peyton Randolph informed the Convention that he had received such a document from a member who was prevented by sickness from attending; and he laid it on the table for perusal.

It was read generally by the members, approved by many, though thought *too bold* for the then state of things. But they printed it in pamphlet form, under the title of "A Summary View of the Rights of British America." It found its way to England—was taken up by the Opposition—interpolated a little by Edmund Burke, so as to make it answer Opposition purposes, and in that form ran rapidly through several editions.

The document thus singularly cast upon the world, without an author's name — though the author never denied but exulted in his production—was the boldest proclamation of American wrongs, and the loudest defiance of the British Government, that had yet emanated from the Colonies. It did not find rapid acceptance—"the leap proposed," as Jefferson remarked, "being too wide for the great mass of the citizens to take." But they reasoned themselves up to it by degrees, as each successive mail from Great Britain brought them news of the obstinacy of the Administration. There was no mincing the matter in these celebrated "Instructions," which became in the end instructions for the people, rather than for their representatives as at first intended. They went fearlessly over the whole ground of dispute and difference, and spoke of the King and his authority in a manner that shocked the loyal, and made the timid ask themselves whether the author were not damaging his cause by his vehemence. He represented to the King that these, his "*States*" (it was the first time in American history that this word was used instead of Colonies) had often individually made humble applications to the throne to obtain redress of wrongs, without even receiving the courtesy of an answer; and hoping that their collective application—not penned in the language of servility, as if they were asking favours, but demanding rights — would obtain the respectful acceptance to which they were entitled from one "who was no more than the chief officer of the people, appointed by the laws, and intrusted with definite powers, to assist in working the great machine of Government, erected for their use, and consequently subject to their superintendence." He went on to remind the King of the fate which had befallen the Stuarts for their treasonable practices, and to enumerate the various aggressions and encroachments of King and Parliament in restricting the free commerce of the States—in controlling, and, in some instances, prohibiting, interior manufactures; and especially accusing the King of negligently or wilfully refusing his assent to measures duly passed by the local legislatures; and, "for the most trifling reasons, and sometimes for no conceivable reasons at all, vetoing laws of the most salutary tendency."

But viewed in the light thrown upon the subject by all the aftercourse of American affairs until the outbreak of the Civil War in 1861, Jefferson's declarations in this State paper, with reference to negro slavery and the slave-trade, and the blame fairly attachable to the British Government for introducing and endeavouring to perpetuate slavery, are such as to reflect the highest honour on his statesmanship, and to mark him out, in this as in other respects, as a man far in advance of his time. "The abolition of domestic slavery is," he said, "the great object of desire in these Colonies, where it was unhappily introduced in their infant state. But previous to the enfranchisement of the slaves we have, it is necessary to exclude all further importation from Africa. Yet our repeated attempts to effect this by prohibiting, and by imposing duties which might amount to a prohibition, have been hitherto defeated by his Majesty's negative—thus preferring the immediate advantages of a few British corsairs to the lasting interests of the American States, and to the rights of human nature, deeply wounded by this infamous practice."

Jefferson was not only thus far in advance of British public opinion on one great question of the future, but quite as far in advance of it on another — that of Free Trade. In his eloquent peroration, after disclaiming any wish of separation from the mother-country, provided justice were done, he said: "We are willing on our part to sacrifice everything which reason can ask, to the restoration of the tranquillity for which all must wish. On their part (the British Government) let them name their terms; but let them be just, and accept of every commercial preference it is in our power to give, for such things as we can raise for their use or they make for ours. But let them not think to exclude us from going to other markets, to dispose of those commodities which they cannot use, nor to supply those wants which they cannot supply. Still less let it be proposed that our properties within our own territories shall be taxed or regulated by any power on earth but our own. The God who gave us life gave us liberty at the same time. The hand of force may destroy, but cannot disjoin them. This is our last, our determined resolution!"

The instructions to the delegates appointed by Virginia to the great Philadelphia Congress of the same year, which were carried in Jefferson's enforced absence, were very much milder in tone and language, although Jefferson was not so obstinately wedded to his own ideas as not to confess that possibly the preference given to the tamer and more courteous document was wise under the circumstances. But Jefferson's resolutions coming back from England with the impress of British acceptance upon them, and the great name of Edmund Burke as their supposed author—or, if not their author, their editor and approver—had a more powerful effect on American opinion than could have been anticipated.

Patrick Henry's oratory wrought in the same direction. In the second Virginia Convention (1775), of which Jefferson was a member, he received a greater number of votes than any other nominee. The separation between the Moderates, who did not wish to take the irrevocable leap and break with the mother-country, and the fiery spirits, who saw no remedy but Independence, grew wider and wider. Henry, with the impulsiveness of his character, made up his mind to bring affairs to a crisis, and pledge Virginia to resistance. For this purpose he moved that the colony be immediately put into a state of defence, and that certain members be a committee to prepare a plan for embodying, arming, and disciplining such a number of men as might be sufficient for that purpose. Henry introduced this resolution in one of his most fervid bursts of semi-Irish, semi-Saxon declamation, the leading idea and peroration of which were in words familiar to every American schoolboy: "We must fight, sir. I repeat it—we must fight. An appeal to arms and to the Lord of hosts is all that is left to us." Jefferson seconded the resolution, which was carried by a decided majority, and was appointed one of the committee to carry it into effect.

An opportunity for fighting occurred much sooner than was anticipated, though fortunately, perhaps, for Patrick Henry, his wish to avail himself of it was overridden by cooler heads than his own. In pursuance, as was the opinion of the time, of a pre-concerted scheme for disarming all the colonies, the commander of a British man-of-war, lying in the James River, acting under the orders of Lord Dunmore, sent a party of armed men into Williamsburg, and forcibly carried off all the gunpowder in the public magazine, except a few barrels, which were left with the supposed intention of blowing up the building. While the public mind was greatly excited by this circumstance, news arrived of the battle of Lexington. The discontented spirits of Virginia could no longer restrain themselves, and several hundreds of men flew to arms. The volunteers of the county of Albemarle assembled at Charlotteville, and addressed a message to Colonel Washington, in which they offered, if he approved, to march upon Williamsburg, to enforce the return of the public property (the gunpowder seized by Lord Dunmore's orders), or "perish in the attempt."

As they did not make the attempt, it has been conjectured that Washington, whose reply has not been preserved, counselled inaction as the better policy. Patrick Henry, however, was less prudent, and desired to precipitate a conflict which Washington was anxious to avoid. Calling together the Independent Military Company of the county of Hanover, of which he was captain, Henry marched upon Williamsburg. His numbers increasing at every step, at last amounted to nearly 5000 men. The Moderates, as well as the Loyalists, were alarmed; and Lord Dunmore, thoroughly awakened to the seriousness of the crisis, took measures of defence,—sent Lady Dunmore and family to the protection of the Fowey man-of-war, at anchor in the river, and ordered the sailors and marines, under the command of Captain Montague, ashore, to aid the loyal inhabitants in repelling aggression. Either his lordship apprehended defeat, or had misgivings as to the legality of his act in seizing the gunpowder, for he sent a messenger to Patrick Henry, who was then sixteen miles from Williamsburg, at the head of his little army, with a bill of exchange for the value of the property. At this triumph—for such it was—Henry's volunteers began to disband, and an armed collision was avoided.

In England the state of public opinion, as influenced by the Opposition, was growing so favourable to the Colonial cause, that the Prime Minister (Lord North) deemed it advisable to try the effect of conciliation. But his conciliation left the principle at issue exactly where it stood. He still insisted on the theoretical right of Great Britain to tax the Americans, which was the very point that Americans of every shade of politics, except the ultra-loyalists, had determined to resist at every hazard. He consequently failed in the attempt to bring about a better understanding. To Jefferson was confided, on the part of the Legislature of Virginia, the task of replying to the Minister; and he accordingly prepared a paper, which the House of Burgesses adopted with but slight modifications. After setting forth all the reasons which induced Virginia to persist in her original demands, and to make common cause with the sister colonies, he concluded by saying : "We [the Virginians] have exhausted every mode of application which our invention could suggest as proper and promising. We have decently remonstrated with Parliament. It has added new injuries to the old. We have wearied our King with supplications. He has not deigned to answer us. We have appealed to the native honour and justice of the British nation ; their efforts in our favour have hitherto been ineffectual. What, then, remains to be done ? That we commit our injuries to the even-handed justice of that Being who doeth no wrong, earnestly beseeching Him to illuminate the councils and prosper the endeavours of those to whom America has confided her hopes."

When Jefferson shortly afterwards took his seat in Congress, he found that his reputation as the author of so many admirable State papers had preceded him. He was the youngest member but one, and had no oratorical power. But he had an old head upon young shoulders, and a mastery of diction and of logic with his pen, which more than atoned for all his deficiencies as a speaker. He was cordially welcomed by the more ardent spirits, and with curiosity, if not respect, by the more moderate politicians. John Adams was particularly struck by his talents and his manner. "Though a silent member in Congress," he afterwards wrote, "he was so prompt, frank, explicit, and decisive upon committees and in conversation, that he soon seized upon my heart." Five days after Congress had assembled, he was placed upon the committee charged with the duty of drawing up a "declaration of the causes of taking up arms." It was believed at the time, and for more than a quarter of a century afterwards, that this document was mainly the work of John Dickinson of Philadelphia; but Jefferson, in his autobiography, claimed all the essential parts of it as his own. The declaration was adopted by Congress, and largely circulated in Great Britain and the colonies.

When the second Congress assembled in 1776, it was evident to nearly all America that no further negotiation was possible with the mother-country except at the point of the sword. At the commencement of the year—when this conviction was beginning to spread, and when even the timid and those who loved England the most were becoming reconciled to it—a pamphlet was published, which did more than any similar work had ever done in any country to stimulate public opinion, convince the wavering, strengthen the weak, and create a general adhesion, almost amounting to unanimity, to the principles it enunciated and the course of proceeding which it recommended. This was " Common-Sense," by Thomas Paine, an Englishman, who some years previously had been induced to settle in America by the recommendation of Dr Franklin. Its effect was instantaneous. " Its tone, its manner, its Biblical allusions," says Dr Randall, the biographer of Jefferson, "its avoidance of all openly impassioned appeals to feeling, and its unanswerable common-sense, were exquisitely adapted to the audience to whom it was addressed."

John Adams somewhat disparaged the work ; but Jefferson was loud in approval. Edmund Burke, in an address to the electors of Bristol, spoke of it as " the celebrated pamphlet which prepared the minds of the American people for independence." The Legislature of Pennsylvania voted Paine £500 for his pamphlet, and the other colonies vied with each other to do him honour. Congress was not sitting at the time ; but when it assembled, public opinion in and out of that body had become riper for decisive action than the most sanguine could have anticipated. The memorable Declaration of Independence was the first fruit of its labours—a document which is alone sufficient to perpetuate the name of Thomas Jefferson, and to cover it with glory in the estimation of his countrymen. It came from his mind, clear, shapely, complete, as Minerva from the brain of Jupiter, and received no essential additions or important alterations from other hands, except such slight verbal modification as added little or nothing to its essential symmetry, its force, or its perspicuity. John Adams and Benjamin Franklin, as members of the committee intrusted with the task of preparing it, had the right of revision. But they found no scope for any important criticism. Dr Franklin suggested the substitution of the words " absolute despotism " for " arbitrary power "; and recommended that the phrase, " foreign mercenaries to invade and deluge us with blood," should be altered to " invade and destroy us "; and made a few other emendations which Jefferson adopted. Mr Adams substituted for the words " his present Majesty," the " present King of Great Britain," and made a few other alterations equally trivial. Thus the body as well as the soul of the document was Jefferson's alone, and there were none who could claim or contest with him the credit of its authorship. Nevertheless, the gad-flies and mosquitoes who always buzz about celebrity, anxious to sting for the gratification of their own malevolence, discovered that Jefferson was indebted not only for many of the ideas, but for much of the phraseology, to the English pamphlet of Edmund Burke! . Jefferson was much amused by the accusation, and allowed the little critics to revel unmolested in the mire of their own spite, without taking the trouble to contradict them.

He had at this time, in addition to his public business, many important private affairs that demanded his attention. His household at Monticello —including his own family, his mother, his sister, and the whites in his employ—numbered thirty-four persons. In addition to these, he had to manage on his estate, by himself or his agents, no less than eighty-three slaves. There was also his law business, so that altogether he had irons enough in the fire to have justified him, had he been so inclined, in abandoning the thankless cares and duties of public life. But, like the tiger who has tasted human blood, and never afterwards reconciles itself to tamer food, he had drunk of the intoxicating draught of politics in a perilous time, and could not content himself with the milk-and-water of domesticity. His heart as well as his intellect was in the strife, and he decided to abandon law rather than the cause of his country in the crisis of its fortunes. It was well for America—perhaps not so well for himself—that such was his determination.

Nevertheless, after the adoption of the Declaration of Independence, and its enthusiastic proclamation in all the colonies, he declined a renomination to Congress and a foreign mission.   To his mind, as to that of all other Americans of the time, the first allegiance of a citizen was due to his own State. He was an American, it is true; but he was more particularly a Virginian.   The Union of the States seemed to him—who had so much to do in framing it—to be but a partnership, of which the main object and sole justification was to prevent and resist foreign aggression, especially that of Great Britain, of which alone there was at that time the slightest probability.   For all domestic purposes he considered the State to be supreme.   The Union was a bridge of many arches to cross the stream of foreign enmity, and the destruction of any one of them would bring down the whole edifice.   Such was then the view of all native-born Americans, and such continued to be the view of the great Democratic party, of which Jefferson was the founder, until the outbreak of the Civil War of 1861 administered to the principle the rude shock from which it has not yet recovered, and possibly never may. But with these views clear in his mind, Jefferson, partly for the convenience of attending to his home affairs, withdrew from Federal or Union politics for nearly three years, after the Declaration of Independence, and mainly devoted himself to those of Virginia. His friend, Patrick Henry, was now Governor of the State, appointed by the people in succession to Lord Dunmore, the last British and royalist Governor; and he and Jefferson had thus constant opportunities of meeting and of working together.

Elected a member of the House of Delegates, Jefferson became the avowed and active leader of the Reform party, and advocated and introduced a variety of measures, which, by their boldness, startled the feudal and conservative sections of the House. He prepared Bills for " the abolition of the laws of entail and primogeniture," and for " a general revision of the laws of Virginia," both of which excited violent opposition, but were ultimately carried. He also introduced measures for the disestablishment of the Episcopal Church, formerly the Church of England,

and for placing all religious sects on the same footing of freedom and equality; and two measures
still more remarkable for their time, in which public
opinion declined to follow him, but which were
nevertheless destined to be partially successful,
though not until after many years. The first
related to the education of the people, the second
to the abolition of negro slavery, on both of which
great and essential measures of public wisdom he
towered in clearness and breadth of view far above
all his contemporaries. To provide for the better
education of the people, he prepared three Bills—
for "the more general diffusion of knowledge," for
"amending the constitution of the College of William
and Mary," and for "establishing a public library."
The first of these Bills might serve as a model in our
day, did the religious differences of the British
people permit, for the establishment of a system
more truly national than that so recently carried
under the auspices of Mr Forster, or than any that
timid politicians or arrogant theologians would con-
descend to discuss.

Mr Jefferson broadly laid down the principle
that it was the "duty" of the State to provide
for the proper education of the children of all
its citizens who were too poor to educate their

progeny themselves; and in accordance with this fundamental idea, prepared a project whereby such instruction was to be assured for three years certain to every child of Virginia. The peculiarity of his scheme was, that after instruction of the children for the proposed term, at the public expense, in reading, writing, and arithmetic, and the reading of such books as would make them acquainted with the main facts of Grecian, Roman, English, and American history, there should be an annual examination by the overseer or school inspector—sworn to act without favour or affection—who should select a pupil of at least two years' standing, of the best and most promising talent and disposition. This pupil was to be sent to the grammar-school of the district, to be there *boarded* and educated at the expense of the State for at least one year. Among the pupils thus selected a further choice was to be made at a stipulated time, and those on whom the choice fell, after examination, were to be denominated "seniors," and eligible to remain for four years on the public foundation. From these "seniors," the visitors were annually to select one, and send him to the College of William and Mary, to be boarded, clad, and educated for three years further at the expense of the State—by this means securing all the advantages of a collegiate education for the child of the poorest citizen, provided such child had merit and ability enough to pass the required examinations.

His opinions on the question of negro slavery were too much in advance of the prejudices of his age to be accepted. He did not propose to give the then existing generation of slaves, ignorant and demoralised by their slavery, the liberty which he thought they were unable to turn to beneficial account, and which, in his opinion, would only have been the liberty to be neglected, to starve, and to die uncared for, like wild animals whose labour was valueless to man; but he proposed to pass an Act for the emancipation of all the children of slaves born after a certain time, and providing for the maintenance of such children by their parents or their masters, until their arrival at the age of fourteen. They were then to be brought up at the public expense, to tillage and handicraft, fitting them to earn their own livelihood by wages, the females to the age of eighteen, the males to the age of twenty-one. After this time they were to be " deported " under proper guidance to such territorial possessions of the United States as might be available, provided with arms, implements of husbandry, seed, and farm stock. They were then to be organised into independent communities and republics, under magistrates of their own race, and under the protection of the United States.

"Nothing," he afterwards said in relation to this subject, "is more certainly written in the Book of Fate, than that these people [the negroes] are to be free ; nor is it less certain that the white and the black races cannot live together in the same government. Nature, habit, and opinion have drawn indelible lines of distinction between them. It is still in our power to direct the process of emancipation and deportation, peaceably and in such slow degree as that the evil shall wear off insensibly, and the place of the negroes be filled *pari passu* by free white labourers. If, on the contrary, slavery be left to itself, our human nature must shudder at the prospect before us." Happy would it have been for the United States if these sage counsels had been followed ; still happier for the negroes, emancipated by the great Civil War, which has given them a liberty for which they are unsuited, and which may yet lead to what Jefferson called a "deletion" of the race, by a servile war of which the premonitory symptoms are only too apparent.

Jefferson, in eloquent words, denounced the slave- .

trade with all the fiery indignation he could summon
into his pen in the first rough draft of the Declaration of Independence.   He only committed the fault
of attributing to George III. personally the acts for
which the British Government and Parliament,
and the public opinion of the time, were mainly
responsible.   "He" (the King), said the document,
" has waged cruel war against human nature itself,
violating the most sacred rights of life and liberty
in the persons of a distant people who never offended him, captivating and carrying them into slavery
in another hemisphere, or to incur miserable death
in the transportation thither.   This piratical warfare, this opprobrium of *infidel* powers, is the warfare of the *Christian* King of Great Britain, determined to keep open a market where men should
be bought and sold.   He has prostituted his negative for suppressing every legislative attempt to
prohibit or restrain this miserable commerce.   And
that this assemblage of horrors might want no
fact of distinguished cruelty, he is now exciting those very people to rise in arms amongst us,
and to purchase that liberty of which he has deprived them by murdering the people on whom he
first obtruded them,—thus paying off former crimes
committed against the liberties of one people, with

crimes which he urges them to commit against the lives of another."

This passage, directed against the foreign slave-trade more than against domestic slavery, was unfortunately expunged by the House,—partly perhaps for the reason that it accused the King of Great Britain of guilt for which he was not personally responsible, and partly because there was no sufficient evidence to show that either he or his Government had incited the slaves to rise in insurrection against their masters. It would have been better had the passage been amended and corrected, instead of being expunged altogether.

In June 1779, Patrick Henry having served for three years as Governor of Virginia, Jefferson was elected in his stead. The events of these years in Virginia relate more to the personal history of George Washington, and to the progress of military operations against the British, than to the career of Thomas Jefferson. While in office, Washington always found in him a steady supporter, and one infinitely more ready to aid and comfort him in his arduous duty, against odds that at times seemed wellnigh insurmountable, than to join the ranks of the dissatisfied, and of those who clamoured for a change of military chieftainship, whenever the progress of hostilities seemed to be unfavourable.

But the office of Governor of a State, continually exposed to the warlike operations of the British, was neither a sinecure nor a bed of roses. Thrice during this term, the State was in danger of hostile occupation by the troops of Benedict Arnold, the American traitor, and of the British generals, Phillips and Cornwallis, besides being harried by the cavalry of the dashing Colonel Tarleton—a man who was as much hated by the Virginians as Claverhouse was by the Scottish Covenanters, and for the same reasons. Once Jefferson himself had a very narrow escape from capture by a detachment of Tarleton's horse in his own house of Monticello. One of his plantations, called Elk Hill, was occupied for ten days by that ruthless soldier. The owner, forewarned of the enemy's approach, had time to remove some portions of his effects; but Tarleton destroyed all the growing crops of corn and tobacco, burned all the barns, let loose all the stock of cattle, sheep, and hogs, carried off all the horses capable of service, and, as Jefferson complained, "cut the throats of all that were too young for military purposes." He also broke down all the fences, converted the place into an absolute waste, and carried off thirty slaves. "Had this been to have given them freedom," said Jefferson, "he would have done right; but he only assigned them to inevitable death from small-pox and putrid fever, then raging in his camp. This," he added, "I afterwards knew to be the fate of twenty-seven of them. What became of the other three I never learned."

And worse than these losses and privations, and the hardships inflicted upon his wife, now grown delicate in health, and forced to remove from place to place with her young family for safety from a marauding soldiery, was the discontent, fast ripening into ingratitude and formal complaint against his administration, of the Legislature and people of his beloved and sorely harassed Virginia. The Legislature, summoned to meet at Charlotteville, alarmed at the approach of the redoubtable, and at times almost omnipotent, Tarleton, adjourned to Staunton, west of the Blue Ridge mountains. Nor were the members in the estimation of the majority safe even at this place. On a false alarm of Tarleton's approach, they adjourned *sine die* in a panic, leaving power to the Speaker to convene them "when and where he pleased." A cry was raised that in such a state of affairs a dictator would be of more value to the State than a constitutional gover-

nor and a timid House of Assembly; and Patrick
Henry was distinctly pointed out as the man for the
emergency.   One Mr Cary of Ampthill, a relation
of Mr Jefferson, hinted that any such dictator would
be more likely to receive the dagger of Brutus than
the support of the public.   The very thought, in
the opinion of Jefferson, was treason against the
people and against mankind, and would be trump-
eted through the world as a proof of the inability
of a republican form of Government in times of
public danger to shield the State from harm.   The
idea never took the shape of a formal proposition to
the Legislature; but towards the close of Jefferson's
career as Governor, and when he had positively declined a renomination, the malcontents put forward
a young member to make a series of charges
against him in reference to his official conduct, and
to demand a public inquiry.   Jefferson's friends,
instead of opposing, expressed their willingness to
meet the inquiry on every particular.   Their
promptitude somewhat disconcerted his opponents.
No vote was taken, and the subject was adjourned
by general consent.   The charges resolved themselves into five: first, that he had not, when advised by General Washington, put the country into
a proper state of preparation and defence; second,

that during successive invasions he did not use all available means of resistance; third, that he too much consulted his personal safety; fourth, that he ignominiously flew from Monticello at the near approach of Tarleton's dragoons; and fifth, that he abandoned the office of Governor as soon as it became one of difficulty and danger. All these charges came to nothing; the young member, a Mr Nicholas, was not present to bring them forward at the appointed time. Mr Jefferson refuted them *seriatim*, and the House of Delegates unanimously passed a vote of thanks to him for his impartial and upright administration, declared the charges against him to be wholly unfounded, and placed this public avowal upon record, to obviate all future and remove all former censure. But although Mr Jefferson was thus triumphant, the accusation rankled in his mind, and gave him a distaste for public life, which it took a long time to remove, and infused a tincture of bitterness into his thought.

During these ungracious discussions in his native State, the Federal Congress—uninfluenced by the calumnies against the author of the Declaration of Independence—nominated him to act in concert with Mr Adams and Dr Franklin on behalf of the

United States at the proposed Congress of Vienna. He respectfully declined the appointment, partly because the charges against him were at the time in abeyance, partly because he was disheartened at the treatment he had received, and partly—perhaps chiefly—on account of the increasing illness of his wife, to whom he was devotedly attached. Many attempts were made by his political friends to induce him to alter his determination, but without effect; and some went so far as to deny the right of a man so able and so eminent to withdraw from public life when the State required his services.

But he was not to be shaken even by the flattery conveyed in the reproof, and remained quietly at home, reading, writing, and fiddling, working in his garden, and sitting at the bedside of his wife, to administer to her the medicines which she preferred to take from his hand. She had borne children too rapidly for her delicate health, and died in September 1782, four months after having given birth to her sixth child, a daughter, that only survived two years. His eldest daughter, Martha, afterwards Mrs Randolph, described how, for four months during which her mother lingered, her father was never beyond call, and passed most of his time at her bedside, or in a small room adjoining. A moment before the closing scene, he was led from the room almost in a state of insensibility by his sister, who with great difficulty got him into the library, where he fainted. He kept his room for three weeks, during which he walked about almost incessantly night and day, only lying down occasionally when nature was exhausted. When at last he was able to leave his room, he rode out on horseback, and rambled about the mountains in the least frequented roads. In those melancholy wanderings his daughter was his constant companion, a solitary witness to many a violent burst of grief.

As is usual with fervent natures when bereaved of those they love, he found a relief to his heart in increased love for those still left to him, as well as in mental occupation. An accidental fall from his horse, a few months before his wife's death, having confined him to the house for several weeks, he commenced a series of replies to inquiries, statistical and others, which had been put to him, in reference to the soil, climate, and productions of Virginia, by the French Secretary of Legation at Washington. To the completion of this work—afterwards published under the title of 'Notes on Virginia'—he applied himself, after Mrs Jefferson's

death, with redoubled assiduity. He also commenced
an anxious examination of the state of affairs on
his plantations, and found—what he expected—that
his private means had greatly suffered by his devotion to the business of the State. For two years
he found ample employment in setting right what
was wrong; in looking into his accounts of profit
and loss; in reforming and retrenching; in exam-
ining, along with his farm bailiffs and overseers,
into the management of every part of his estates;
but always managing to spare time for the pursuits
of literature and music, which he loved, and never
wholly losing sight of the political world which he
had temporarily abandoned.

In May 1784, he was for the third time appointed by Congress, notwithstanding his previous refusals, to a European mission, and was
associated with Franklin and Adams in the negotiation of treaties of commerce with foreign nations—more especially with France. The belief
that he could be useful, together with the urgent
entreaties of friends and former political associates, and particularly the desire to give his
daughters a European education without being separated from them, induced him at last to forego his
purpose of abandoning public life. His mind being

made up, he completed his arrangements with un-usual rapidity, and arrived in Paris within two months after acceptance of the mission.

His career in the French capital was the pleas-antest episode of his public life. Dr Franklin, in his snuff-coloured suit, his shoe and knee buckles, his quaint manners and agreeable conversation, was, and had long been, the favourite in the brilliant circles of French society, and in the gay Court that dreamed not of the evil days that were coming, nor thought what influence the sympathy of the old French monarchy for the American Republic was doomed to exercise upon the whole current of European thought and politics. But popular as Franklin was, Jefferson not only rivalled but out-stripped him in the race of fame and fashion. The literati, the philosophers, the wits, the poets, the musicians, the painters — as well as the fair ladies who reign supreme in fashionable circles— all found in the celebrated American a man with whom it was a pleasure to converse, and to whose intimacy it was an honour to be admitted. Jeffer-son knew how to " be all things to all men," and was an admirable listener as well as talker. His modesty was only surpassed by his merit; and it was noticed of him, not without secret approval, though possibly with open wonder, by the fast men and women of the day—for the "fast" are of all epochs and of all countries that claim to be civilised —that the least spoken or acted indelicacy caused him to blush like a boy who had never been at school.

The prevalent ideas of religion, which owed so much of their scepticism and cynicism to the teachings of Voltaire and the Encyclopedists, found in Jefferson not only an apt pupil but even a master; for he had thought out for himself in America, from his boyhood upwards, a system of theology more akin to Platonism than to modern Christianity. Though not a scoffer, like Voltaire, he took so little trouble to conceal his opinions that he drew upon himself the accusation of atheism. But in those days, as to a certain extent in our own, the essential difference between atheism and theism was never admitted by those who assume the monopoly of orthodoxy; and Jefferson's alleged atheism, which he indignantly denied, was continually charged against him, after his return to America, to injure his public character and overweight him with unpopularity in the political race. But in the congenial society of the French capital, where ultra-scepticism was the fashion, and where the Abbé de Talleyrand thought it necessary to explain to the English ambassador, Lord Gower, that neither he nor the Archbishop of Paris was a Christian, the accusation either of deism or of atheism would have done him no harm, and consequently no one thought it worth while to make it. But it was the political rather than the religious *debâcle* of thought,—the ominous rumblings of the approaching earthquake, that was to throw down so much that was good along with so much that was evil in France,—that attracted the leading spirits of the French capital to Dr Franklin in the first instance, and to Mr Jefferson in the second.

The rising men of France considered the independence of America as due in a great measure to French support, as it unquestionably was, and looked with admiration upon the stand which the Americans had made in support of a principle, no doubt vital in itself, but trivial in comparison with the oppressions, exactions, and every form of corruption and misgovernment which France, without exhibiting the courage of resistance, had endured for ages. Not only officers who had served under Lafayette, Rochambeau, and L'Estaing in America, but the younger scions of the *noblesse* who had never stirred from home, and knew not what aid they were rendering to the downfall of their own order by advocating the rights of man after the American fashion, thronged the evening receptions of Franklin and Jefferson. It was the leavening of the lump, and produced a fermentation greater and more violent than the philosophers foresaw.

It was not in Jefferson's nature to do things by halves, or give semi-assent to great principles; and he had not been many months in Paris before he applied to the events occurring around him the same sharp scrutiny that he had given to those of his own country, and clearly defined to himself the shape and the direction of the revolution that he saw not only to be inevitable, but of near approach. The republicanism of which he was the apostle at home, he preached to his intimates abroad. He seems to have loved the French people, and appreciated the many admirable traits in their character, while wondering at the patience they had so long exhibited under misgovernment which would, ages before, have driven the Anglo-Saxons to rebellion. Feudalism and all its results, hereditary aristocracy and monarchy, laws of entail and primogeniture, class privileges and monopolies, he held in equal abhorrence, but reserved for monarchy the expression of his deepest dislike. The extravagance of his animadversions against kings often bordered upon the ludicrous, especially when he alarmed himself, as he often did, with the idea that a large party in the United States would willingly supersede republicanism by a hereditary monarchy after the British fashion.

He wrote to General Washington in August 1788 a letter on the alarming state of affairs in France, in which he spoke of "the evil passions of kings and of those who would be kings." On the same day he wrote to another correspondent: "So much," in reference to French affairs, "for the blessings of having kings, and magistrates who would be kings! From these events our young Republic may learn useful lessons: never to call a foreign Power to settle their differences; to guard against hereditary magistrates; to prevent their citizens from being so established in wealth and power as to be thought worthy of alliance by marriage with the sisters, nieces, and cousins of kings; and, in short, to besiege the throne of Heaven with eternal prayers to extirpate from creation this class of human lions, tigers, and mammoths called kings. From whom, let him perish who does not say, 'Good Lord, deliver us!'" In another letter of the same year, he declared that "no race of kings had ever presented above one man of common-sense in twenty generations!" But these violent denunciations, and many others of a similar kind that are scattered through his correspondence, were intended more for home than for foreign use.

The amended constitution of the United States was under discussion. Jefferson, who would certainly have been elected a member of the Convention had he not been abroad in France, could not reconcile himself to complete silence on the subject, apprehensive as he was of the efforts of the Federal party to establish something like a hereditary chief-magistracy, and a legislative peerage, which he considered to be involved in the appointment of life-senators. He was even opposed to the re-eligibility of the President to a second term of office, and would have reduced the term from four to three years. Monarchism was, in fact, his *bête noire* — his favourite aversion — the red flag by the waving of which before his eyes any athlete in the *tauromachia* of politics could drive this fine bull frantic. Yet, notwithstanding all his hatred of kings, whether it were real or assumed, he had no very hard words to launch against poor Louis the Sixteenth, when the throne of France was tossed about on the waves of revolution like a cork upon the billows. In describing in his Memoirs the taking of the Bastille, the declaration of the Republic, and the execution of the King and the Queen, he dwelt not only without severity but almost with favour on the King's character, and made more ample allowance for the appalling difficulties of his position than any writer of the time.

"The King," he said, in reference to the events of 1789, "was now become a passive machine in the hands of the National Assembly, and had he been left to himself, he would have willingly acquiesced in whatever they should devise as best for the nation. A wise constitution would have been formed, hereditary in his line, himself placed at its head, with powers so large as to enable him to do all the good of his station, and so limited as to restrain him from its abuse. This he would have faithfully administered, and more than this I do not believe he ever wished. But he had a queen of absolute sway over his weak mind and timid virtue, and of a character the reverse of his in all points. This 'angel,' so gaudily painted in the rhapsodies of Burke, with some smartness of fancy, but no sound sense, was proud, disdainful of restraint, indignant

at all obstacles to her will, eager in the pursuit of
pleasure, and firm enough to hold to her desires, or
perish in their wreck.   Her inordinate gambling
and dissipations, with those of the Count d'Artois,
and others of her *clique*, had been a sensible item in
the exhaustion of the treasury, which called into
action the reforming hand of the nation ; and her
opposition to it, her inflexible perverseness, and
dauntless spirit, led herself to the guillotine, drew
the King on with her, and plunged the world into
crimes which will for ever stain the pages of modern
history.   I have ever believed that had there been
no queen, there would have been no revolution.
No force would have been provoked, nor exercised.
The King would have gone hand in hand with the
wisdom of his sounder counsellors, who, guided by
the increased lights of the age, wished only, with
the same pace, to advance the principles of their
social constitution.   The deed which closed the
mortal course of these sovereigns I shall neither
approve nor condemn.   I am not prepared to say
that the first magistrate of a nation cannot commit
treason against his country, or is unamenable to its
punishment ; nor yet, that where there is no written
law, no regulated tribunal, there is not a law in our
hearts, and a power in our hands, given for righteous

employment in maintaining right and redressing wrong. Of those who judged the King, many thought him wilfully criminal, many that his existence would keep the nation in perpetual conflict with the horde of kings, and that it were better that one should die than all. I should not have voted with this portion of the Legislature. I should have shut up the Queen in a convent, putting harm out of her power, and placed the King in his station, investing him with limited powers, which I verily believe he would have honestly exercised, according to the measure of his understanding."

When, on the motion of the Vicomte de Noailles, the brother-in-law of Lafayette, the National Assembly abolished all privilege of classes in the State, Jefferson, who in the Legislature of his native Virginia had introduced and carried a series of similar measures, was highly gratified with the contagion of his example. "Thus," he wrote, "went down at one sweeping blow all the abusive privileges of feudalism, the tithes and casuals of the clergy, all provincial privileges, and, in fine, the feudal regimen generally." As if in acknowledgment of the fact that the American revolution was the parent of that in France, and that the example set by the authors of the Declaration of Independence was stimulating the French to establish their nascent liberties on as broad and lasting a foundation,—the committee of the National Assembly appointed to draw up a constitution, officially invited Mr Jefferson to attend and assist in their deliberations.   This was an extraordinary request to make to a foreigner, as well as a very high compliment; but Mr Jefferson, with a prudent eye to the effect which his compliance might have had on his political character at home, excused himself " on the obvious consideration, that his mission was to the King as chief magistrate of the nation; that his duties were limited to the concerns of his own country, and forbade him to intermeddle with the internal transactions of that in which he had been received in a specific character only."

But the Marquis de Lafayette — who, at this early period of the revolution, deceived himself with the hope that he could safely ride the political whirlwind—was too fresh from his American battle-fields, and too fully imbued with the principles he had imbibed from the teachings of Washington and Jefferson, not to desire the participation of the latter in the great work of constitution - making, that might, he thought, be as successful in the Old World as in the New.   If Jefferson would not, or could not decently, lend his formal aid to the business in hand, might he not help informally? Lafayette thought that he might, and wrote a note to the American Minister, to say that on the following day he should bring a party of six or eight friends, "to ask a dinner of him." Jefferson wrote back to assure Lafayette and his friends of a hearty welcome. The Marquis came at four o'clock, the then fashionable hour of dinner in Paris, and brought with him Barnave, Lameth, and four other members of the National Assembly, whom he described as leading patriots of honest but divergent opinions.

The cloth having been removed, and wine placed on the table after the American manner, the Marquis introduced the subject of their friendly conference by summarily reminding the gentlemen present of the unsatisfactory state of affairs in the National Assembly, of the danger incurred by the disagreement of the patriots among themselves, and the probability that in consequence the aristocratic party would carry everything before them. Though he also had his opinion, he was ready to sacrifice it to that of his brethren in the patriotic cause; and whatever was agreed upon, he at the head of the national force would maintain.

Jefferson records that the discussions lasted for six hours, during all which time he was "a silent witness to a coolness and candour of argument unusual in the conflicts of political opinion; to a logical reasoning and chaste eloquence disfigured by no gaudy tinsel of rhetoric or declamation, and truly worthy of being placed in parallel with the finest dialogues of antiquity as handed down to us by Xenophon, Plato, or Cicero. The result was, that the King should have a suspensory veto on the laws; that the Legislature should be composed of a single body only, to be chosen by the people. This *concordat* decided the fate of the constitution." But as Jefferson had been in a manner entrapped into taking a part—though he says it was a silent one—in this great historical conference, he thought it his duty to explain next morning to the Minister of Foreign Affairs, the Count de Montmorrin, in what manner he had become involved. The Count already knew all that had passed, and paid Mr Jefferson the compliment of saying, "that so far from being displeased at the use made of his house on the occasion, it was his earnest wish that Mr Jefferson would often assist at such conferences, being convinced that he would be useful in moderating the warmer spirits, and promoting a wholesome and practicable reformation only."

The influence that Mr Jefferson might thus have exercised on French politics he was not destined to employ, and the mighty Revolution, in which he took so warm and almost paternal an interest, knew him and his counsels no more. His private affairs in Virginia required his presence after a long absence, as his estates and plantations, exceeding ten thousand acres in extent, were suffering from the neglect or malfeasance of the overseers to whom he was compelled to entrust their management. In June 1789, General Washington informed the Senate of the United States that he had granted Mr Jefferson leave of absence from his post in Paris, and in September the American Minister bade farewell to Lafayette and all his French friends, with the expectation of returning towards the middle of the following year.

He took with him the most pleasing recollections of the French people of all classes, of the hospitalities, graces, and amenities of the rich and the learned of Paris, and a feeling strong in his mind that, next to being an American, the best thing in the world was to be a Frenchman. It was his desire to return to a position which he had enjoyed so long and appreciated so highly; but it was one that was not destined to fulfilment. His own country claimed his services, and he never again beheld either France or Europe. On leaving France, accompanied by his two daughters, he passed a few weeks in England, where he does not appear to have had, or to have cared to have, many friends or acquaintances, and arrived off the Capes of the Chesapeake, after a passage of nearly two months, in the packet-ship Clermont, bound from London to Norfolk in Virginia, and which put in for him at Cowes in the Isle of Wight.

The voyage was of fair average for the time, and unattended with danger until the moment of arrival. When off the Capes of the Chesapeake, the vessel lay in a thick fog for three days, when the captain, seeing no chance of a pilot, determined to run in at a venture. The risk was great, but it was successfully accomplished, though not without a smart collision with a brig coming out of Norfolk, which tore away a part of the rigging. Two hours after Jefferson and his daughters had landed, the Clermont, on board of which they had left all their luggage, was discovered to be on fire. Luckily, however, their effects, including his valuable historical papers, were rescued from the flames. After short delays, and a few visits paid to friends on the line of route, the party arrived at Monticello on the 23d of December 1789.

The overseers on the plantations and the negro slaves had received notice of the great event, and gave him a reception such as the tenants on great English estates were accustomed in the olden time to give their landlords after long absence, or on attaining majority, or on occasion of a marriage, or the birth of an heir to the family honours. The relations between the Virginia planters of Jefferson's day and their slaves were generally of a paternal character. The planter was the patriarch, and the slaves, especially those of pure African blood, looked up to him as the visible representative of power and beneficence. He was their king, their lawgiver, their benefactor, their friend, their father, their physician; and if hardship were inflicted or wrong done by overseer or underling, he was the Judge of Appeal, who was sure to do them justice. Jefferson was too great an enemy of slavery to deal harshly with the slaves whom it was his misfortune to possess, and whom he could not emancipate, however willing to do so, in opposition to a force of public opinion that would have made an end of his public, and possibly of his private life, had he dared to brave it. The negroes at that time had not learned that wrong was done them, and no white apostles had appeared among them to excite insurrection against their masters. Jefferson was personally as kind-hearted a man as ever lived, and his negroes knew it, and lavished upon him, on those rare occasions when his public duties allowed him to come among them, an amount of affection which no white and free labourers ever exhibit, or perhaps are capable of exhibiting, to their employers. His daughter Martha afterwards described the scene. When the carriage arrived at Shadwell—Mr Jefferson's birth-place—the negroes determined to draw it up the mountain-side by hand to Monticello. " When the door was opened they received him in their arms and bore him to the house, crowding round and kissing his hands and feet, some blubbering and crying, some laughing. It seemed impossible to satisfy their anxiety to touch him and the earth which bore him." This ebullition of feeling was by no means unusual, and at all times the negroes were most devoted in their attachment to him. " They believed him," says his daughter, " to be one of the greatest, and they knew him to be one of the best of men, and the kindest of masters." They spoke to him freely in all their difficulties, and he watched over them in sickness and in health, interested himself in all their concerns, ever showing esteem for the good, and indulgence to them all.

On his way from Norfolk to Monticello, Mr Jefferson received a communication from General Washington which influenced the whole course of his future life, involved him anew and more violently in the vortex of politics, and rendered his dream of ease a dim possibility of the future, rather than a present possession. He was offered the high position of Secretary of State; and after much earnest thought and many misgivings, he accepted it.

On the 19th of February 1801, Jefferson wrote to his son-in-law, Mr Randolph, that exactly after a week's balloting, ten of the States had recorded their votes in his favour for the Presidency of the United States, in succession to Mr Adams—that four States voted for Aaron Burr. The opposition of the minority to Jefferson had been violent and protracted; but his great celebrity, and the eminent services he had rendered to the Republic, if it were only for drawing up the masterly Declaration of Independence, were too great to be ignored in those early days, when personal distinction and public

achievements for the national good or the national
renown were passports—as unhappily for America
they have ceased to be in the present time—to the
love and favour of the people, and to the highest
honour in their power to bestow.

It is not the object of these pages to narrate the
history of the United States after they had become
independent of Great Britain,—thanks to the efforts
of Washington, Jefferson, and their great, though less
celebrated and possibly less illustrious compeers,
Benjamin Franklin and others; or much might be
said of Jefferson's cautious and successful statesmanship and prudent management of public affairs
during his first Presidency, from 1801 to 1805.
It was during his first occupation of the Presidential chair that Louisiana was purchased from
the French — a purchase which Jefferson highly
approved, if he did not originate.   Burr, who was
Jefferson's competitor for the Presidency, was not
a popular man.   His unpopularity was afterwards
amply justified by a disgraceful private and public
career; and Jefferson's victory was therefore hailed
with enthusiasm by all—and they were the great
and overwhelming majority—who desired that the
Presidential office should be reserved for respectable
men, especially if the respectable men were pos-

sessed of brilliant talents and capacity. Great rejoicings were held in all the principal cities of the
Union; and a song written for the occasion, of
which the chorus was "Jefferson and Liberty,"
took possession of the fancy, or perhaps the heart,
of the multitude, and was heard on every side *ad
nauseam*, until its constant repetition partook of
the character of a public nuisance. The new
President gave such general satisfaction in his high
office, that he was elected for a second term in
1805, and would probably have been re-elected to
a third term in 1809, if he had been disposed to
accept the burdensome honour, and the still more
burdensome responsibility. But his mind on the
subject had long been made up. In a letter
written to an intimate friend in January 1805,
after his election to the second term, and but two
months previous to his inauguration, he wrote:—

"My opinion originally was, that the President
of the United States should be elected for seven
years, and be for ever afterwards ineligible. I
have since become sensible that seven years is too
long to be irremovable, and that there should be a
peaceable way of withdrawing a man midway when
he is doing wrong. The service for eight years,
with the power to remove at the end of the first

S

four, comes nearly to my principle as corrected by experience; and it is in accordance with that, that I am determined to withdraw at the end of my second term. The danger is, that the indulgence and attachments of the people will keep a man in the chair after he has become a dotard, that re-election through life shall become habitual, and that election for life will follow. General Washington set the example of voluntary retirement after eight years, and I shall follow it. . . . I had determined to declare this intention; but I have consented to be silent, on the opinion of friends who think it best not to put a continuance of office out of my power, in defiance of all circumstances. There is but one circumstance which could engage my acquiescence in a third election—to wit, such a division about a successor as might bring in a monarchist. But that circumstance is impossible. While, therefore, I shall make no public declaration of my purpose, I have freely let it be understood in private conversation. In this I am persuaded that my friends generally will approve of my views. And should I, at the end of my second term, carry into retirement all the favour which I acquired in the first, I shall feel the consolation of having done all the good in my power, and expect with more than composure the termination of a life no longer valuable to others, or of importance to myself."

Jefferson's second inauguration took place in 1805, on the customary day, the 4th of March, when he was in the sixty-second year of his age. The inaugural address which he delivered on the occasion was only remarkable for the pathetic paragraph with which it concluded :—

" In entering upon the duties to the exercise of which my fellow-citizens have again called me, I have no fear that any motives of interest will lead me astray. I am sensible of no passions which can seduce me knowingly from the paths of justice; but the weakness of human nature, and the limits of my own understanding, may produce errors of judgment injurious to your interests. I shall need, therefore, all the indulgence I have hitherto experienced ; and the want of it will certainly not lessen with increasing years. I shall need, too, the favour of that Being in whose hands we are, who led our forefathers, as He led Israel of old, from their native land, and planted them in a country overflowing with all the necessaries and comforts of life, who has covered our infancy with His providence, and our riper years with His wisdom and power, and to whose goodness I ask you to join with me in supplication that He will so enlighten the minds of your servants, guide their counsels, and prosper their measures, that whatever they may do shall result in your good, and secure to you peace with, and the friendship and approbation of, all the nations of the world."

A few days before the expiration of his second term of office, addresses poured in upon him from all parts of the country, expressive of the highest approval of his administration, and his wise conduct of public affairs. But that which pleased him most of all was an address voted by an overwhelming majority of the Legislature of his native State of Virginia, on the 6th of February—less than a month before the installation of his destined successor, Mr Madison. "We have to thank you," said the gratifying document, "for the model of an administration conducted on the purest principles of republicanism, for pomp and state laid aside, patronage discarded, internal taxes abolished, a host of superfluous officers disbanded, the monarchic maxim that a national debt is a national blessing renounced, and more than thirty-three millions of our debt discharged, and, without the guilt and calamities of conquest, a vast and fertile region added to our country, far more extensive than her original possession, bringing along with it the Mississippi and the port of New Orleans, the trade of the West to the Pacific Ocean, and, in the intrinsic value of the land itself, a source of permanent and almost inexhaustible revenue. . . . How blessed will be the retirement into which you are about to go! How deservedly blessed it will be! You carry with you the richest of all rewards, the recollection of a life well spent in the service of your country, and proofs the most decisive of the love, the gratitude, and the veneration of your countrymen. That your retirement may be as happy as your life has been virtuous and useful; that our young men may see in the happy close of your days an additional inducement to form their minds on the model of yours,—is the devout and earnest prayer of your fellow-citizens who compose the General Assembly of Virginia."

Jefferson, thankful to be free of the heavy responsibilities of the Presidential office, attended as a spectator the inauguration of Mr Madison, and two days afterwards set out on his return to his farms, his plantations, his library, and his dearly beloved violin, at Monticello, which he reached in the middle of March. He wrote to Madison on the 17th an account of the journey, which he declared to have been very fatiguing, over roads which were so trying to wheel-carriages that he found it more comfortable to ride on horseback, which he had done for eight hours, during as thick and disagreeable a snowstorm as he had ever witnessed. He was now in his sixty-seventh year, and felt no inconvenience from his ride except fatigue—a result which gave him "more confidence in his *vis vitæ* than he had ever before entertained." His personal appearance at this time has been described by his biographer, Dr Randall, who wrote his life in three large volumes. "Jefferson was 6 feet $2\frac{1}{2}$ inches in height. His movements were unrestrained, swinging, and bold. Calm authority sat in his eye, and lurked in the firm intonations of his voice. In a crowd, or in any situation, he at once attracted notice. He was recognised by high and low as a leader of men. The impression which his looks conveyed was that of great firmness and gentleness combined, of powerful energy in perfect repose. His conversation was always pleasing to the listeners, though he made no effort at sustained brilliancy, and he utterly lacked wit."

In 1810, Jefferson, in a letter to the great Polish

patriot Kosciusko, thus described his course of life at his farm at Monticello :—

"My mornings are devoted to correspondence. From breakfast to dinner I am in my workshop, my garden, or on horseback among my farm-labourers. From dinner to dark I give to society and recreation with my neighbours and friends; and from candle-light to early bed-time I read. My health is perfect, and my strength considerably re-inforced by the activity of the course I pursue. I talk of ploughs and harrows, of seeding with my neighbours, and of politics, too, if they choose, with as little reserve as the rest of my fellow-citizens. I feel the blessing of being able to say and do what I please without being responsible to any mortal. A part of my occupation, and by no means the least pleasing, is the direction of the studies of such young men as ask me for it. They have the use of my library, and make a part of my society. In advising the course of their reading, I endeavour to keep their attention fixed on the main objects of all knowledge—the freedom and happiness of mankind; so that, coming to bear a share in the councils of the country, they will learn to keep in view the sole objects of all legitimate government."

Jefferson, during his quiet retirement, had few troubles to contend with—but one of them afflicted him greatly. In removing his effects from Washington, a large trunk, sent round by water for the sake of economy, was broken open by robbers on the Jame river, and its contents, valueless to the thieves, were thrown into the stream. He was particularly fond of philology, and had spent thirty years in collecting and making vocabularies of the various Indian tribes, which were not then so nearly extirpated as they have since become. He had fifty of such vocabularies in manuscript, which were all thrown into the river, destroyed or lost, with the exception of a very few leaves, that were afterwards discovered in the mud of the river. What made the loss harder to bear, was the fact that many of the dialects, of which the records thus destroyed—and to all appearance preserved by a hand well competent for the task—had become extinct, and that others were fast perishing with the tribes that had employed them. The loss was irreparable, and Jefferson never ceased to lament it during the remainder of his life.

A letter preserved by Dr Randall, and written by one of the granddaughters of Jefferson some years after his death, gives so interesting a picture of this great Cincinnatus of the Western world, that no sketch of the life and character of the philosopher, the scholar, and the statesman would be complete without it :—

" With regard to the tastes and wishes which he carried with him into the country, his love of reading alone would have made leisure and retirement delightful to him. Books were at all times his chosen companions, and his acquaintance with many languages gave him great power of selection. He read Homer, Virgil, Dante, Corneille, Cervantes, as he read Shakespeare and Milton. In his youth he had loved poetry; but by the time I was old enough to observe, he had lost his taste for it, except for Homer and the great Athenian tragics, which he continued to the last to enjoy. He went over the works of Æschylus, Sophocles, and Euripides, not very long before I left him. Of history he was very fond, and this he studied in all languages, though always, I think, preferring the ancients. In fact, he derived more pleasure from his acquaintance with Greek and Latin than from any other resource of literature; and I have often heard him express his gratitude to his father for causing him to receive a classical education. I saw him more frequently with a volume of the classics in his hands than with any other book. Still he read new publications as they came out, never missed the new number of a review, especially of the 'Edinburgh,' and kept himself acquainted with what was being done, said, or thought in the world from which he had retired. He loved farming and gardening, the fields, the orchards, and his asparagus-beds. Every day he rode through his plantation and walked in his garden. In the cultivation of the last he took great pleasure. Of flowers, too, he was very fond. One of my early recollections is of the attention which he paid to his flower-beds. He kept up a correspondence with persons in the large cities, particularly, I think, in Philadelphia, for the purpose of receiving supplies of roots and seeds, both for his kitchen and flower garden. I remember well when he first returned to Monticello, how immediately he began to prepare new beds for his flowers. He had these beds laid off on the lawn, under the windows, and many a time I have run after him when he went out to direct the works, accompanied by one of his gardeners, generally Wormley, armed with spade and hoe, whilst he himself carried the measuring-line. I was too young to aid him, except in a small way, but my sister, Mrs Bankhead, then a young and beautiful woman,

. . . was his active and useful assistant. I remember the planting of the first hyacinths and tulips, and their subsequent growth. The roots arrived, labelled each one with a fancy name. There was Marcus Aurelius and the King of the Gold Mine, the Roman Empress and the Queen of the Amazons, Psyche, the God of Love, &c. Eagerly, and with childish delight, I studied this brilliant nomenclature, and wondered what strange and surprisingly beautiful creations I should see rising from the ground when spring returned, and these precious roots were committed to the earth, under my grandfather's own eye, with his beautiful granddaughter Anne standing by his side, and a crowd of happy young faces, of younger grandchildren, clustering round to see the progress, and inquire anxiously the name of each separate deposit. Then when spring returned how eagerly we watched the first appearance of the shoots above ground. Each root was marked with its own name written on a bit of stick by its side; and what joy it was for one of us to discover the tender green breaking through the mould, and run to grandpapa to announce that we really believed Marcus Aurelius was coming up, or the Queen of the Amazons was above ground! With how much pleasure, compounded of our pleasure and his own, on the new birth, he would immediately go out to verify the fact, and praise us for our diligent watchfulness! Then when the flowers were in bloom, and we were in ecstasies over the rich purple and crimson, or pure white, or delicate lilac, or pale yellow of the blossoms, how he would sympathise in our admiration, or discuss with my mother and elder sister new groupings and combinations and contrasts! Oh, these were happy moments for us and for him!"

Jefferson's declining years were harassed and over-clouded by pecuniary difficulties—not brought upon him by personal or family extravagance, or by his mismanagement of his own or his paternal resources, but by his good-natured folly in becoming security for a lifelong friend, in whom he trusted,—not wisely but too well, and too much. But though Jefferson, like all other men who have made themselves eminent in political contests, and the inevitable animosities engendered in the antagonisms of public life—especially in such gigantic crises as those which accompanied and followed the birth of the young Republic—had made many and powerful enemies, he had made a greater number of equally and more powerful friends. These latter were eager to come to his rescue, and offers of assistance poured in upon him from all quarters; but all of these that were of a private nature he respectfully but positively declined. Those of a public nature he gratefully accepted. From New York the sum of 8500 dollars was forwarded; from Philadelphia, 5000 dollars; from Baltimore, 3000 dollars; and from other less important cities, considerable sums, and large in proportion to their wealth and population. A scheme of a lottery for his benefit, proposed by some of his friends, but never thoroughly approved by himself, was brought forward only to be abandoned. "Mr Jefferson," says his biographer, Dr Randall, "had the inexpressible satisfaction of believing that his debts would be paid; that his hearthstone would descend to his children; and that his family would be left independent. Happily he died in that delusion."

To the permanent disgrace of his contemporaries and colleagues—many of the latter being powerful and rich—the grave had only closed over the remains of the great patriot, when his goods and chattels, and the whole of his landed property, were sold by public auction to clear off his liabilities; and his unmarried daughter was left without a place in which to lay her head. Kings, it has been observed, are too often ungrateful; but Democracies and Republics are quite as often forgetful of the merits and necessities of their greatest benefactors.

Mr Jefferson had been a sufferer for many years from severe chronic diarrhœa—a malady which, with over-sensitive delicacy, he concealed from his family, and which he endeavoured to conceal from his medical attendants. The weakness thus occasioned, which would have told severely upon him, even if he had been a younger man, told with crushing force upon him as he approached fourscore, and which, combined with other infirmities and old age, proved fatal at eighty-two. In the spring of 1826 his strength became seriously impaired, his appetite diminished, and the little food he was able to take failed to afford him adequate nutrition. His mind, however, retained all its usual energy and lucidity. He knew himself to be fast failing, and was quite resigned to death, though in the month of June in that year he had a lingering hope that death would not strike him until after the 4th of July—the anniversary of the Independence of the United States— which he had done more than any man, Washington alone excepted, to secure and establish. On the 3d of July, wrote Dr Dunglison, the physician who attended him, his slumbers were evidently those of approaching dissolution. He slept until evening, and on awaking, thought the night had passed, and said faintly, " This is the 4th of July." On learning that the day had not arrived, he quietly sank to sleep again, but woke several times in a state of semi-consciousness, which lasted until fifty minutes past noon — on the anticipated 4th — when he breathed his last, without a sigh or a struggle. Thus his wish was gratified, and his life was prolonged to the memorable 4th, rendered still more memorable that day by the fact that the great Republic, of which he was one of the founders, then completed the fiftieth year of its independence.

This circumstance was well calculated to operate powerfully and pathetically on the imagination of the American people. The event, impressive in itself, was rendered still more impressive by the death, on the same day, of John Adams, his firm friend and predecessor in the Presidential chair. The circumstances have been already recorded in the life of that statesman (see p. 204), and were commented upon in all the pulpits of the land on the following Sunday, in terms befitting the singular solemnity of the occasion.

Thus lived and thus died the great Thomas Jefferson—a man who, taken all in all, was the most remarkable man of his age and country, and towered high above all his contemporaries, Washington himself not excepted. Washington did more than Jefferson, but he worked physically and successfully; while Jefferson, with a far higher range and capacity of mind, worked intellectually and often unsuccessfully. All his ideas were in advance of his time. Had his plans for the gradual abolition of slavery been adopted, as they ought to have been, and would have been if his contemporaries had been half as wise and far-seeing as he was, they would have prevented the stupendous Civil War that from 1860 to 1865 imperilled the existence of the Republic, and rendered impossible the false issues that led to it, the shedding of the brave blood which was poured out like water on both sides during that fratricidal struggle, —not for liberty, as has been asserted, but for power and dominion, and the right of the North to play against the South the part attempted to be played, but without success, by George III. and his Ministers against the unwilling colonies. Neither Washington nor Jefferson, nor the leading Southern statesmen of their day, upheld slavery for the love they bore it, or maintained it except temporarily, and with the greatest regret and compunction, as an evil to be eradicated in due time; but the means to accomplish which, with safety to all whose interests were involved directly or indirectly in its continuance, even to the unhappy negroes themselves, whose very existence might be imperilled by sudden freedom, were not apparent to anybody—Jefferson alone excepted. It is a common error, and a cruel calumny, to assert that the Southern States in the late war took up arms for the sole purpose of maintaining negro slavery. The real motive power of the war was the denial of the Southern States that the Northern States had any right to meddle with the question except within their own boundaries; that as the Northern States had abolished negro slavery, one by one, in the exercise of their undoubted rights as States,—Massachusetts at one time; New York at another; Pennyslvania, and all the rest, at such times as suited their own convenience and supposed interest, and the will of their several legislatures, all sovereign in the matter,—the same rights belonged to each State of the South, which would, in all likelihood, have abolished the pernicious institution when the time was ripe, if they had not been goaded into obstinacy by what they considered the illegal interference of the North, in matters which were for the decision of the South alone.[1] Mr

---

[1] The whole question ultimately turned upon a side issue, and was

Jefferson—as befitted the author of the immortal
Declaration of Independence, which contains the
noble words, that " *all* men " were born free and
equal—was an enemy of slavery, either of the
white man or the black, and was with all his heart
and mind desirous of its abolition in America,—
immediate, if that were possible; gradual, if immediate emancipation were impossible or even
greatly dangerous,—as he proclaimed in his early
manhood, when he was not in possession of power
or office, and which he reiterated more emphatically

not wholly due to philanthropic or humanitarian, but mainly to
political motives. Politically, the North disapproved of slavery ;
socially, it disapproved of the negro. The new States that were
carved out of the great and almost illimitable Western territories of
the Union were colonised by the overflow of Northern men and by
European emigrants, and negro slavery was not permitted in them.
The Southern slave States did not furnish emigrants to the West, and
were consequently, in default of their occupation of new territories,
in danger of being continually outvoted and rendered powerless in
the great Congress of the nation. As the North, for political
reasons, extended the area of free States westwards to the Pacific
Ocean, so the South, for political reasons, and for the conserva-
tion of the equipoise between the two great sections of the Republic, was desirous of creating States southwards in Texas, and to the
west of what was called Mason and Dixon's line of latitude, in
which negro slavery should be permitted. To this arrangement
the North objected—not so much for love of the negro, as for love
of political ascendancy. Hence the war, and hence the abolition of
negro slavery by Mr Lincoln as a war measure, and not as one of
Christian justice and enlightened philanthropy.

and more solemnly after he had twice served as chief magistrate, and consequently spoke with more than common authority and experience. In May 1826, less than three months before his death, he wrote to a friend and relative on the subject of slavery and some others, upon which he had been accused of changing his opinions as he grew older. "My sentiments have been forty years before the public. Although I shall not live to see them consummated, they will not die with me; but, living or dying, they will ever be in my most fervent prayer."

Jefferson's views on the subject of slavery were unhappily without effect on the minds of his countrymen. They were far in advance of the public opinion of his time when first promulgated in 1784; but they nevertheless influenced to a larger extent than is generally admitted the opinion of the Northern States, as they one by one—in their own time, and to suit their own pleasure and convenience—abolished the slavery which they had learned to consider wrong, not perhaps altogether without the leaven of the selfish consideration that in the North free labour was profitable, and slave labour was unprofitable, for the reason that it was far more costly than free labour. In the Northern

States labour was only remunerated while the labourer was able and willing to work; in the South the labourer was maintained at considerable cost during his infancy, as well as in his senile decrepitude, when his labour was without any value.

Mr Jefferson was also in advance of the public opinion of the great majority of his countrymen, who entertained feelings of hostility and ill-will against the British nation, and against Englishmen especially, for the part that the British Government had taken in resistance to the liberty and independence of the American colonies. Jefferson did not blame the British people for the unwise policy of their Government, but constantly, and on every convenient occasion, urged upon the Americans the desirability and the duty of maintaining friendly, and indeed cordial, relations with their brothers on the other side of the Atlantic. In this respect also the opinions of Jefferson have at length begun to prevail more largely than ever among his countrymen, and help to strengthen the estimation in which his memory is held by all right-minded men on both sides of the Atlantic.

BENJAMIN FRANKLIN.

THE part played by Benjamin Franklin in the establishment of the Independence of the United States was eminently great, if not remarkably brilliant. While there was something patrician in the birth, education, conduct, and public services of Washington, and Jefferson, and Adams, his fellow-labourers in the work, Benjamin Franklin was wholly plebeian in origin, and in his avocations for the greater part of his early life. But such mighty plebeians, and such men of undoubted genius as he in later life proved himself to be, in literature, in science, and in statesmanship, the world has rarely seen. He was born in Boston, Massachusetts, in 1706, the son of a tallow-chandler in very humble circumstances, but a man of decided opinions in religion and politics, and of very considerable ability. Franklin in his childhood developed a great love for reading,—and books

of travel and adventure at sea being more abundant
than any other in his father's scanty library, the
boy's thoughts took a seaward turn, as is customary
with boys of an enterprising spirit, eager to see
what the world may be like beyond the boundaries of their native town or village.   But as his
access to a wider range of literature was facilitated
in due time, his enthusiasm for a sea-life gradually
diminished, and his tastes took a more intellectual
turn.   He had an elder brother established in
Boston as a master - printer, and to him he was
apprenticed by his father.   The brothers, however,
did not agree.   The elder brother was too severe,
and the younger too proud and independent to
endure control which he considered to be unreasonable, if not unjust.   He finally broke through the
covenants of his indenture of apprenticeship, to the
great displeasure and annoyance of his brother, who
resolved that the illegality of the act should be
made known to all the master-printers in Boston
and the neighbourhood, so as to prevent the young
man from obtaining employment at any of their
offices.   His efforts in this direction were successful, and Benjamin left Massachusetts and emigrated
to New York—then a comparatively small city—
where he obtained work, though not without diffi-

culty, in the office of an obscure printer, a German,
named Keimer. He was then only seventeen years
of age; but like Lady Macbeth, as described by
her husband, he was of "undaunted mettle," and
confident in his own strength and resources. He
worked for Keimer during a year and a half at
miserable wages,—on which, however, he managed
to subsist without running into debt. At the end
of this time he was induced by the representations
of a friend—or perhaps he was no better than an
acquaintance, to whom the name of friend was not
strictly applicable—to try his fortune in London.
He obtained employment as a compositor at an
office in Great Wild Street, Lincoln's Inn Fields,
where he set an example of temperance and abstin-
ence from alcoholic drinks to his fellow-workmen,
which they ridiculed and sometimes resisted. The
case or desk at which he worked at this office is
still preserved in London. He remained in England for little more than a twelvemonth, when
he was induced by a Mr Denham, a well-to-do
merchant in Philadelphia, to return to America
and establish himself in that city, as clerk or secretary to that gentleman. He retained that employment until the death of Mr Denham, which occurred
in 1727, when Franklin had just passed his twenty-

first year.   Finding no chance of gaining a livelihood in Philadelphia, or any other career open to
him, he returned to his old business of compositor,
and served with his former master, Keimer, at New
York, for two years, at wages somewhat higher than
he had previously earned, but still not over liberal.
But liberal or scanty, he made them sufficient,
acquiring reputation and credit in the meantime,
and making friends on every side.   The result was,
that he was enabled to set up business in Philadelphia in a small way, and to marry a young
woman whose acquaintance he had made before his
journey to London.

From this time forward his career was one of
slowly growing but steady prosperity.   He established,
edited, and printed 'Poor Robin's Almanack'—
a publication which speedily became celebrated all
over America, and attained a large and remunera-
tive sale.   It was continued for more than twenty-
five years with increasing success, and recommended
itself to the taste of the multitude by the homely
wisdom, as well as the plain and homely language,
of the proverbs and maxims of thrift, prudence, and
domestic economy, which formed the staple of the
literature which it provided, not only for the instruction but for the amusement of its readers.

Franklin appeared as an author in other directions —especially by his pamphlets on public affairs. His style was broad, simple, and plain—without any trace of affectation or any attempts at "fine writing"—resembling in these respects that of the once celebrated and still remembered William Cobbett. "His style," says an American admirer, "was adapted to all tastes and comprehensions. The scholar admired its compact and nervous simplicity; the uneducated fancied the limpid diction was like that which they themselves used in their ordinary familiar intercourse. It united the characteristics of Bunyan and Defoe with some of those of Swift and Addison. There was an obvious and all-pervading common-sense in its propositions; its illustrations were so inimitably apt and telling; its poignânt but easily understood wit so surely exposed every weak point of an adversary, so surely carried the derisive laugh of the multitude along with it, that it may well be doubted whether a more effective popular writer, on a class of subjects appealing to the understanding on the practical affairs of human life, was ever written in the English language."

As his pecuniary means increased, he became an influential, and made himself a useful, citizen of the growing city of Philadelphia, in which his home was for the future to be fixed. He was the first to propose and the strongest to support the establishment of a public library. He originated the first Fire Insurance Company in Philadelphia; organised measures for an Academy, which afterwards expanded into a University; headed a public subscription for, and afterwards obtained a grant from the Legislature of Pennsylvania to endow, the first hospital ever established in the city; and made himself conspicuous either in purse or person in the furtherance of every work of public usefulness and philanthropy.

In the year 1747 he was elected one of the representatives of Philadelphia in the Legislative Assembly of Pennsylvania—his first appearance in the public life of politics—in which, on a still larger scale, he afterwards played so distinguished a part. He spoke but seldom in the Assembly. He was a doer, not a talker; and on the rare occasions when his voice was heard, his remarks—they could not be called speeches—were few and short, but always to the point. He made no pretensions to oratory, which he looked upon, when studied with the view of creating an effect, with something like contempt. In this respect he was of the opinion of a very rich and philanthropic Scotsman in Philadelphia, whose purse was always open for charitable and patriotic purposes, who, being appealed to for a subscription to aid in the endowment of a Chair of Elocution in the University of Pennsylvania, replied, in broad Scotch, to a deputation which waited upon him for the purpose: " Na, na ! I'll no gi'e a dollar—no a red cent even—to help in the establishment of such a pernicious institution. I consider the gift of the gab the curse of all free countries, especially of England and America ! "

During the time that Franklin sat in the Assembly, a somewhat bitter controversy was raised by the heirs of the great William Penn, the founder of the State of Pennsylvania, who claimed immunity from the payment of all State taxes on the ground of the public services of their ancestor. Franklin opposed their claim with all his characteristic energy ; and made himself so conspicuous by his antagonism to a demand which he asserted to be absurd, as well as selfish, unjust, and unpatriotic, that he was soon looked upon as the leader of the anti-Penn movement. The question assumed such dimensions, that the Assembly thought it desirable to send a delegate to London to plead the cause of the people of

Pennsylvania against the heirs of Penn before the
Privy Council, with whom the ultimate decision
rested.   They made choice of Franklin for the
honourable post; and he went to London, pursuant
to his instructions, and pleaded the cause so successfully, that it was decided that the estates of
the Penn family were equally liable with those of
all the other citizens and inhabitants of the State,
and were therefore adjudged to pay their fair share
of the public burdens.   The result gave such
satisfaction to his Philadelphian friends, that
Franklin was requested to remain in London until
further orders, as agent - general for the colony.
Three other of the colonies—Massachusetts, Maryland, and Georgia—shortly afterwards intrusted
him with similar functions in their behalf, each of
them paying him a salary.   In this responsible
position he remained for five years in London,
during which time literary and scientific honours
were bestowed upon him by many learned bodies.
He was chosen a member of the Royal Society,
Foreign Associate of the Academie des Sciences
of Paris, and appointed D.C.L. or LL.D. by the
Universities of Oxford, Cambridge, and St Andrews.
It was not, however, wholly to his literary fame that
these honours were attributable.   His scientific at-

tainments—especially in the knowledge and application of electricity—had made him famous in every country of Europe. He was known and honoured as the most eminent and able man that America had yet produced. He bore his honours meekly, while accepting them as his due; and on his return to America, found that his countrymen were as ready as foreigners to greet him with well-merited acclamations.

He was a second time appointed the agent-general of Pennsylvania in London, and while acting in that capacity, in 1766, was examined at the bar of the House of Commons in relation to the Stamp Act, of which he was a strenuous opponent. The Stamp Act sowed the first seeds of the unhappy estrangement, soon to take a revolutionary shape, which occurred between the colonies and the mother-country. Franklin observed the first symptoms of the coming rupture, and endeavoured to act the part of peacemaker. But his efforts were unfruitful; and the rude rebuffs which he experienced from men in office during his second mission to England somewhat soured his usually placid temper, until ultimately he became as vigorous an opponent of the British connection as he had formerly been its warm friend.

In the House of Lords, shortly after Franklin's return to America, the great Lord Chatham replied to an insinuation of the Earl of Sandwich, that his conciliatory views with regard to the dissatisfied colonies had been inspired by Benjamin Franklin. His lordship, while asserting that his plans and opinions were entirely his own, spoke of Franklin in highly eulogistic terms. " If," said his lordship, " I were the first Minister of this country, and had the care of settling this momentous business, I should not be ashamed of publicly calling to my assistance a person so perfectly acquainted with the whole of the affairs of America as the gentleman alluded to. He is one, I am pleased to say, whom all Europe holds in high estimation from his knowledge and wisdom, and ranks with our Boyles and Newtons — an honour, not to the English nation only, but to human nature." Edmund Burke, in the House of Commons, spoke in similarly laudatory terms of the character of the distinguished American, stating " that his life had brightened every hour it continued."

But though an opponent of the immediate separation of the colonies from Great Britain, he was too acute and far - sighted a student of life and history, not to foresee the day when such separation would become inevitable. Three months before the final outbreak which led to the famous incident of the destruction of the tea in the harbour of Boston, he wrote to Mr Winthrop, an influential inhabitant of that city: " According to the Boston newspapers, there appears to be some violent spirits among them who are in favour of an immediate rupture. I hope that a spirit of prudence will govern the country, and enable it to avoid a struggle, under the operations of which the colonies might be crushed, and prevent their recovering their former position for a whole century. As among friends every affront given or received does not necessitate a duel, so among nations a war is not required for the redress of every wrong or encroachment. At present, according to my notions, it will suffice if we assert our rights on every proper occasion."

Not that he ever recognised the right of Great Britain to levy taxes, but always opposed the exercise of what he called illegal tyranny. In a letter to Lord Kames, dated in April 1767, he wrote: " I have passed a considerable portion of my life in England, and there formed so many relations of friendship, that I love and esteem this country, and form many sincere wishes for its prosperity. I desire, therefore, to see the establishment of a union with the colonies, which I look upon as the condition of her prosperity. As regards America, if such a union do not appear to me the less evident, America may at present suffer under the weight of the arbitrary power of Great Britain, and might suffer for a long time from separation. Scotland and Ireland are in a different position. Surrounded by the sea, they cannot increase sufficiently in population, in wealth, or in power, as England can. But with an immense territory, favoured by nature with all the advantages that can result from soil and climate, with great navigable rivers and lakes, America cannot fail to become a great, populous, and powerful country. From this time forward, a shorter period than is generally anticipated, she will be capable of shaking off the fetters that bind her, perhaps of binding some of them on those who placed them upon her. . . . There still remains among the American people so much respect, veneration, and love for Great Britain, that if Great Britain will only treat us prudently and with due regard to our rights and privileges, she may govern us easily for several centuries, without force, and nearly without expense. But I do not observe in America the necessary amount of wisdom, and I deplore the absence of it."

To avoid the necessity of taxing the colonies without their consent, Franklin, as early as 1754, proposed to Governor Shirley of Massachusetts a plan for authorising and enabling them to elect and send members to the British Parliament. It was a long and able State paper, but not altogether original; for nearly a hundred and twenty years previously, in 1637, seventeen years after the landing of the pilgrims of the Mayflower, the magistrates of Connecticut proposed a confederation of all the colonies, to be followed, when completed, by the sending of members to represent them in Westminster.

After Franklin's return to America, the anti-British agitation had assumed a formidable shape, and had divided the colonies into two irreconcilable parties—the enemies and the friends of the King of England and of the British connection. Franklin's side was taken, and, although the fires of his youthful activity burned somewhat dimly in 1775, when he was upwards of sixty-eight years of age, he engaged in the cause which he had espoused with an ardour which many more youthful competitors might have envied. The very day after

U

his return from London he was elected a member
of the first Congress, then about to meet in Philadelphia — that very Congress which afterwards
voted the separation of the thirteen colonies from
Great Britain, and their erection into thirteen independent States.   In this crisis, to Franklin's great
sorrow and permanent distress of mind, his only
son took the side of the British, and made himself
as conspicuous as a loyalist as his father was as a
unionist.   Franklin's sorrow deepened into anger.
He ceased to hold any communication with his
son, and never forgave him for his partisanship
until a few days before his death, when the for-
giveness which he expressed appears to have been
nominal rather than real, and to have dwelt less in
his heart than upon his lips, or at the point of his
pen, when he wrote of it.

Franklin's son William, born in 1731, was a
man of some distinction and public service.   He
was appointed by Lord Fairfax in 1763 as Governor
of New Jersey, and acted in that capacity until the
dispute between the colonies and the mother-country
had become so embittered, that no Governor appointed by royal authority could be permitted to
hold his place.   In 1775 William Franklin was
declared to be an enemy of his country, and sent

as a prisoner to a fort in Connecticut, where he remained for nearly three years. During his imprisonment, in 1777, he applied to General Washington for permission to visit his wife, who was lying dangerously ill a few miles distant from his place of captivity. Washington referred the request to Congress, who refused it. Mrs William Franklin, who died the year afterwards, attributed as long as she lived this hard refusal to the influence of her husband's father. The suspicion, under the circumstances, was not altogether unnatural, but appears to have been wholly unfounded. A tablet erected to the memory of this lady in St Paul's Church, New York, records that, compelled to part from the husband whom she loved, and despairing of the soothing hope of ever seeing him again, she sank under the accumulated burden of that and other sorrows.

While the rough draft of the Declaration of Independence was under the consideration of Congress, Franklin sat next to Jefferson, and noticed that he writhed a little under the acrimonious criticisms to which it was subjected by some of the hypercritical, as well as some of the really judicious members of that assembly. But none of the criticisms attacked the spirit or substance, but merely the occasional phraseology, of the immortal document. But Jefferson nevertheless winced under it; and Franklin, with a view of distracting his attention and amusing him, told him that he made it a rule, whenever it was in his power, to avoid becoming the draftsman of any document that was to be passed under verbal review by any public body whatever. "When I was a journeyman printer," said he, "one of my companions, who had served out his time as an apprentice, resolved to set up in business for himself, not as a printer, but as a hatter. His first concern was to set up a handsome signboard, with a proper inscription. He composed it in these words: 'John Thompson, hatter; makes and sells hats for ready money,' with the picture of a hat subjoined. He thought he would submit the inscription to his friends for their approval or amendment. The first man he showed it to thought the word *hatter* tautologous, because it was followed by the words 'makes hats,' which sufficiently showed that he was a hatter. It was struck out. The next person observed that the word *makes* might as well be omitted, because his customers would not care who *made* the hats: if the hats were good and to their mind, they would buy, by whomsoever they were made.

He struck it out accordingly. A third person said he thought the words *for ready money* were useless, as it was not the custom of the place to sell on credit. Every one who purchased expected to pay. The words were expunged, and the inscription now stood, ' John Thompson sells hats.' *Sells hats?* said his next friend. Why, nobody expects that you will give them away! What, then, is the use of those words? ' Sells hats ' was therefore obliterated. The signboard was ultimately reduced to the name John Thompson, with the painted figure of the hat subjoined." [1]

Towards the end of the year 1776, when the Declaration of Independence was published for the admiration and astonishment of the world, Franklin was appointed envoy to Paris, where, in 1778, in conjunction with Silas Deane and Arthur Lee, his brother Ministers, he negotiated with the French

[1] *Apropos* of this anecdote, it may be recorded that the pedestal of the statue of General Sir Charles James Napier, that now stands in Trafalgar Square, Charing Cross, originally bore the inscription, "Erected by public subscription of all classes, civil as well as military." I objected, in a published letter, that "if the statue were erected by public subscription, *all classes* subscribed to it, and that if *all classes* subscribed, there must have been *civil and military* men among them." The criticism found its way into all the London newspapers, and the words "of all classes, civil as well as military," were ultimately deleted. —C. M.

Government a treaty of alliance, offensive and defensive, between France and the United States. The treaty stipulated that should war arise between France and England, neither the United States nor France should make truce or peace with Great Britain without the consent of the other, nor either of them lay down their arms until the independence of the United States was formally recognised and established.

"It would be difficult," says the Count de Segur, in his 'Memoires,' "to express with what cordiality, with what favour, were received in France, in the bosom of an ancient monarchy, these envoys of a people who were in insurrection against their sovereign. Their simplicity of dress, and unaffected but dignified demeanour, contrasted with the magnificence and artificial formalities of Paris and Versailles, gave them the antique air, which seemed to transport within our walls, in the midst of the over-refined and senile civilisation of the eighteenth century, some of the sage contemporaries of Plato. Even before they were officially received by the Government, they were visited daily and eagerly by the most distinguished people of the Court and the capital, as well as by all the *savans*, the philosophers, and celebrated literary men."

This important treaty was unanimously ratified by Congress, and enthusiastically approved and applauded by the American people. Its promulgation was celebrated by public rejoicings throughout the whole of the thirteen " States," no longer " colonies." Washington, who was still at Valley Forge with his army, set apart a day for a grand military parade in honour of the occasion. " The army," says Washington Irving, in his life of the national hero, " was assembled in its best array. There were solemn thanksgivings by the chaplains at the head of each brigade, a national discharge of thirteen guns (one for each State of the Union), a general *feu de joie*, and shouts of the whole army— Long live the King of France ! Long live all friendly European Powers ! Huzza for the American States ! A banquet succeeded, at which Washington dined in public with all the officers of his army, attended by a band of music. Patriotic toasts were given, and heartily cheered. ' I never was present,' wrote a spectator, ' where there was such unfeigned and perfect joy as was discovered in every countenance.' "

After the signature and ratification of this treaty, which was the crowning achievement of his life, Franklin, who had now attained his seventy-second year, remained in Paris for five years, and retained during that time the influential and brilliant position which he occupied in the French capital, and might have retained it as long as he lived, till, in 1785, the increasing infirmities of age, and his desire to die at home among his own people, induced him to ask the President to recall him.   His residence in Paris was both a diplomatic and a social success.   He was a universal favourite among the courtly circles amid which his life was spent.   To be an American in Paris in those days was to possess a passport to everybody's goodwill; and Franklin, in his plain costume, his snuff-coloured coat, his blue worsted stockings, his simple manners, his transparent *bon-hommie*, his quaint, dry humour, and his skill as a *raconteur* of jokes and good stories, rendered him *the* American *par excellence*.   He was loved, though often laughed at; and, notwithstanding the smiles that his harmless and sometimes assumed eccentricities provoked, was esteemed and respected by everybody.   The leading politicians of the day esteemed him for his successful statesmanship; the Republican party — then in the throes of the nascent liberty which they afterwards brought forth amid blood and tears—admired him for the liberty which he had so greatly helped to secure for the

American people; the learned bodies looked up to him with veneration for his brilliant scientific attainments; and the leaders of fashionable society, more especially the ladies, admired him for the charm of his conversation. But it was not female society alone that he fascinated by his talk. President Madison, who only made his acquaintance after his final departure from Paris, wrote in after years: "Franklin's conversation was always a feast to me. I never passed half an hour in his company without hearing some anecdote or some observation worth remembering."

He had earned his leisure by his long and eminent public services, but he was not suffered to enjoy it undisturbed. Shortly after his return to Philadelphia, he was elected President of the Supreme Executive Council of the city; and two years afterwards was appointed delegate from the State of Pennsylvania in the Convention appointed to revise and amend the Articles of Union, and to draw up a Constitution. The Convention sat for upwards of four months—from May until September—under the presidency of General Washington. Difficulties and serious differences of opinion on vital points arose, as had been foreseen, within the first week of its meeting, and increased in acerbity as the

discussions proceeded.   Three of the thirteen States
declined originally to send delegates, or to be otherwise represented in the deliberations; though ultimately, and at the last moment, they consented to
take part—though they did not cordially agree—
in what was enacted by this, the most important
public body, next to that which voted the Declaration of Independence, which had ever assembled in
America.

It was asserted many times during his long
career that Dr Franklin had renounced Christianity
in his youth, and never believed in its historical
truth, its supernatural origin, or its dogmas.   However this may have been, it is certain that he
always believed in and asserted its great fundamental doctrine of love to God and to mankind,
and the duty of loving your neighbour as yourself,
and of doing as you would be done by.   Yet he
never paraded his religious views before the public.
But towards the close of his life he departed from
his usual reticence, for, during the stormy sittings
of the Convention, he was so painfully impressed
with the wide and apparently irreconcilable differences that prevailed among the delegates, and the
serious consequences which they seemed to threaten,
that he invoked with much solemnity the influence

of prayer to Almighty God to calm and to enlighten their councils. "In the situation of this Convention," he said, in the course of a short and impressive speech, "which is groping, as it were, in the dark to find political truth, and scarcely able to see it when presented, how has it happened that we have never once thought of applying to our Heavenly Father to illuminate our understandings? In the beginning of our contest with Great Britain, when we were sensible of danger, we offered daily prayers to Him to grant us His divine protection. Our prayers were heard, and they were graciously answered. I have lived a long time; and the longer I live, the more convincing proofs I have of the truth that God governs the affairs of men. We have been assured in the sacred writings that, except the Lord build the house, they labour in vain that build it. I firmly believe this; and I as firmly believe that, unless God aid us, we shall succeed in this political building no better than the builders of the Tower of Babel. We shall be divided by our little partial local interests; our projects for union will be confounded, and we ourselves shall become a byword and a reproach to the nations down to future ages. And, what is worse, mankind may hereafter from this unfortunate instance despair of establishing government by human wisdom, and leave it to chance, war, and conquest."

At the close of his speech he moved that henceforth prayers imploring the assistance and blessings of Heaven should be offered up in the Convention every morning before the commencement of business, and that one or more of the clergy should be requested to officiate.   This proposition was not favourably received or acted upon, from an apprehension that, as the Convention had not hitherto invoked the aid of Heaven at the daily commencement of its deliberations, the adoption of religious services at so late a period, and as a mere after-thought, would create uneasiness in the public mind with regard to the issue, concerning which much disquietude was already felt.   This incident —whatever may be thought of the action of the Convention—ought to relieve Franklin's memory of the charge of irreligion so often brought against him, though it may not dispose of the charge that Franklin disbelieved in the divine origin of Christianity.

At last all the various articles and sections of the Constitution having passed, either with or without amendments, a committee of five was appointed on the 8th of September to revise the style of and

arrange the articles agreed to by the Convention.
Their report did not give entire satisfaction, and
Mr Randolph, one of the delegates from Virginia,
expressed the pain he felt at differing from the body
of the Convention, on the close of the great and
awful subject of the future constitution of the
Union. Anxiously wishing for some accommodat-
ing expedient which would relieve him from his
embarrassments, he submitted a proposition that
another general Convention should be asked to
decide on any amendments that might be offered
by the delegates. This proposition was strongly
opposed by Mr Charles Pinckney of South Carolina. "Nothing but confusion and contrariety," he
said, "will spring from the experiment of a second
Convention. The States will never agree in their
plans, and the delegates, coming together under the
discordant impressions of their constituents, will
never agree." He was not without objections to the
draft. He objected, in the first place, to the con-
temptible weakness and dependence of the Executive; and in the second, to the power of a majority
of Congress over the commerce of the whole of the
States. Washington threw the great weight of his
name, authority, and influence on the other side;
and the proposal of Mr Randolph for a new Con-

vention was ultimately negatived, and the Constitution as it stood was ordered to be engrossed.

When this document in its final form was read on the 17th of September, Franklin rose and addressed the Convention. "I confess," he said, "that there are several parts of this constitution which I cannot at present approve. But I am not sure that I shall *never* approve them. For, having lived long, I have experienced many instances of being obliged, by better information or fuller consideration, to change opinions even on important subjects which I once thought to be right. The older I grow, the more apt I am to doubt my own judgment, and to pay more respect to the judgment of others. Holding these sentiments, I agree to this Constitution, with all its faults, if there be such, because I think a general Government necessary for us. There is no form of Government but what may be a blessing to the people if well administered; and I believe further that this is likely to be well administered for a course of years, and that it can only end in despotism, as other forms of Government have done before it, when the people shall become so corrupted as to need a despotism, from being unfit for any other." Dr Franklin concluded his effective speech, unadorned

in its eloquence, as Sir Robert Peel more than half
a century afterwards declared the eloquence of
Richard Cobden to be, by expressing the hope that,
"for their own sakes, as a part of the people, and
for the sake of posterity, the delegates would act
heartily and *unanimously* in recommending the Constitution for the approval of Congress."

Several other delegates supported the appeal of
Franklin, but without effect. Three members, whose
objections to the proposed Constitution were of an un-
compromising character—Colonel Mason, Governor
Randolph, and Mr Gerry—remained recalcitrant,
and absented themselves while the other delegates
affixed their signatures. Franklin, with the view,
no doubt, of making apparent a unanimity which
was not real, proposed that the members should
sign the instrument in the following form: "Done
in Convention by the *unanimous consent of the States
present*, this 17th day of December, in the year of
our Lord 1787, and of the Independence of the
United States, the 12th." The words, "the States
present," savoured somewhat of jesuitry; but they
served their purpose, and deceived nobody.

Franklin played no conspicuous part after this
in public affairs, though he still continued to take
an interest in and make himself useful in the civic

affairs of Philadelphia, where his venerable and picturesque appearance, his long white hair, his healthful countenance, and his plain attire, were familiar to everybody.

Franklin died at his house in Philadelphia on the 17th of April 1790, at the advanced age of eighty-four years and three months, mourned and respected, not only by his own countrymen for his eminent public services, but by foreign nations for the variety of his attainments and the brilliancy and usefulness of his career. Five days afterwards, James Madison, who had served the high office of President, moved in Congress, "that the House [of Representatives] being informed of the decease of Benjamin Franklin, a citizen whose native genius was not more an ornament to human nature than the various exertions of it were precious to science, to freedom, and to his country, do resolve, as a mark of veneration due to his memory, to wear the customary badge of mourning for one month." In Paris, where he was so well known and highly appreciated and beloved, Mirabeau in the National Assembly, Condorcet in the Academie des Sciences, and Larochefoucauld before the "Society of 1789," paid eloquent tributes of respect to the genius and character of the great American plebeian. Mirabeau,

when the news of his death arrived in Paris on the
18th of June 1791, said in the Assembly : " Franklin is dead. The genius which gave freedom to
America, and shed torrents of light upon Europe,
is returned to the bosom of the Divinity. The
sage whom two worlds claim for his services to
science and the history of empires, holds most undoubtedly an elevated rank among the human
species." He concluded by proposing that the
National Assembly should wear mourning for three
days, which, being seconded by General Lafayette
and M. de Larochefoucauld, was carried unanimously. " All things considered," says Mr Rives,
formerly American Minister in Europe, " Franklin
was perhaps the most remarkable man of his age.
Born in comparative obscurity, bred to a mechanical
employment, without patronage, and without education, except that which by a marvellous husbanding
of his time and mental resources he bestowed upon
himself, he came to stand before kings and Parliaments and learned assemblies in the native majesty
of superior intellect and genius. The great and the
wise of all lands did him homage. The friend and
correspondent of Hume, of Robertson, of Kames, of
Buffon, Vergennes, Condorcet, and Larochefoucauld,
courted and flattered by Voltaire, honoured by the

x

warm and cordial applause of Chatham and Burke, elected by an eager rivalry of adoption into all the learned societies of Europe, as well as of his own country, his blended services to science and freedom were immortalised in that pregnant line of classical antithesis, which the genius of Turgot annexed inseparably to his name——

Eripuit cœlo fulmen, sceptrumque tyrannis."

To this eloquent and well-deserved eulogium nothing need be added.

JAMES MADISON.

JAMES MADISON, the fourth President of the United States, played no very great or leading part in the struggle that freed the North American colonies from the yoke of the mother-country; but the influence which he brought to bear on the consolidation of the newly acquired liberties of the New World, and the drawing up of the constitution, was of the highest value and importance. He was the youngest of the five great men to whom the United States were mainly indebted for their liberty and the establishment of their independence upon a basis firm enough to defy all possible attack from without; and only vulnerable, as all human institutions are, from inherent rottenness and corruption. Against the inroads and growth of these, Madison and Jefferson, and their colleagues in the mighty work, took such precautions in settlement of the articles of union, and in the provisions of the constitution, as have reduced to a minimum the dangers which beset all human governments, whether republican or autocratic.

James Madison was born in March 1751, the son of a large landed proprietor in Orange County, Virginia, who held the position of " County Lieutenant," equivalent in dignity and influence to that of Lord Lieutenant in England. He never, however, took any very decided part in politics, being too exclusively engrossed with the management of his plantations, of which he possessed several, situated at considerable distances from each other, to spare time for public affairs.

The young Madison received the rudiments of his education at the paternal home in Montpelier, and was in due time sent to Princeton College. Here he became the favourite pupil of Dr Wotherspoon, an eminent Scotsman, who had emigrated to Virginia. He remained for three years with this accomplished preceptor, and received a sound classical and general education. He returned home at the age of twenty with the degree of Bachelor of Arts, not a scholar merely, though his scholastic acquirements were highly creditable to his talents and industry, but a keen politician, taking an enlightened interest in all the public questions of the time.

The action of Governor Gage in Massachusetts on the 19th of April 1775, in destroying some military stores at Concord in that State, on the pretext that they were about to be employed by the colonists in hostile operations against the constituted authorities, and a similar outrage in Virginia on the following day, excited considerable indignation whenever the events became known. The almost simultaneous attack ordered by Lord Dunmore, the Governor of Virginia, on the powder-magazine at Williamsburg, was universally believed to have been prearranged with his brother Governor in Massachusetts. By his lordship's directions, a party of marines from the British sloop of war, the Magdalen, lying in the James River, landed at Williamsburg under cover of the night, and took forcible possession of between fifteen and twenty barrels of gunpowder, which they conveyed to their vessel. As soon as information of what had been done reached Fredericksburg, a meeting of the Independent Light Horse Company of the town was held, at which it was resolved to march upon Williamsburg on the 29th, in order to recover the gunpowder, and to protect the remainder of the military stores in the magazine. Invitations to the independent companies of all the neighbouring towns and counties were forwarded, with the

result that six hundred horsemen declared themselves in readiness to join the movement. The
crisis looked so serious that the venerable Randolph
Peyton, late speaker of the Virginian Legislature,
and president of the Continental Congress, became
alarmed, and wrote to the leaders of the movement,
advising that they should proceed no further in the
business, inasmuch as Lord Dunmore had given
"full assurance" that due satisfaction should be
given to the colonial authorities for the outrage that
had been committed. A meeting of the principal
people was hastily summoned, at which it was resolved to adjourn indefinitely the further consideration of the subject; but, "considering the just rights
and liberty of America to be greatly endangered by
the violent and hostile proceedings of an arbitrary
Ministry, and being firmly resolved to resist such
attempts at the utmost hazard of their lives and
fortunes, they pledged themselves to each other to
be in readiness at a moment's warning to reassemble,
and by force of arms to defend the law, the liberty,
and the rights of Virginia, and of any sister colony,
from unjust and wicked invasion." This spirited
declaration, instead of concluding with the customary formula of "God save the King," appended to
the usual proclamations of the Governor, ended with

the significant, and, under the circumstances, the minatory words, " God save the liberties of America." This was one of the earliest mutterings of the popular storm that was so soon to burst over the colonies ; nor was it the only warning to the Governor, nor the only lesson he received from the outraged colonists. Within a week after these proceedings, Mr Patrick Henry, at the head of the Independent Company of Hanover, marched towards Williamsburg, to demand compensation for the gunpowder which had been wrongfully seized, or in default " to make reprisals upon the King's property, of sufficient value to replace the powder." Lord Dunmore, averse from pushing matters to an extremity, and conscious that his action had been illegal, very reluctantly yielded to the threat, and ordered the Receiver-General of the Colony to send Mr Henry his bill of exchange for £330, the estimated value of the powder. Mr Henry gave his receipt in due form for the amount, and immediately disbanded his force, and returned with his comrades in triumph to their homes, meeting wherever they passed an enthusiastic reception from the people.

It was upon this occasion that young Mr Madison took the first prominent step in a political career that was destined to be so memorable and distinguished. He was charged by a meeting, of which his father was chairman, to draw up an address of thanks to Captain Patrick Henry and his brave companions for their successful exertions in exacting redress from Governor Dunmore, which he signed along with ten other citizens. This curt but emphatic document concluded with the words, that the signatories gave it as their opinion that the blow struck originally at the government of Massachusetts (and afterwards at that of Virginia) was a hostile attack on every one of the colonies, and a sufficient warrant for a resort to such acts of violence and reprisal as may be expedient for the security and welfare of the American people.

During the twelvemonth next ensuing, the breach between the Colonies and the mother-country continued to widen. A continental Congress had been summoned to meet at Philadelphia, which had unanimously resolved to put all the colonies in a state of defence, and the great George Washington was appointed to command " all the forces raised and to be raised in defence of American liberty." Mr Madison was not a member of that Congress; but in May 1776 he was elected, being then in his twenty-fifth year, as a delegate to the Virginia Convention, charged with the duty of instructing the

Congress, to draw up the Declaration of Independence.

On the same day and by the same act by which the Convention pronounced its decision in favour of the independence of the Colonies, a committee was unanimously appointed to prepare a Declaration of Rights, and such a plan of Government as would be most likely to maintain peace and order in the State of Virginia. A committee of twenty-eight members, among whom was Mr Madison, was appointed for the purpose. The leading spirit of the committee was Mr George Mason, whose original draught of the Declaration, in fourteen articles, is still preserved. It received during its consideration a few verbal and not very important alterations, the most important of which was one proposed by Mr Madison. The last article of the fourteen related to the all-important subject of religious liberty, and set forth that "as religion, or the duty which man owes to his Creator, and the manner of his discharging it, can be directed only by reason and conviction, not by force or violence, all men should enjoy the fullest *toleration* in its exercise." Mr Madison strongly objected to the word "toleration," on the ground that it implied the possession of superior power, and that it granted as a favour and a boon that which was an inherent and indefeasible right. He therefore proposed to strike out the words, that " all men should enjoy *the fullest toleration* in the exercise of religion," and to substitute, " that all men are equally entitled to the free exercise of religion, according to the dictates of conscience." The amendment, after some discussion, was finally agreed to. This was the first great legislative triumph achieved by the young statesman, but not the last; and procured for him the applause of many of the leading spirits of the time, both in America and in the mother-country.

In the year 1777 he was chosen by the first ballot of the two Houses of the Virginian Legislature to the Council of State, a body which consisted of eight members, which participated with the Governor in the exercise of all executive powers, and without whose advice he could perform no official act. He was elected without his knowledge or consent,—a rare honour to fall to the lot of so young and so modest a man. Captain Patrick Henry was then the Governor of Virginia, and in the second year of his incumbency, and a man considerably older than Mr Madison. The Governor knew no language but English, and the services of Mr Madison, who had an adequate knowledge of French, were often called into requisition as an interpreter among the French officers who had volunteered into the military service of Virginia, or followed the Marquis de Lafayette in their enrolment under the banners of General Washington. These adventurous volunteers were mostly, like Lafayette himself, young sprigs of aristocracy, without the slightest knowledge of the democratic observances that were necessary in a popular Republic; and Madison, in after-life, used often to relate how amused he was to have to translate for Governor Henry letters addressed to him as " Son Altesse Royale, Monsieur Patrick Henry, Gouverneur de l'État de Virginie."

In December 1779, Mr Madison, then twenty-eight years of age, was chosen by the General Assembly of Virginia to represent that State in the Congress of the confederation,—the supreme and central authority, on which depended the conduct of the war against Great Britain, the establishment and recognition of American Independence, and all the collective interests of the thirteen confederated colonies, now claiming to be sovereign States. It possessed the powers of peace and war, conducted foreign negotiations, received ambassadors and ministers, appointed diplomatic agents as well as all civil and military officers of the higher grades employed in the service of the United States, exercised a general superintendence and control over the operations of the war, determined the amount and description of the land and sea forces to be raised by the several States, and fixed the sums of money to be contributed by each for the common defence. It was at the same time declared to be a fundamental canon of the confederacy that "each State should retain its sovereignty, freedom, and independence, and every power, jurisdiction, and right, which was not by the articles of this confederation expressly delegated to the United States in Congress assembled."

"Nothing," says Mr W. C. Rives, the author of the uncompleted history, in three large volumes, of 'The Life and Times of James Madison,' "could have been more gloomy and discouraging than the aspect of public affairs when Mr Madison entered upon his national career. The main body of the American army was still in winter quarters at Morristown, and almost on the verge of dissolution, from the combined effect of short supplies of food and clothing, short terms of enlistment, and the spirit of dissatisfaction, approaching to mutiny, which those causes naturally produced. These brave men were

by turns and for weeks together without meat or
without bread, and in the extremity of their dis-
tresses could not always be restrained from ir-
regular modes of supplying their wants, which the
law of self-preservation seemed to excuse if not to
justify."

On the 20th of March, Mr Madison took his
seat in this Congress that met at Philadelphia; and
on the 27th he wrote to Mr Jefferson, who had
been elected Governor of Virginia in succession to
Mr Patrick Henry: "Among the various conjunc-
tions of alarms and distress which have arisen in
the course of the Revolution, it is with pain
I affirm to you that no one can be singled out
more truly critical than the present. Our army is
threatened with an immediate alternative of dis-
banding or living on free quarters. The public
treasury is empty, and public credit exhausted.
Congress is complaining of the extortion of the
people, and the people of the improvidence of Congress, and the army of both. . . . These are
the outlines of the picture of our public situation.
I leave it to your own imagination to fill them up.
As things now stand, if the States do not vigorously proceed in collecting the old money, and
establishing funds for the credit of the new, we

are undone; and let them be ever so expeditious in doing this, still the intermediate distress to our army, and hindrance to public affairs, are a subject of melancholy reflection. General Washington writes that a failure of bread has already commenced in the army, and that for anything he sees to the contrary, it must inevitably increase. Meat they have only for a short season; and as the whole dependence is on provisions now to be procured, without a shilling available for the purpose, and without credit for a shilling, I must confess that I look forward with the most painful apprehensions."

The dark clouds lifted at last. The arrival of powerful reinforcements from France, under Generals Lafayette and Rochambeau, and of the Count de Grasse with a French fleet in the Chesapeake, filled American statesmen with hope and courage. Affairs speedily took a turn for the better; and the surrender at Yorktown, in October 1871, of the British army, under the Marquis of Cornwallis, gave the revolted colonies for the first time the well-founded hope—almost approaching to a certainty—that they would be finally triumphant, and that their independence was virtually secured.

The colonies, during their long and arduous

struggle, had always commanded the sympathy and support of a large and influential portion of the British people, not only out of Parliament, but in the House of Lords and Commons; and had perhaps no such obstinate enemy as the King himself, and such of his Ministers as agreed with him upon the merits, or yielded their opinions to his for the sake of his favour, and for the enjoyment of the offices which depended upon it.

After the surrender of the Marquis of Cornwallis, the war still lingered, amid the growing impatience of the British nation; but it was not until after a series of military events—which it is no part of the purpose of these pages to describe—that peace was finally declared in 1783, and that Sir Guy Carleton, the British commander in New York, received instructions from the British Government to evacuate that city. On the 18th of October in that year, the Congress of the United States issued a proclamation discharging the troops who had been enlisted for the war, and returning to the whole army the thanks of the country for their long, eminent, and faithful services. "In the progress of an arduous and difficult war," said the impressive document, "the armies of the United States have displayed every military and patriotic virtue, and are not

less to be applauded for their fortitude and mag-
nanimity in distress, than for a series of heroic and
illustrious achievements, which exalt them to a
high rank among the most zealous and successful
defenders of the rights and liberties of mankind."
At the same time a second proclamation, either
wholly drawn up by Mr Madison or largely inspired by him, was issued for the appointment of
a day of public thanksgiving to Divine Providence
for bringing to so auspicious and glorious an issue
a contest which at its commencement had apparently
been so unequal.   The document impressively and
eloquently set forth that the Almighty "had been
pleased to conduct the American people in safety
through all the perils and vicissitudes of the war;
that He had given them unanimity and resolution
·to adhere to their just rights; that He had raised
up a powerful ally [France] to assist them."   And
then, looking forward to the future, it invoked the
same divine aid "to give wisdom to the councils of
the nation; to inspire the people with an earnest
regard for the national honour and interest; to
enable them to improve the days of prosperity by
every good work, and to be lovers of peace and
tranquillity; to bless them in their husbandry,
their commerce, and navigation; to smile upon

their seminaries and means of education; to cause pure religion and virtue to flourish amongst them; to give peace to all nations; and to fill the world with His glory."

With the expiry of the legal term of this Congress, Mr Madison's public career came to a temporary close. At the age of thirty-two, in December 1783, he retired to his father's estate, and devoted himself to the legal and other studies which had been interrupted by his public duties. But though he studied law assiduously, he never was called upon to practise it professionally, mainly for the reason that he did not depend upon it for subsistence, and was quite contented to live the life of a planter or country gentleman, looking after his crops and governing his slaves, to whom, in principle, he would gladly have given their freedom, had public opinion or the imperative force of circumstances allowed him to do so. He was too eminent a man, and his public services had been too valuable and conspicuous, to allow him to indulge for a long time in the expectation that he would not be once again summoned to take part in public affairs. He was not therefore surprised that, at the annual election to the House of Delegates for the State of Virginia, he was chosen to represent his native county in that body.   This occurred in April 1784, or little more than six months after his retirement from the higher and more influential sphere of Congress.

During three years he took an active part in all the politics of his State, without ceasing, however, to take an enlightened interest in those of the whole confederacy.   At the end of that term, during which he could not legally sit in the general Congress, he was once again elected to that body. There was still much difficult and embarrassing work to be done in the consolidation, not so much of the liberty or the independence of the States, as of their stable and cordial union.   The separatist spirit was still powerful and aggressive, and many, if not all, of the States thought much more highly of their separate rights, as independent, self-sustaining, and self-governing commonwealths, than of their duties and liabilities as component parts of a great, powerful, and united nation.   This was the great danger that now and for long afterwards confronted the statesmen of the Union, and all who desired to weld and fuse it into a strong homogeneous power and nationality, formidable in its unity against the whole world.   So early as 1783, the New England States—which had been mainly colonised by the

Puritans and the Pilgrim Fathers, who had brought with them in the Mayflower their spiritual pride and intolerance, and their sturdy spirit of independence—had begun to talk of establishing a separate confederacy, without the admission of New York, Pennsylvania, or any of the Southern States. This feeling had not diminished in the progress of time; and in 1786, as Mr Rives records in his life of Madison, the dissatisfaction of these States with the Federal Union had grown to such a height, "that, according to the testimony of a distinguished contemporary actor having the best opportunities of information, a project was actually matured for their withdrawal and formation into a separate confederacy." Mr Fisher Ames, a leading man of the time, publicly proclaimed his want of faith in his countrymen,—proclaiming that they were too corrupt and too democratic for liberty, and that the States were too extensive for union.

The discontent of a large portion of the people of Massachusetts found a leader in the autumn of 1786, in the person of one Captain Shay, who had served under Washington in the army of Independence, who got together a considerable force, with the object of establishing a separate Eastern Confederacy *vi et armis.* He expressed his determination to attack the arsenal at Springfield, and seize the arms and ammunition that were there stored in very considerable quantities.   Affairs looked so threatening that Congress instructed General Knox, the Secretary of War, to proceed to Springfield at the head of a sufficient force, and take such measures as he deemed necessary for the safety of the Federal powder-magazine at that place.

A Committee of Congress on the 21st of October reported, "that from the facts stated in the letter from the Secretary of War, and other authentic information, it appeared that a dangerous insurrection had taken place in various parts of the State of Massachusetts, which was rapidly extending its influence; that the insurgents had already, by force of arms, suppressed the administration of justice in several counties; that though the Legislature of the said State was in session, it would undoubtedly defeat the object of the Federal interposition, should a formal application be made for the same; and that it consequently appeared to the Committee that the aid of the Federal power was necessary to stop the progress of the insurgents." The Committee added, "that there was the greatest reason to believe that, unless speedy and effectual measures were taken to defeat their designs, the insurgents would possess themselves of the arsenal at Springfield, subvert the Government and not only the Commonwealth of Massachusetts to a state of anarchy and confusion, but probably involve the United States in the calamities of a civil war."

Additional troops were needed for the purpose; but the Committee, apprehensive that if the purpose were openly avowed, a very ill feeling would be created all over the Union, applied for the necessary increase to Congress, on the plea that the troops were needed—as they partially were—for hostilities against the Indians on the western frontiers of the Union, who were giving the settlers considerable trouble. The troops asked for were accordingly raised; and a portion of them were despatched under General Lincoln to Springfield. Shay attacked the arsenal, but was repulsed with considerable loss in killed and wounded, and the capture of 150 prisoners.

The rebellion—for such it was—never took collective form after this defeat, but continued in detached efforts in various parts of Massachusetts, and lasted with more or less violence for several months. Many of the insurgents, dreading the penalties of the law if they were captured, took refuge in the adjoining States of Connecticut, Vermont, and New Hampshire, the authorities of which refused to deliver them up on the demand of the legal authorities of Massachusetts.

General Washington was very painfully impressed by the Massachusetts rebellion, and the sympathy which it excited in several other States; and wrote a letter to Mr Madison on the subject, in which he said: "How melancholy is the reflection, that in so short a time we should have made such large strides towards fulfilling the prediction of our transatlantic foes, that if we were but left to ourselves, our Government would soon dissolve! . . . What stronger evidence can be given of the want of energy in our Government than these disorders? If there is not power in it to check them, what security has a man for life, liberty, and property? To you, I am sure, I need add nothing on this subject." Mr Madison, in his diary of the proceedings of Congress, under date of February 1787, stated "that all the members agreed that the Federal Government in its existing shape was inefficient, and could not last. The members for the southern and middle States were generally anxious for some republican organisation of the system which should preserve the Union, and impart due energy to its Government. Mr Bingham of Philadelphia alone avowed his wishes that the Confederacy might be divided into several distinct confederacies, on the ground that its great extent and various interests were incompatible with a single Government."

A Convention met in 1787 to consider the vital and growing question of a real union of the States, and the affirmation on a basis too firm to be shaken of the central or Federal power. Of this important body, Washington, Jefferson, Franklin, and Madison were members, and all of them lent their talents, influence, and energy to the Federal or Union cause. Mr Madison felt very strongly on the subject. In a letter to Judge Pendleton, addressed to him a few days before taking his seat, he expressed his fears that if the Convention did not agree to a remedy, the propensity towards the establishment of a monarchy, which already existed, would grow and strengthen; and that the bulk of the people would probably prefer the lesser evil of a partition of the Union into three more practicable and energetic confederacies, to the downfall of a republican form of Government, in favour of a monarchy. "At present," he said, "no money is paid into the public treasury; no respect is paid to the

Federal authority; not a single State complies with the requisitions made upon it; some of them pass the requisitions over in silence, and others positively reject them.   The payments ever since the peace have been decreasing, and of late have fallen short of the pittance necessary for the civil list of the Confederacy.   It is not possible that a Government can last long under these circumstances."

This Convention, as has already been recorded in these pages, in the narratives of the part taken by Washington, Adams, Jefferson, and Franklin respectively, was as much indebted to Madison as to any of these for the happy issue of its labours in the establishment of the constitution of the United States.   Under that constitution the States prospered until the great Civil War of 1861-1865 placed it for a while in abeyance; only to be restored, with some modifications, on the defeat of the Southern confederacy in 1865.   These modifications confirmed by legal enactment the abolition of negro slavery, decreed without legal or constitutional authority, and solely as a war measure by President Lincoln, and introduced a few other amendments, having for their only objects the strengthening of the central authority, and the curtailment of the State rights which, pushed to their logical conclusions, had justified and might hereafter justify the secession of any State or States from the Federal Government.

In those early days of the Republic, before the first President had been elected, and the constitution finally established, eminent public service either in the camp or the cabinet was not held to be a disadvantage to the candidate who aspired to the highest office in the gift of the people. On the contrary, it was a passport to their favour, as was proved by the successive elections of Washington, Adams, and Jefferson, and as was proved at a later time on two memorable but exceptional occasions. The first was when Abraham Lincoln, who was elected to the Presidency in 1861, on account of his harmless mediocrity, was nominated a second time for his safe though not brilliant talents as a statesman. The second occurred when the same distinction was conferred on General Grant, as an acknowledgment of his victorious campaign against the South in the Civil War, and who received on two separate occasions the suffrages of the nation. The services of Mr Madison in Congress, during the early struggles of the Colonies against King George III. and the Ministry and Parliaments of the mother-country, were too conspicuous to be ignored by an appreciative country, and in 1809 he succeeded Mr Jefferson in the Presidency, obtaining 122 votes out of a total of 176.

He gave such general satisfaction during his incumbency, that he was elected to a second term in 1813. His tenure of office during eight years was chiefly memorable for the war declared by the United States against Great Britain, on the question of the rights of neutrals, which the American Government and people held to have been unjustifiably invaded. Mr Madison was personally opposed to the war—having reason, as he thought, for believing that the British Ministry had resolved to revoke the Orders in Council which had given so much offence to the American people, had time been allowed, and more patience and management exhibited. But passions had been excited, and violent counsels prevailed. The moderate and peaceable opinions of the President were overruled, and war was declared. It lasted with varying fortunes until 1815, without producing any tangible results, except a few barren victories—first on one side and then on the other—leading to no ulterior consequences of any great importance, except the creation of national animosities that it required the lapse of more than a generation to soften, but not to extinguish.

The most notable incidents of the war were the naval engagements between the Chesapeake, an American, and the Shannon, a British man-of-war, in Hampton Roads, off the mouth of the Chesapeake, in which, after a hard-fought battle, the victory remained with the Shannon. On board of the American ship 48 men were killed and 98 wounded; the British loss amounted to 24 killed and 59 wounded. The American captain was fatally wounded, and died of his injuries five days afterwards, at Halifax, in Nova Scotia.

Still more notable and deplorable was the attack upon the city of Washington in August 1814, by a British force of 5000 men—believed by the Americans to be 10,000—under the command of General Ross. The American force, under General Winder, was badly commanded and ill-disciplined. "There were no funds," says Ingersoll, an American historian, "though the city banks proffered a few hundred thousand dollars of their depreciated and in a few days destined to be inconvertible paper currency. There were no rifles nor flints enough: American gunpowder was inferior to English. There was not a cannon mounted for the defence of the seat of Government; not a regular soldier in the city; not a fortress, breastwork, or military fortification of any kind within twelve miles. The neighbouring militia of Maryland and Virginia were worn down by mortifying and disastrous service, routed and disheartened. The proportion of regular troops—all of them mere recruits, never tried in fire—was like that of coin to paper in the wretched currency, so small an infusion of the precious metal that there was scarcely any substance to rely upon."

At the first notification of the approach of a British force of well-disciplined troops, the utmost alarm prevailed in Washington, and in the councils of the President and the Administration. The Secretary of the Navy, fearing that they might fall into the hands of the enemy, set fire to a new sloop-of-war with ten guns, afloat on the Potomac, to a new schooner, to a large frigate on the stocks, and to a vast quantity of stores and machinery. On the appearance in Pennsylvania of great numbers of affrighted fugitives, flying from Bladensburg and Georgetown before the advancing British, a panic seized upon Washington. Mr Madison fled in all haste across the Potomac, but secured some of the most precious Cabinet papers, some clothing, and other important articles, including a full-length portrait of General Washington which adorned the principal public room of the White House. The city, before the arrival of the British, was plundered by gangs of escaped slaves and other ruffians, and much damage was done. But the damage, great as it was, was small in comparison with that inflicted by the British. General Ross sent forward a flag of truce, with a view of negotiating for the ransom and consequent preservation of the public buildings and other property. General Ross himself accompanied the party bearing the flag; but the party was fired upon from the windows of one of the houses in the avenue, and the General's horse was shot under him and killed. Every thought of accommodation or truce was now dispelled. The furious soldiery broke into the house from which the shots were fired, put all the people they found inside to the sword, and afterwards set the place on fire. Nothing stopped their fury after this until they had burned down the Capitol, with the valuable library of Congress, the War Office, and every other public building that was pointed out to them. The Americans themselves, fearing pursuit, set fire—by order, it was said, of Mr Madison—to the two ends of the long wooden bridge over the Potomac.

The third most memorable incident of this unhappy war was the defeat of the British forces under General Pakenham at New Orleans, on the

8th of January 1815, by General Jackson, who was afterwards elected to the Presidency, mainly in consequence of the reputation he had acquired by this victory.   Jackson was the first of the grossly illiterate Presidents,—a rough, a rowdy, a duellist, a profane swearer, and a fire-eater, without any pretensions to culture or refinement, but an honest and straightforward man, with no false pretence or affectation about him.   He had an abundance of the uncommon quality known as common-sense. For the possession of this quality, but principally by his defeat of a British general in the unhappy second war between the mother-country and her proud offshoot, he acquired the favour and support of the electoral body at a time of political excitement.

At the close of his second presidential term, when he was succeeded by Mr Monroe, Mr Madison was glad to retire to his patrimonial estate and farm at Montpelier, in his native county of Orange, in Virginia.   He was weary of the buffetings of politics and the animosities of party strife, that were alien to his gentle and peaceable nature, and only too happy to devote himself to the amenities of congenial society, and the cultivation and the consequent improvement of his private fortune, which had suffered from his long devotion to the

public service. He managed to find time for the
study of natural history, of which he had always
been particularly fond. He also recommenced the
study of law—in which he was no mean proficient
—and of literature, which he had never wholly
neglected, even in the midst of engrossing public
business. He was temporarily summoned, in 1829,
after nearly twelve years of seclusion, to serve
as a member of the Convention that met to revise
the constitution of the State of Virginia; and also
acted as Rector of the University of that State.
But the infirmities of age were pressing severely
upon him; and after serving for a few months in
the Convention, he finally returned to his estates,
and steadfastly refused all future participation in
public affairs—whether local or general—in Virginia or in Washington. But though he lived a
retired, he by no means endured a lonely life.
His house at Montpelier was the resort of all the
celebrated men of his time, more especially of the
leading politicians of his own party. His conversation was particularly fascinating, not only for its
wit and humour, and the fund of anecdote at his
command, but for his reasoning and argumentative
power, and his sound, temperate, and comprehensive views upon public affairs, and all the leading

questions of the time.   He died in 1836, in the
eighty-fifth year of his age, being survived by his
wife—a general favourite in all society—to whom
he had been united for forty-two years.   He left
no family, but a reputation second to that of no
statesman or public functionary of his age and
country, Washington and Jefferson alone excepted.

With these remarks may be concluded the personal history of the five principal founders of the Independence of the United States, each differing from
the other in character, acquirements, and achievements, but none differing from his fellows in
zeal and utility in the building up of the great
edifice of American liberty, which already begins to
overshadow the world.

THE DANGERS OF ULTRA-DEMOCRACY.

In tracing the lives and the work of the five great men who were mainly instrumental in founding the Republic of the United States, and who endeavoured so to shape its laws and mould its destinies as to secure for it not alone an independence able to withstand all probable attack, but a stability equal, if not superior, to that of the oldest empires and monarchies of Europe and Asia, we have shown that their work was one of the most difficult recorded in history. But when they rested from their labours, they each and all entertained doubts, misgivings, or fears of the durability of the apparently splendid edifice of democratic liberty which they had reared for the world's wonder. The independence of the thirteen colonies, or, as they afterwards called themselves, " States," was not secured without painful and long-continued struggles, which, without the aid of France, then engaged in a war with Great Britain, might, after all, have proved abortive. The union which they formed amongst each other was not established on such a firm and satisfactory basis as to allay jealousies, prevent all future animosities, dissensions, and disagreements, or to reconcile conflicting ideas and interests. The opinions of these five men were by no means in complete accord, and were shared, in their several degrees of divergency, by large classes of the people. Unanimity was impossible; but compromise, difficult though it appeared during many stages of the parturition, was attainable. And it was attained, with more or less willing adhesion, on the part of all the thirteen States.

The form of the future Government presented no difficulty of choice. A kingdom or an empire was impossible, and, if possible, would have been impolitic and unwise. The man did not exist out of whom the Americans could have fashioned either a king or an emperor, unless it were George Washington, whom nineteen out of twenty Americans would have refused to acknowledge in either of those capacities, and who was, besides, much too wise, prudent, and far-seeing a statesman to accept the perilous and uncertain responsibility. A Dictator might have been more easily found; but the bold ambition and the high genius necessary in the man who would strive for the dictatorship, and be able to retain it, were non-existent. Even the materials of a Cromwell were wanting. Washington, if he had been a younger and more ambitious man, might have afforded a not very distant approximation to the character. Even a Republic on the model of the republics of antiquity and of the middle ages was not possible, on account of the absence of the aristocratic element in American society—that element which formed the main ingredient of all the ancient democracies. There was but one form of aristocracy in America, and that was the aristocracy of colour— by the unwritten laws and usages of which every white citizen was a virtual aristocrat, compared with his dark-skinned brother.

Each of the thirteen original States was of necessity a pure democracy, after it had thrown off the yoke of Great Britain; and it was absolutely necessary that the union of those States should rest on a democratic, and indeed on an ultra-democratic basis. The democratic form of government is theoretically the best, wisest, and most natural that a people or a nation can establish. Government by the people and for the benefit of the people is the perfection of civilisation; but it is necessary before such a government can be established, if any length of life is to be expected for it, that the people, in the broadest sense of the word, should be virtuous and intelligent. Virtue and intelligence, notwithstanding the old classical assertion that the voice of the people is the voice of God, are not found to a conspicuous extent among the multitudes of any nation. The hewers of wood and the drawers of water may be virtuous in their degree, and as far as the sordid and engrossing cares of their hard lives will permit; but intelligent in any high sense of the word—intelligent from education and the cultivation of their noblest faculties of mind—they never have been in any age or country, and in all probability never will be, notwithstanding all the efforts which the church, the chapel, the college, and the school board may empirically employ to make them so. In a new country, such as the British Colonies were when the colonists revolted against British rule, sparsely peopled by the pioneers of civilisation, who had to struggle hard with nature for the means of subsistence, and with the Red Indians, the legitimate possessors of the soil, for their lives and safety, the ruder virtues of humanity flourished more vigorously than they could have done in the crowded cities of the old world. Intelligence born of necessity, and the sharpening of the faculties by contact with the wilderness, fitted them for self-government, and made republicans of them naturally. A Republic was thus, not theoretically alone, but practically, the best, even although it might not have been the only form of government which they could establish. The greatest danger which such a republic either inherited or incurred, lay in the probability, if not in the certainty, that, with the progress of time and the increase of population, the primitive virtue would disappear, and that the intelligence still existent would be perverted to base uses by the struggle for existence and the desperate and immoral competition for wealth and position, the invariable concomitant of an over-ripe and over-populous civilisation.

The founders of the American Republic were aware of these dangers, and did their best to provide against them, by recognising the thirteen small republics to be each complete in itself, and therefore easily governed, and setting themselves resolutely against the plan, which found considerable favour at the time, of consolidating the thirteen into one, and calling the consolidation a " Union," and not a sole entity. The first idea, however, was not that of "Union," but of "Confederation." But the name found no support among the people.

One party—not led by Washington, but of which Washington was the most illustrious and influential, and Alexander Hamilton the most eloquent adherent—desired to nationalise and to concentrate authority, so that the several commonwealths should not only be one and indivisible against the outer world, but one and indivisible among themselves,— in other words, that the congeries and agglomeration of republics, each self-existent and self-governed, should become one great Republic, and be as much a unit as France or England, Spain or Russia. It is true that the very name or designation of the new power described a different political fabric; for in a nationality, properly so called, there can be but one State, and not many States. This discrepancy, however, between the fact and the designation, did not appear very formidable, and the statesmen and philosophers of those days reconciled themselves to the only name that was then possible for the new Commonwealth, and trusted to the future to make practically right what might be theoretically wrong.

The opposite party—the true founders of repub-

licanism in America, led by the illustrious Jefferson, as great a man in his sphere as Washington
—insisted that the centralisation of power was incompatible with liberty; that the thirteen States
were even then too large to be well governed from
one centre; that each State was a true republic,
with its own constitution, its own legislature, and
its own method of administering its own affairs.
The Washingtonians, Federalists, and Centralisers so
far prevailed as to supersede the temporary confederation by what was called "a more perfect union."
This new compact was by turns approved and
attacked by all parties, as whim or necessity suggested. It was tolerated rather than beloved, and
held its ground after a certain unstable fashion, till
the election of Mr Lincoln—a period of seventy-
three years.

From the very first the friends of these conflicting principles were at variance, and on more than
one occasion the upholders of the rights of the
several States and commonwealths that claimed to
be supreme within their own boundaries, and called
themselves Democrats, was at issue with the Washingtonians and Federalists, who called themselves
Republicans, and would have established what was
virtually an autocracy, and not a democracy, if

their idea of the one Republic, paramount to the
thirteen commonwealths, found acceptance.   Thus,
as has been truly said, the founders of the Republic
and the people of their day went wrong from the
beginning.   They started upon a treacherous basis,
inasmuch as the contracting parties had opposite
designs as to the results of their agreement, and
conflicting notions as to their intentions in acceding
to it.   The one party thought republican liberty
was secured by unlimited local and limited central
action; the other imagined that a central Government in any shape was a point gained, and that
time and opportunity might be relied upon to increase its authority, and eventually to fuse into one
grander nationality than the sun had ever shone
upon, the incongruous and widely-extended commonwealths of the Atlantic seaboard, and eventually
the still more incongruous and more widely-extended
populations that sooner or later would extend to the
Pacific, and overflow the whole of the North American continent.

The idea was splendid and inspiriting.   What
mattered it to those who indulged it, and would have
given it form and substance, if its realisation could
only be achieved by the sacrifice of the republican
liberty on which the whole scheme was founded?

Nothing.   They accepted all contingencies; and for the sake of unity, the first place among the nations, and the consequent power to overawe Europe, would have yielded everything to the central power which they created.

The disruption of the Union—in order that the rights or desires of any one State, or any combination of States, might prevail over the central authority of the Republic—was continually threatened, and always possible from the earliest period. In 1803, when the Central Government purchased Louisiana from the French and incorporated it with the Union, Mr Josiah Quincy—a very eminent citizen of Massachusetts, and member of Congress— advocated in that assembly the repudiation of the transaction, and contended that Massachusetts had a right to withdraw from the Union,—for the reasons, among others, that its people had been taxed, without their consent, to pay their share of the purchase-money, and that it extended the area of negro slavery.   At the Hartford Convention in 1814, when the whole of the New England and several of the other Northern States were vehemently opposed to the continuance of the war with Great Britain, a far more serious disruption of the Federal compact was threatened.   New York and

the New England States—comprising Massachusetts, Connecticut, Rhode Island, Vermont, and New
Hampshire—suffered greatly in their foreign trade
by the blockade instituted and rigidly maintained
by Great Britain, and complained that their ships
remained idle in their harbours and rotted in their
wharves in consequence. The Convention loudly
and all but unanimously expressed its determination to secede from the Union, unless the Central
Government agreed to a peace with the mother-
country ; and the disaffection expressed by the delegates extended all over the Northern States, and
might have produced the disruption which was
threatened, if the war had not been happily terminated, for European rather than for American
reasons.

But a far greater danger threatened the Union
seventeen years afterwards, when a formidable attack was made upon the State Democracies and
the rights claimed and hitherto exercised by all
the States—including the eleven additional ones
that had joined the Union—since the Declaration
of Independence. General Andrew Jackson, twice
elected to the Presidency, was the functionary
under whose auspices the attack was made. He
was a man of the lowest class, born among the

dregs of the people, with none of the education, the feelings, or the manners of a gentleman, or even of an ordinary shopkeeper. But he was brave, resolute, honest, and well-intentioned; and he acquired the goodwill and extorted the admiration of his countrymen by his defeat of a small British force at New Orleans during the war of 1814. He was a profane swearer, a bully, and a drunkard; but a good soldier, an able commander, and an upright, if not an able magistrate. He was scarcely for three months together, during his busy and rough life, out of a street brawl or a duel; always went about armed—carried his life, as it were, in the hollow of his hand—and was ready at all times to risk it against the meanest of his foes for the smallest offences. He was commonly known as " Old Hickory "—a name given to him by the vulgarest of the people, from the toughness of his character—hickory being the hardest wood grown in the American forests.

He was celebrated for three predominating and rampant aversions—a hatred of debt, of paper-money, and of Great Britain. His hatred of Great Britain was partly founded upon the prejudices inherited with his Irish blood, but mainly upon jealousy of its supremacy among the nations of the world. The object of his love was the union of the States—not because such union was conducive to the liberty of the American people, but because he thought, if firmly maintained, it would in the course of time spread itself over the whole North American continent from the Atlantic to the Pacific, from the Arctic zone to the Isthmus of Panama; and not only over the continent, which included Canada, but over the West India Islands, including Cuba, the possession of which is still the dearest wish of the American heart. In this respect he was in complete sympathy with the popular passion and ambition of his contemporaries,—a passion and an ambition which the lapse of time seems to have strengthened, and which has been but partially satisfied by the results of the war which the "Union" wantonly provoked against Mexico, and which resulted in the annexation of Texas on its southern border — a country as large as France—and of California, the richest jewel in the splendid tiara of the Republic.

General Jackson had no respect for the rights of the States, which were supposed and declared to be each sovereign and independent within their own boundaries, if those rights seemed to him to be hostile to the designs of the Union in its collective capacity. The Vice-President — the cele-brated Mr Calhoun — was a man of a different character, and had political ideas entirely at vari-ance with those of his superior. Consequently, after a very short tenure of the office, he resigned the Vice-Presidency in favour of a seat in the Senate. To the other three objects of his hatred, General Jackson speedily added a fourth in the person of Mr Calhoun.

Up to the year 1828—during the first term of General Jackson as President—the expenditure of the Central Government, which was wholly distinct from that of the several States, had been so small, the revenue so large, and the surplus so consider-able, that Federal statesmen had much difficulty in devising a means for disposing of it to the satisfac-tion of the people. The surplus, and consequently unnecessary revenue, was derived from the heavy duties levied by the Protectionists on foreign goods —not, as they said, for purposes of revenue, but for the encouragement of native industries. The Protectionists—quite satisfied with the working of their principle—proposed to continue it in full operation, and to devote the large accruing revenues to distribution, *pro rata*, among all the States in proportion to their population. The Free-Traders—

who were preponderant in all the Southern States, which were purely agricultural, and had few or no manufactures—objected to a protective system, of which the Northern States reaped all the real or supposed advantages ; and proposed, instead of dividing the surplus revenue, to prevent all surplus for the future by reducing the import duties to the lowest rates which would produce a merely sufficient revenue, to meet the small expenses of the Central Government.   Upon this point issue was joined throughout the whole Union,—General Jackson being strong for Protection, his former Vice-President being equally strong for Free Trade.   The Congress declared itself in favour of Protection— though not disinclined to a modification of its stringency by a reduction of the tariff—provided the principle of the duty of the Central Government to protect and encourage native industry were affirmed.

Mr Calhoun, unlike General Jackson, was a man of education and culture, a trained lawyer and statesman, a master of language, both with the tongue and the pen, an acute logician, in his manners and conversation a gentleman, and a natural aristocrat—neither a rowdy himself nor an associate of rowdies, such as was the President ; and when

Mr Calhoun, in the Senate, made himself the mouthpiece of the Free Trade party, the antagonism between him and the President became violently personal as well as political.

The question at issue was formally introduced into Congress in December 1831. Long debates ensued, which lasted for seven months. In the summer of 1832, the measure for continuing the protective duties, vehemently opposed by Mr Calhoun and by the Southern members, aided by a few Northern men, was passed by both Houses—in the Senate by a majority of 32 against 16; and in the House of Representatives by 129 against 65. The result did not astonish but greatly incensed the whole of the agricultural South; and early in the autumn of that year, the State Legislature of South Carolina passed an Act calling for a convention of the whole people, to take into consideration what they thought to be the unconstitutional action of the Washington Congress, and to recommend the course that the State Legislature should in consequence pursue. The Convention met in November, and agreed to the memorable " Ordinance of Nullification," which was passed unanimously amid shouts of bewildering excitement—every man present pledging, by solemn oath, his life and sacred honour in its support. This ordinance consisted of five decrees or parts :—

"That the tariff law of 1828, and the amendment to the same of 1832, were null, void, and no law, nor binding upon this State, its officers, or citizens.

"That no duties enjoined by that law, or its amendment, should be paid, or permitted to be paid, in the State of South Carolina, after the 1st day of February 1833.

"That in no case involving the validity of the expected nullifying Act of the Legislature, should an appeal to the Supreme Court of the United States be permitted. No copy of proceedings should be allowed to be taken for that purpose. Any attempt to appeal to the Supreme Court "might be dealt with as for a contempt of the Court" from which the appeal was taken.

"That every office-holder in the State, whether of the civil or the military service, and every person hereafter assuming an office, and every juror, should take an oath to obey this ordinance, and all Acts of the Legislature in accordance therewith or suggested thereby.

"That if the Government of the United States should attempt to enforce the tariff laws then existing, by means of its army or navy, by closing the ports of the State, or preventing the egress or ingress of vessels, or should in any way harass or obstruct the foreign commerce of the State, then South Carolina would no longer consider herself a member of the Federal Union ; the people of this State would thenceforth hold themselves absolved from all further obligation to maintain or preserve their political connection with the people of the other States, and would forthwith proceed to organise a separate Government, and do all other acts and things which sovereign and independent States may of right do."

Mr Hayne, the then Governor of South Carolina, went even beyond the Convention in his zeal for the democratic rights of his native State, and in the boldness of the language in which he asserted his determination to uphold them. " I recognise," he said, " no allegiance as paramount to that which the citizens of South Carolina owe to the State of their birth or their adoption. I publicly declare, and wish it to be distinctly understood, that I hold myself bound by the highest of all obligations to carry into full effect, not only the ordinance of the Convention, but every Act of the Legislature, and every judgment of our own Courts, the enforcement of which may devolve upon the Executive. I claim no right to revise their acts. It will be my duty to execute them, and that duty I mean to the utmost of my power faithfully to perform." He went even further than this, and declared that "if the sacred soil of Carolina should be polluted by the footsteps of an invader, or be stained with the blood of her citizens, shed in her defence, he trusted in Almighty God that no son of hers, native or adopted, who had been nourished at her bosom, or been cherished by her bounty, would be found raising a parricidal arm against her; and that even should she stand *alone* in the great struggle for constitutional liberty, encompassed by her enemies, there would not be found, in the wide limits of the State, one recreant son who would not fly to the rescue, and be ready to lay down his life in her defence. South Carolina," he added, " could not be drawn down from the proud eminence on which she had placed herself, except by the hands of her own children. She asked but a fair field, and no more. Should she succeed, it would be glory enough for her to have led the way in the noble work of reform. And if, after making these efforts, due to her own honour and the greatness of the cause, she were destined utterly to fail, the bitter fruits of that failure, not to herself alone, but to the entire South, and to the whole Union, would attest her virtue."

The remaining States of the South did not possess at this time a statesman of the high calibre, the courage, and the eloquence of Mr Calhoun, to defend the cause of Free Trade and State rights against Protection and the despotism of the Congress at Washington. Giving South Carolina their fullest sympathy, those States gave nothing else, and left it to fight the battle unaided, apparently deeming the struggle to be more praiseworthy than helpworthy. The South Carolinians were thoroughly in earnest. The young and middle-aged, even the old men, enrolled themselves enthusiastically as volunteers, and submitted themselves to daily drill, to be in readiness at a day's or an hour's notice to support their determination by force of arms. The ladies busied themselves in preparing blue cockades and badges, with the real or imitation palmetto leaf, the State emblem, to be worn in the caps or on the bosoms of the volunteers. Everything presaged the arbitrament of war, if President Jackson and the congressional majority which supported him resolved to push matters to that extremity. The ladies all wore the nullification badge, and placed it on the breasts of their children; and even the negro slaves who acted as nurses, and the negro slaves who worked in the cotton or rice plantations, displayed the badge of hostility to the Central Government. The truculent General Jackson was not alarmed at these threatening manifestations; but the majority that had supported his views, both in the Senate and in the House of Representatives, were fearful of provoking such an outburst of wrath in the whole South as would in all probability have produced a violent disruption of the Union—from causes which would not have estranged the sympathies of Europe, but, on the contrary, would have commanded them, more especially in Great Britain. A Southern Confederacy was even at that time debated; and the idea took such root as to lead to the striking of a medal in commemoration of nullification and of State rights, bearing on one side the head of John C. Calhoun, and on the other the inscription, "First President of the Southern Confederacy."

General Jackson was resolved to support the action of Congress, and lay in wait for the commission of some act on the part of Mr Calhoun that might, by the aid of any unscrupulous lawyer to be found in Washington or the Northern States, be construed into treason; and swore with profane oaths—not only at the times, which were by no means infrequent, when his brain was inflamed by raw whisky, but in the early morning, when he was sober—that if he were found guilty, he would have John C. Calhoun hung " as high as Haman." " By the Eternal ! " he said, " if this kind of thing goes on, our country will be like a bag of meal with both ends open. I'll tie up the ends of the bag, and save the country. By the God of heaven ! I will uphold the laws. They are trying me too much."

These were his private utterances; but, as was to be expected from the fact that he had cooler heads in his counsels, his public utterances were more dignified, though equally resolute. Mr Livingstone, who acted as his Secretary of State, drew up by his advice and inspiration a proclamation, addressed to the whole of the American people, which stated his firm determination to uphold the action of the central power, and to crush by force if necessary the opposition of South Carolina. The Governor of South Carolina immediately issued a counter-proclamation, in which he denounced the doctrines of the President as specious, false, and

pernicious, and tending to uproot the principle
on which the voluntary union of the several States
was founded, thus destroying the liberties not only
of the States, but of their individual citizens, and
which would lead infallibly, if not successfully
resisted, to "the establishment of a CONSOLIDATED
EMPIRE, one and indivisible, the worst of all
despotisms."

Mr Calhoun may or may not have been disheartened by the unwelcome discovery of the fact
that the other States of the South displayed no
inclination to support him, otherwise than by brave
resolutions and flatulent speeches. At all events,
whatever may have been the reason, he favoured in
the Senate, of which he still continued to be a
member, an attempt to compromise the difficulty.
By that compromise—which was at last effected—
the great question of the right of any State to dis-
agree with, or, if need were, to oppose the decrees of
the Central Government, was adjourned, but not
settled. The eminent senator, Mr Clay, whose
name and character were highly respected both in
the North and the South, and whose influence in
the South was second only to that of Mr Calhoun,
introduced a Bill providing that the protective
duties at that time in force should every two years be

reduced by one-tenth until the year 1842, when all duties *ad valorem* should be reduced to twenty per cent, or as much lower as the then sitting Congress should determine. With some difficulty Mr Calhoun was induced to support this measure. South Carolina acquiesced with an ill grace, contented more or less to adjourn for ten years the final settlement of the right of nullification, and the consequent right of secession from the Union, which sought *vi et armis* to impose its will on an independent and recalcitrant community. The President disapproved of this compromise, and would have vetoed it, as he might legally have done, had he not been overpersuaded by cooler heads than his own. During the remainder of his life he cherished a vindictive and unchristian animosity against Mr Calhoun. Being asked by the Rev. Dr Edgar, his spiritual comforter, on his deathbed in 1845, what he would have done with Mr Calhoun and the other nullifiers in South Carolina, if they had proceeded to violence, the old man sprang suddenly up in his bed, his fading eyes flashing with momentary fire, and exclaimed, "Hung them up, sir, as high as Haman! They should have been a terror to evil-doers for all time, and posterity would have pronounced it to be the most meritorious act of my life."

This vital question of State rights was not only held in special favour by the South, but by the North. The abolition of negro slavery by Great Britain in 1835, accompanied by the handsome compensation of £20,000,000 sterling to the slave-proprietors in the West Indies, gave an immense impetus to the question in the Northern States. The enemies of negro slavery were a small but powerful and growing sect, and never lacked zealous and eloquent supporters in the pulpit and on the platform, and to a certain though not great extent, in the press. In the Northern States the free labour of white men was found to be cheaper and more effective than the enforced labour of the blacks; and hard work in the fields was not forbidden by the climate, as it was generally in the South, to all white-skinned workmen. In one phrase—a favourite with all commercial people—slavery in the North "did not pay." One by one the Northern States, for this great commercial reason, strengthened and supported in a minor degree by reasons of religion and philanthropy, as well as by the purely philanthropic and non-commercial example of Great Britain, set about the task of emancipating the negroes.

The North, however, was not by any means unani-

mous in undertaking the great work, nor was the action of the States simultaneous. Every State that
resolved upon the emancipation of the black labourers acted on its own voluntary determination, and by
the legal agency of its own legislature—as a free,
sovereign, and independent State—without asking
for or expecting the co-operation of any other.
The small State of Rhode Island, called affec-
tionately "little Rhody" by its people, first moved
in the matter, without waiting for the example
of Great Britain, or even for the Declaration of
Independence,—and led the way in 1775, by
enacting that all children thereafterwards born
of slave mothers within its boundaries should be
free. Massachusetts followed suit in 1780, as did
the great State of Pennsylvania. Connecticut, without manumitting its actual slaves, decreed that all
the children of slave mothers, born after the 1st of
March 1784, should be free. New York abolished
slavery in 1783; New Hampshire, nine years afterwards, in 1792; while New Jersey, only separated
from New York by the Hudson river, did not see
its way to abolition until 1820. It must be said,
however, in the interests of truth, that although
religion and philanthropy, as well as the meaner
considerations of economic science, prompted these

and other Northern States, there were not wanting among them a class of selfish and hard-hearted slave-owners, who took timely advantage of what they knew to be inevitable, by sending all their young and able-bodied slaves into the South, and selling them to the best available advantage. The abolitionists in these Northern States, not contented with doing the right thing in the right way, were unhappy because the Southern States did not imitate their example, and instituted a zealous propaganda for the coercion of the South. They forgot or ignored the fact that the economic elements of the problem to be worked out were not identical in the two geographical sections of the Republic.

Meanwhile a new and highly important element in the case was yearly assuming larger and more important dimensions. The free Northern States were continually receiving new partners in dominion, by immigration from Europe, and by the invasion of the unoccupied and fruitful territories of the great West by the young and adventurous spirits of the earlier settlements of the Atlantic seaboard, who found the homes of their fathers too narrow for their enterprise, their ambition, and their earth-hunger. The thirteen original States had grown into twenty or thirty, and the new-comers were free of the burden—or guilt as they considered it—of negro slavery. These magnificent accretions strengthened the pre-existent sentiment of the people of the thirteen older States—which had found favour with Washington, Hamilton, and the Federal party—and impressed them with the splendid idea of the advantages that would attend the establishment of one great, glorious, undivided Republic, extending over all the continent, and possessed of resources, agricultural and mineral, far superior to those of Great Britain, France, Italy, Spain, or Germany, or any other of the European monarchies. And this natural growth of the area of the Northern States naturally impressed on the minds of the statesmen of the South that the South ought also to expand, and that its "manifest destiny" was, *per fas aut nefas*, to invade, to conquer, and to possess Mexico and the West Indies,—an idea which, in the course of time, was resolutely acted upon, and led to the forcible acquisition of Texas and California.

The Abolitionist and Anti-slavery party at this crisis took up the idea once entertained by the Free Trade party in the South, and, arguing that their political partnership with the slave States rendered them participators in the guilt of slavery, which they were powerless to abolish, imposed upon them the duty of separation. The idea was present during many long years in the minds of the leading publicists and people of the North; and was expressed in 1848 in emphatic language by Mr W. H. Seward, afterwards the Secretary of State in Mr Lincoln's administration during the War of Secession, in a speech or lecture delivered at Baltimore. He declared to an auditory in that border city—all whose sympathies were in favour of the South—his firm conviction that the separation of North and South was both desirable and inevitable, and that, come when it would, the people of both sections would afford the world "a splendid example of the inherent excellence and utility of republican and democratic freedom, and at the same time read a lesson of peace to the corrupt and rotten monarchies and empires of Europe, by separating amicably, by mutual agreement, and without the shedding of a drop of blood."

Mr Seward published the speech in a pamphlet three or four years afterwards, little dreaming that on this very question time and the course of events would transform the peaceable philanthropist and liberal statesman into the most truculent and bloodthirsty administrator that his country had ever seen.

Mr Horace Greeley, the celebrated editor of the 'New York Tribune,' who exercised a powerful influence over the Anti-slavery and Republican party of the North and West, openly and persistently advocated separation. In lines that were continually recited in speeches and writings by the abolitionists, he described the American flag as a "flaunting lie" and "a blood-stained rag," that ought to be torn down from every battlement and steeple in the North, and that should be hoisted half-mast high in sign of its degradation in every American ship on the ocean. He advocated the independence of the Northern States, or any portion of them; or if independence were not attainable, their incorporation with Canada, and a return to their allegiance to the "Old Country"—anything rather than continuance in a union with the Southern States, that maintained and endeavoured to extend negro slavery.

The Northern States, however, were not unanimous on the subject of slavery or the desirability of its abolition. Their leading statesmen cared more for protection to native industry, and high, if not absolutely prohibitive, duties upon all the manu-

factured goods that Great Britain and Europe could
supply, than for the freedom of men with black
skins, whom they were willing to recognise as men,
but wholly unwilling to recognise as brothers having
equal political and social rights as themselves. Provided that the Southern members of the House of
Representatives and the Senate of the Federal Government would cease their agitation in favour of
the lowering of the duties on foreign manufactured
goods to the minimum that would produce a
revenue, they were willing to lend all their influence in favour of Southern slavery.

With a view to the success of this object, they
entered into an immoral contract with the celebrated Daniel Webster, beyond all comparison the
most eloquent and powerful orator then existent in
America. Webster was an Abolitionist at heart;
but he was a man of luxurious and extravagant
habits, encumbered by a load of debts, and needy
as well as greedy in the extreme. For a large
annual salary, in addition to the payment of all his
actual debts, he sold his advocacy and his soul to
the Northern manufacturers, and fought the battle
of Protection, not wisely but too well, in Congress;
and fought, at the same time, in the same assembly,
with equal unwisdom, and with superior eloquence,

the battle of the slave-owners against the Abolitionists. He continued to fight it with unflinching
courage and zeal until he died broken-hearted. In
spite of the mercenary and corrupt bargain, which
it was suspected rather than known that he had
made, by selling the birthright of his conscience for
a mess of pottage, his death was mourned throughout all America. The people remembered his marvellous eloquence, but did not remember his equally
marvellous venality; and every pulpit and platform
in the land rang with expressions of condolence and
regret at his death.

One only voice was raised in his denunciation,
that of Theodore Parker of Boston, a Unitarian
preacher of great power and popularity, who
launched against his memory a tremendous phi-
lippic, which has seldom been surpassed, or even
equalled, in the annals of political warfare.

Mr Webster, though the most eminent corrup-
tionist of his day, by no means stood alone in political dishonesty. The old patriarchal virtue was
not wholly extinguished in the Southern States,
of which the white inhabitants were the descendants of the early heroes of the War of Independence.
Their ranks had received very few if any accretions
from the large European immigration of Irishmen and

Germans that continued to pour into the Northern and the recently settled Western States. The new-comers were ignorant of, or wholly misunderstood, the foundations on which American liberty rested; and knowing nothing of the thoroughly and essentially democratic self-government of the several States, thought only of the greatness of the Union, and of their own newly-acquired importance and weight in the social and political scale, and as component parts, however poor and mean in worldly circumstances, of the sovereign people.

Mr Fisher Ames, a thoughtful New Englander, foresaw the dangers likely to arise from the growing number of the States and Territories, and from the character of the alien races that invaded them in search of farms, security, and freedom, and declared, in memorable words, that the country was "too big for union, too sordid for patriotism, and too democratic for liberty." Year after year the offices in the gift of the President and the Central Government increased in number, and the candidates increased disproportionately in every State of the Union. Political services—to the total, or almost total, exclusion of merit—were the sole qualifications for Presidential favour; a result that was due to the pernicious doctrine broached by General

Jackson, who maintained that to "the victors belonged the spoils." This doctrine is still in force,
though condemned by all thinking Americans, for
the reason that, however useful and efficient these
wrongly-appointed State officials may prove to be,
they are expelled from office at the end of four
years, along with the Presidents who appointed
them, to make room for the friends of the incom-
ing President, who claim, as their predecessors did
before them, an indefeasible right to the "spoils."[1]

---

[1] President Lincoln, a man of strong common-sense, singleness
of mind, and sturdy honesty, saw the evils of this system, and
would have remedied it had it been in his power. He sometimes
told, with great gusto, when he unbent among his intimate friends,
an anecdote in proof of the unconquerable thirst for the "spoils"
that afflicts the venal intriguers, high and low, who pull the dirty
wires of which the successful manipulation often elects a previously
obscure man to the Presidency.

"I hadn't been settled a week in the White House," said the
good, plain man, "when I was visited by a strong, hearty, dirty-
looking fellow—from Kansas, I think, he said—who gave me a
powerful grip of the hand, and informed me that he had made
me President. 'Many people have told me the same thing,' said
I; 'but how did you make me the President, if you really did
so?' 'My vote carried my State in your favour, and my State
carried your election; therefore I made you President. And I
want you to do something for me in return!' 'But what do
you expect me to do?' I asked him. 'I want you to give me the
Embassy to London or Paris,' he replied. 'Impossible,' said I;
'both embassies have been filled up already.' 'Well, then,' said
he, 'I have no objection to Vienna or Berlin!' 'Bespoke,

There never was a time between the great
" Nullification" alarm in 1832, until the election
of Mr Lincoln in succession to Mr Buchanan in

bespoke,' said I. 'It's rather hard,' said he ; 'but I'll take Constantinople, if you've nothing better to give me.' 'All the
embassies have been filled up long ago,' said I. 'The Collectorship of Customs at New York would suit me capitally,' said he,
turning a quid of tobacco in his mouth ; 'or if that be disposed of,
I would accept the collectorship at Boston or elsewhere.' 'Utterly
useless to expect a collectorship anywhere,' said I. 'It's cussed
hard,' said he, 'after I have made you President, that I can't
get anything for my trouble. Can you give me a lighthouse?'
'Nary a lighthouse,' said I. 'Nor a post-office ?' 'Nary a post-
office.' 'Well, Mr President, all I can say is, that it is an infernal
shame that you can't give me anything at all. Can you loan me
twenty dollars ?' 'I have parted with my last dollar,' said I,
'and can't do it.' 'Well,' he rejoined, 'though I'm greatly disappointed, I'm not proud. Can you give me an old coat, or an old
pair of boots ?' I found him an old pair of boots, with which he
.went away ; and I afterwards learned that he had pawned them at
a liquor-store for half a bottle of whisky."

A kindred story found currency and favour among the cynics of
the Northern States during the earlier months of the War of
Secession in 1862. The Federal army had been defeated by the
Confederates at Bull Run, and made a somewhat precipitate retreat,
which excited much unfavourable comment at the time. "It is
quite a mistake," said a Northern politician, who doubtless wished
well to the Confederates, "to say that our army was defeated at
Bull Run. The fact is, that a rumour circulated in the ranks that
several vacancies had unexpectedly occurred in the New York
Custom-house. The report no sooner reached the ears of the
officers than they turned towards New York, in order to be first
in the field as candidates ; and the whole army, filled with the
same hopes, followed them."

1860, when the cry of secession was unheard.
During the interval it was not so much the
question of Free-trade as that of Negro Slavery
that created the antagonism between the two sections, although the question of the prohibitory
tariff was never wholly lost sight of. The per-
sistent agitation, kept up by the press, the platform,
and the pulpit in the North, on the subject of
negro slavery, together with the refusal of the
Northern people in many afterwards celebrated
cases to surrender to their Southern masters the
fugitive slaves that had sought and found refuge
in the New England States, by what was called
the "Underground Railway," kept alive the discontent in the South as well as in the North
and West. The unwise abrogation of what was
known as the "Missouri Compromise," which sought
to prevent the extension of the slave-holding
area beyond the geographical limits of the latitude of that State, added fuel to the flame of
agitation, and rendered the North more aggressive
and the South more defiant than they had previously been.

In 1857, when the State of Kansas was not
only theoretically but actually the battle-ground of
the supporters and the opponents of the extension

of slavery into any of the territories that might afterwards become States of the Union, the question of disruption was openly discussed by the chief members of the Democratic and Republican parties.

Mr Buchanan, the elect of the Democrats, occupied the Presidential chair; and the Republicans, having little or no hope of electing a President of their party to succeed him, spoke more loudly of the necessity of a disruption than the opposing faction, who were quite contented with the Union as it stood, if they could but be masters of it, and rule it on Free-Trade and Pro-Slavery principles. Besides, their party were in the majority, which was composed of the whole voting power of the South, and supported by a very large and influential section in the older States of the North, being only in a minority in the newer States of the North and North-West, where the immigrants from Europe, and especially from Germany and Scandinavia, were mainly in favour of the Republican party, and more or less allied in feeling with the Abolitionists. The Democratic party was, in fact, too reliant on its undoubted strength, and too contemptuous of the supposed weakness of the opposite party, to claim from impartial history the praise of prudent management of its resources, or of the wise generalship that sees and calculates the strength of its adversary in order to defeat him.

At the Presidential election of 1860 it committed the suicidal folly of allowing itself to be divided into three sections, who each put forward a candidate, instead of concentrating its forces upon one. Its opponents, who were weaker numerically, were wiser, and united in support of an unknown and very humble man, whose name had scarcely been heard of beyond the limits of the State of Ohio, and was not held in great estimation even there, except by a very few who knew the sterling worth of his character, and the solid honesty that had marked his career. The three candidates whom the Democratic party foolishly allowed to fight the battle of State Rights and old-fashioned American liberty in their behalf, were Messrs Douglas, Bell, and Breckenridge—the latter being the actual Vice-President of the time under Mr Buchanan. At the final declaration of the poll, the numbers stood as follow :—

Mr Douglas, . . .	1,375,157
Mr Bell, ...	590,631
Mr Breckenridge, . .	847,953

amounting in all to 2,813,741 votes cast by the

Democrats. On the opposite side the numbers were for the single candidate,—

Mr Abraham Lincoln, . 1,866,452

This was nearly a million less than the total votes cast by the Democrats, but nearly half a million more than were cast for Mr Douglas, the highest on the list of his opponents. Thus Mr Lincoln, though he was the elect of the minority, succeeded legally to the Presidential chair. Thereof sprung woes innumerable to his unhappy country, and a civil war, unsurpassed in its magnitude in any free country.

Mr Lincoln, though a Federalist, a Republican, and an Abolitionist, was not an enemy of State Rights, which he justly considered to be the true foundation of American liberty. He was often urged by some of his supporters, during the first three years of the war, to issue an edict or proclamation against negro slavery, in order to gain the sympathies of Europe, which, during that time, inclined to the Southern side. He invariably refused, stating that he might issue an edict against the moon or a comet with equal effect; that the abolition of slavery concerned the Southern States alone, and that it was for them to deal with the evil in their own time, in their own way, and

by the legal action of the several States, as the
New England and other Northern States had done.
This was the contention of the whole Democratic
and State Rights party of the North, but was
steadily opposed by the Republicans and Abolitionists, as inconsistent with their favourite project
of creating a great Republic, one and indivisible, to
rise upon the ruins of the small separate republics
that formed an unstable and incohesive Union,
which had been in continual danger of disruption
ever since its establishment.

The inevitable conflict, that unfortunately culminated in one of the most sanguinary wars of
modern times, was hastened by two incidents—the
one of Northern, the other of Southern origin. The
first was the daring invasion of Harper's Ferry, in
Virginia, by a mad enthusiast named John Brown,
who thought—at the head of a handful of negroes,
and a few white comrades as crazy as himself—to
provoke a rising of the slaves in Virginia, and of
all the Southern States, against their owners. John
Brown's followers were speedily overpowered by
the local authorities, and Brown himself brought to
trial for high treason against the sovereign State
of Virginia.

Being found guilty, he was hanged, meeting his

fate bravely like an apostle, and not like a madman, and was forthwith elevated by his white admirers and sympathisers throughout the whole North to the honours of martyrdom, almost of canonisation. His memory was enshrined in a song, afterwards sung by countless thousands of black and white abolitionists, to a popular hymn tune, borrowed from the chapels and conventicles:—

> "John Brown's body lies mouldering in the grave,
>   But his soul is marching on."

The second incident was of more immediate and fearful consequence. It gave the signal for the outbreak of the war which, before it occurred, might possibly have been averted, but which, in the highly inflammable temper of the Abolitionist and Union party, then became inevitable. The Southern leaders virtually commenced hostilities, when General Ripley, the officer in command of the small military force of South Carolina, attacked Fort Sumter, in the harbour of Charleston, and, in the inflated language of the day, "fired the heart of the whole North" by directing his shots against the "sacred flag of the Union," which the zealous abolitionist, Horace Greeley, had called "a polluted rag," and causing it to be hauled down ignomini-

ously from the walls of the fortress, which the
South Carolinians claimed as their own, though it
was erected for Federal and not for State purposes.

The action on the part of the South was planned
and deliberate, but it had the effect on the Northern
mind of a torch applied to a powder - magazine,
and caused an instantaneous explosion of wrath
in the Republican party, shaking the edifice of
American liberty to its very foundations. The
war thus inaugurated cost the Union, before it was
concluded, upwards of five hundred millions sterling
(£500,000,000),—a sum which would have paid
for the manumission of the slaves twenty times
over, with compensation to the slave-owners, such
as Great Britain had given to the West Indian
proprietors,—a compensation which would have been
all the more glorious because unattended by human
suffering and the horrible bloodshed and countless
miseries that are the inevitable concomitants of war,
even when waged in the most righteous of causes.

The time has come when the whole truth should
be told, not alone as to the real origin, but as to
the conduct of this unfortunate and needless war.
The North had for years done its best to provoke
not war, but secession; and the South, in like
manner, had continually insisted upon its right to

dissolve a partnership which it found unprofitable, distasteful, and oppressive. But it was the South and not the North which, at the last moment, inaugurated what might otherwise have been a peaceful and legal separation, by an act of war; while the attack upon Fort Sumter cannot be considered by impartial history as anything but a rash and unwise appeal to the *ultima ratio* — long erroneously considered to be the favourite argument of desperate and ambitious kings and emperors, but which the event in America proved, not for the first time in the world's history, to be equally a favourite with ambitious democracies. But though it must be conceded that the Southern States provoked the war, it must be conceded, at the same time, that they provoked it in defence of what they considered to be their freedom and independence, and that the North, in accepting the challenge, accepted it for purposes of mastery and dominion, and violent coercion of an unwilling brother having equal rights with itself.

Mr Seward, the Secretary of State, who virtually wielded more autocratic power than the President, was ever sanguine as to the success of the Northern arms. He had predicted and recommended, many years previously, as we have already seen, the peaceable and bloodless disruption of a Union distasteful to both of the great sections which composed it; but no sooner had the signal-gun been fired against Fort Sumter, than he became as fierce an enthusiast for war as he had been previously zealous for peace, and rendered himself conspicuous for his truculence amid the many truculent statesmen of his party. He underrated the powers of resistance possessed by the South and the powers of aggression possessed by the North; and was never weary of predicting that the North would end the war by the conquest of the South in "ninety days" at the furthest. The phrase of "ninety days" became proverbial, even after nine times ninety days had passed in sanguinary battles, leaving the South still unconquered and defiant.

The South fought under disadvantages for which its own unreasoning pride and indomitable self-reliance were responsible. All its soldiers were volunteers, enthusiastic in the cause, and fought without resort to the aid of foreigners and paid mercenaries. It was too proud to accept the aid of its slaves, of whom it might have easily raised an army of 200,000 fighting men, brave, and trained to obedience, if it had but promised them freedom at the close of the war as the reward of their services.   But this course, though often urged upon the Southern leaders, and which, if adopted, would have secured them the sympathy of all Europe, and converted many of the European enemies of slavery into friends, was uniformly rejected.   It was not from mistrust of the fidelity of the negroes that the South remained deaf to all recommendation and remonstrances on this vital subject, but from unconquerable pride, and a rooted faith, entertained by the meanest white citizen, that independence would lose its value if it were acquired either in whole or in part by negro auxiliaries.   While the South thus knowingly restricted the ranks from which it could recruit its defenders—having no aid from the copious immigration from Europe, of which it never had any large share, and which the strict blockade of its coasts rendered impossible, even if it had been desirable,—the North was able to draw almost *ad libitum* upon the superabundant population of the Old World for mercenary soldiers.   By an all but reckless amount of bounty money, which it offered to every Irish, German, or other needy immigrant who landed at New York or Boston, it secured what promised to be a limitless supply of fighting men.   The bounty that commenced at 100 dollars a man, went on increasing as the struggle proceeded, until 200, 300, and even as much as 500 dollars, or £100, was freely offered. But though the North expended its money, it did not secure the service of a fourth part, or even of one-half, of the men for whose fighting powers it had paid so lavishly.

Civil war in the best of cases generally produces more scoundrels than it kills — a fact of which the North, during the years 1863 and 1864, had ample proof in the enormous prevalence of what was called "bounty jumping." By the operation of this system of State robbery, an immigrant who had received his 100, 200, or 500 dollars in one town, district, or division of the country, made his way in all haste to another, and received the bounty money a second, third, or even tenth time. A systematic villain of this class fell tardily into the hands of justice during the height of the war in 1864, and was shot in New York, after proof that he had received the bounty money no less than seventeen times, and had "jumped" it sixteen times, until at the seventeenth he was "jumped" into eternity by operation of the law which he had so often outraged. General Grant, under whose relentless strategy the war was brought to a close in 1865, knew the all but limitless resources of men on which he could rely while the bounty system remained in force. He felt that he could have managed to outnumber the Southern legions even if one-half of the men receiving the bounty had been " jumpers "; and boasted that, in his sanguinary encounters with General Lee, he could afford to lose ten men, while Lee could scarcely afford to lose one. The Democratic party in the North—which never ceased to sympathise covertly with the South during the whole course of the struggle—had no better name to bestow upon the ruthless General than the " Butcher," under which cognomen the more outspoken journals of New York and other cities persisted in designating him. Thus the Southern States were defeated, after a gallant struggle, by the overwhelming superiority of the numbers opposed to them, and by their own obstinacy in refusing all help from the negro auxiliaries, who would have been most willing to support their cause for the gift of their freedom, or for that of their unborn children, even if manumission had been withheld from them in their own persons.

The government of the people by the people and for the people, has been for ages considered by sanguine believers in the innate goodness and wisdom of mankind to be the best of all possible forms of government; but neither poets nor philosophers have ever strictly defined what they meant by the " people " who were to form the ideal democracy. When pressed upon the subject, they have been forced to admit that their ideal democracy excluded one - half of mankind in the persons of women, and another large portion in the persons of all the youth of both sexes who were under twenty-one years of age. Nor were these the only restrictions, comprehensive as they were, which kept the so-called democracy within comparatively narrow bounds. From the governing classes were rigidly excluded convicted criminals, lunatics, idiots, and habitual paupers, maintained at the cost of the general community. It follows, from a due consideration of these facts, that a true democracy, in its widest sense, never did and never will exist in any age or country, and that no form of government — whether it be democratic or aristocratic—can be established or maintained without large restrictions. Liberty itself, if it be true liberty, cannot exist without restraint of law, or it would speedily degenerate into licence, and consequently into anarchy. In other words, a democracy is really an

aristocracy in the occult and unavowed estimate of
those who constitute it, inasmuch as the males of
full age, and in adequate possession of their mental
faculties, consider themselves to be the *best* for the
purposes of governing the greater portion of their
fellow-citizens.   Were all the males of full age wise,
temperate, calm, and judicious, unswayed by passion,
prejudice, and inordinate self-interest, and knew what
was best for the State, for themselves, and for their
fellow-citizens, without distinction of sex, rank, or
worldly circumstances, good government would be the
result, and the need of the strong arm of extraneous
authority to maintain peace and order would be
wholly unnecessary.   But this state of things is non-
existent anywhere; and among the multitude in all
countries—whether the form of government be free
and constitutional, or autocratic and despotic—the
mass of mankind cannot justly be accredited with
political wisdom or unselfish virtue.   The hard and
engrossing toil which is their inevitable lot; the
desperate competition for the means of bare subsistence which, as their numbers increase, is forced
upon them by natural causes, against which it is
in vain to struggle; and the ignorance of high
State policy, which the conditions of their daily
existence prevent them from conquering by in-

telligent study and enlarged experience,—all these causes combine to render them unfit for the government of their wiser fellow-citizens.

The greatest worshippers of the people, in the widest sense of the word, cannot claim for the vast majority—counted by heads, and man for man—the purity of motive and the high intelligence that should rule a great nation. They cannot claim for them even the adequate comprehension of their own true interests, or assert, if they would hope to be believed, that either in theological or in commercial matters they would not and do not strive to enforce their will against that of the possibly wiser minority who do not agree with them. The will of a bigoted and cruel majority led, in Europe and in America, to the burning of witches, and to the relentless persecution of dissentients from established doctrine; and to a tyranny, a self-seeking, and a corruption, on the part of the arrogant, the needy, and the greedy, that form the majority—the *imperium in imperio*—in all countries, and more especially in countries that are supposed to be free, and whose opinions find expression in newspapers, caucuses, and in public meetings, where fluent oratory, rather than sound common-sense and cogent reasoning, sways the passions and flatters the prejudices of the multitude. In all widely extended or ultra-democracies—such as the United States are, and as Great Britain threatens to become at no distant period — the power of popular speakers, endowed with what is vulgarly but emphatically called "the gift of the gab," is on the increase, and bids fair to supersede wise, silent, or ineloquent statesmanship, both in legislative assemblies and in the caucuses that strive to override them.

Another evil, in addition to that of ignorance of the art of and object of governments, which necessarily prevails among the great bulk of an ultra-democracy, composed for the most part of poor and struggling men, is that of their subserviency to mere wealth, and the preference of rich men over men who are eminent for their genius or their public virtues. To the mob of voters — who are ever flattered and carried away by the ornate and bewildering eloquence of professional talkers—the man who is known to be rich, and the manufacturer who employs hundreds, or perhaps thousands, of workpeople, has a chance infinitely greater of securing their votes than falls to the lot of the purest saint or the greatest intellectual giant who might solicit their suffrages. But greater even than the most consummate master of language, or the most powerful possessor of large realised wealth, is the successful soldier—the conquering general, the hero of some great victory over a foreign or domestic enemy. In the estimation of the rank and file of all widely extended democracies, he stands supreme above all possible competitors; and if circumstances are favourable, he develops into the Autocrat or the Emperor, and the destroyer of the liberties of his country. Ultra-democracy produced a Bonaparte in France, and twice elevated to the Presidential chair in the United States an Andrew Jackson and a Ulysses Grant, whose principal if not only pretensions to the support of their country-men were derived from their military achievements; and whose claims, such as they were, proved suffi-cient to render nugatory those which were founded upon the culture, experience, and wise statesmanship of the vastly superior men who were opposed to them. Force and money far surpass public virtue, in the estimation of the multitude in all countries, as qualifications for the highest office in their gift.

The wealth which an ultra-democracy greatly reverences, the members of an ultra-democracy will do their best to acquire—honestly if they can; but if honesty is difficult, inopportune, and slow or un-certain of fructification, they will acquire it by the contrary method, and at the expense, if occasion offers, of the country which their suffrages help to govern, and of which they are virtually the masters.

The corruption of American officials of all but the highest class—that only includes the President, the Judges of the Supreme Court, and a few others that may be counted on the fingers of both hands—is proverbial.   The members of the several State Legislatures, and of the Washington Congress, are composed for the most part of men to whom the salaries of membership are an essential object, without which few of them could pay their way.   It cannot with justice, or even propriety, be said of them all that they are open to corrupt influences, and accessible to bribes, either in cash or in kind; but it cannot be denied that, as a rule, men who are poorly paid for legislative work are naturally liable to pecuniary temptation, and often too weak or too unprincipled to resist it.   The shameful leniency displayed to criminals by popularly elected judges is notorious in every State of the Union, though more extensively prevalent in New York and the Northern and Western States, that absorb for the most part the stream of European immigration, than in the older States of the Union, where the land is preoccupied, and farms are not easily obtainable, as in the South and in the small States of New England.   To apply to a man engaged in any honest business or profession—a well-to-do farmer, merchant, shopkeeper, lawyer, or medical practitioner—the opprobrious epithet of a politician, is to insult him as much as if he were called a swindler or a scoundrel.   The pursuit of politics as a profession is generally, though in many cases unjustly, considered in America what Dr Johnson more than a hundred years ago in England declared " patriotism " to be, —the last resource of a scoundrel.

If any justification of the well-merited odium into which professional politicians have fallen in America were needed, the evidence, in glaring superabundance, of unblushing corruption, is ready to the hand of any one who chooses to inquire, in the Report of the House of Representatives, issued at Washington in December 1861, a few months after the commencement of the great Civil War.   The Report is that of " the special committee appointed to inquire into all the facts and circumstances connected with contracts and agreements by or with the Government, showing all of its operations in suppressing the rebellion."   It was resolved by the House that 5000 copies of the Report, with all the evidence on which it was founded, and 10,000 extra copies of the Report without the evidence, should be printed and circulated. The Report and evidence fill a closely printed volume of 1109 pages. A copy of it lies before me as I write—one of several hundred which were bound and distributed gratuitously by a leading citizen of New York, a lover of rational liberty and of honest government, who gave it the alliterative and suggestive title of 'Political Putrification Portrayed.'

At this period the Federal Government was greatly in need of steam-vessels, and was willing to pay somewhat in excess of the fair market price for such commodities, in consideration of the extreme urgency of the public service. An agent named Starbuck, appointed by, and supposed to be acting for the benefit of, the Government, and to be paid by a commission of $2\frac{1}{2}$ per cent on the purchases he effected, acquired on his own account, on the pretence that they were required in his private business, two steamers for the sum of 6500 dollars. He sold them, within a few days, to the Government for 14,500 dollars, on which latter sum he had the effrontery to demand, and the conscience to receive without blushing, a percentage of $2\frac{1}{2}$ per cent, or 3625 dollars, or nearly £700, in addition to the

8000 dollars which he had already surcharged the Government. " It is proper to state," says the Report, p. 20, " that after this testimony was taken by the Committee, it was by them laid before the United States District Attorney in New York, and such steps were taken as resulted in the refunding by Starbuck of 6166 dollars (more than £3000) of the money thus obtained. The ships themselves were found, when delivered at the Navy Yard, to be totally unfit for the service for which they were required, and the Government was again subjected to a further expense of several thousand dollars in repairs, and a delay of several weeks in their use."

The purchasing of vessels for the needs of the State, in its sore emergency, was taken in May from the heads of the Navy Department in Brooklyn and the port of New York, and transferred to Mr G. D. Morgan, a wholesale grocer in that city, and brother-in-law of a member of the Federal Government, the Secretary of the Navy. The following extract will show how the new arrangement worked to the disadvantage of the Government, and that it was no more preventive of peculation and robbery, under the management of so high an official, than the isolated case in the hands of Mr Starbuck had proved itself to be.

"Although the Committee," says the Report, p. 23, "have occasion at this time more particularly to call attention to the remarkable arrangement which existed between the Secretary of the Navy and Mr Morgan, as to the compensation he was to receive for his services, they desire to notice, in passing, a single instance of deception practised upon Mr Morgan in the sale to him of a new vessel, the 'Stars and Stripes,' which had been afloat less than two months. This vessel cost its owners but $35,000 to build her, had earned, under a charter to the United States, in that two months $15,000 nett, and was then sold to Mr Morgan for $55,000, making a clear profit to her owners of $34,400. This was done by making Mr Morgan believe that it cost $60,000 to build her. It is difficult to see how such a deception could have been practised upon a man of the acknowledged business capacity and shrewdness of Mr Morgan, except that he had been called to a service in which he had had no experience, and was ignorant, from any personal knowledge, of the cost of the article he was sent out to purchase.

"The Committee quote from the testimony, not only to show how easy it is to practise, even upon men otherwise shrewd, when dealing in matters of which they have no personal knowledge, but also to expose the shameful manner in which the *character of members of Congress and other officials* is traded upon. Mr Benedict, one of the owners of the 'Stars and Stripes,' testifies as follows (p. 333) :—

"*Question.* Do you know anything about the steamer 'Stars and Stripes'?

" *Answer.* Yes, sir; I was a stockholder and director in the company that owned her.

" *Question.* What has become of her?

" *Answer.* She was sold to the United States Government.

" *Question.* For how much?

" *Answer.* $55,000.

" *Question.* Through whom was the purchase made?

" *Answer.* I cannot tell. The business was done by the president of the company, C. S. Bushnell. He was the president of the New Haven Propeller Company, which owned the 'Stars and Stripes.'

" *Question.* When was the sale made?

" *Answer.* I cannot tell exactly. I think it must have been about the last of July. The reason I think so is that the Treasury notes in which we received our pay were dated the 6th of August.

" *Question.* Had the 'Stars and Stripes' been previously chartered to the Government?

" *Answer.* Yes, sir.

" *Question.* For how much?

" *Answer.* At $10,000 for thirty days; and it was optional for the Government to keep her or not at $9000 a-month after the expiration of that time.

" *Question.* What was the original cost of that boat?

" *Answer.* About $35,000.

" *Question.* And how much was she sold for?

" *Answer.* $55,000. We considered that we built her cheap. She was a very excellent vessel.

" *Question.* Who were the parties that made the negotiation with the president of your company?

"*Answer.* To tell the plain truth, the company knew little about it. The president always declined to tell us much about it.

"*Question.* What idea had the directors in relation to the transaction?

"*Answer.* The directors thought, at least, that it was pretty heavy share.

.   .   .   .

"*Question.* He intimated that he had to pay large sums in Washington to effect the sale?

"*Answer.* He said distinctly that he did not himself get a copper of the $8000. We did not like to believe it, but he asserted it over and over again. He said that his relations to the persons to whom he was obliged to pay this money were such, that he could not and would not reveal their names. He finally so far succeeded in satisfying the stockholders, that they agreed to pay him the $8000.

. "*Question.* After paying him that sum, your company received the $47,000 for the boat?

"*Answer.* Yes, sir.

"*Question.* With which the stockholders were very well satisfied?

"*Answer.* Yes, sir.

"*Question.* They would have been satisfied to have got $35,000?

"*Answer.* I think they would.

.   .   .   .

"*Question.* What assistance did he represent that he was obliged to get?

"*Answer.* He stated to us that *it was impossible to*

*approach the heads of department at Washington without
letters of introduction,* and that it was necessary to get
men of influence to approach them.

" *Question. Did he represent that he was obliged to pay
for letters of introduction?*

" *Answer. He said he was obliged to pay persons in
Washington for their influence.*

" *Question.* More than one person?

" *Answer.* He spoke of persons.

" *Question.* Did he speak of having to pay for the
influence of persons residing in Washington?

" *Answer. No, sir; he spoke as if they were members of
Congress, or ex-members, or something of that kind, whom
he paid for their influence.* I will not say positively
whether he spoke of ex-members.

" *Question.* And he stated that he was obliged to pay
out this entire $8000?

" *Answer. Yes, sir; at least he stated that this two
and a half per cent to Morgan was to be taken out of it.

" *Question.* But beyond that he gave you no information to whom it was paid?

" *Answer. None whatever.*

" *Question.* Upon what ground, then, did the stockholders, after he refused to give them that information,
vote to allow him $8000?

" *Answer.* He told them a long story about the matter.
He satisfied them that he could not approach the Government directly, that it was necessary to have assistance,
and that in all probability he had spent this money."

Enough, and perhaps more than enough, has been

quoted to show the scandalous corruption that
prevailed at a time of public danger and calamity,
when all good citizens should have been zealous to
support the Government.   The report emphatically
condemned the whole of this particular transaction—which was only a sample of many others that
were similar—by the statement that the Committee
did not " find anything less to censure in it, from the
fact that this transaction between the Secretary
of the Navy and Mr Morgan was one between
brothers-in-law,—a family arrangement which re-
flects great discredit upon the public service."

Similar extortions, effected by similarly dishonest
means, were exposed by the Committee, with regard
to the purchase of arms, ammunition, horses, mules,
and military stores of all kinds—a mere recapitu-
lation of which would weary and disgust the
reader.   It may suffice to state that, at a time
when the military forces of the Federal Government, of whom a large portion were Irish and
German mercenaries, who had enlisted for the sake
of the enormous bounty money that was given to
them—raw recruits, and growing lads, unable to
bear the hardships of the campaign—amounted and
approximated to 500,000 men in the field and in
the military hospitals, *pay and rations were drawn for*

710,000 !   Into whose pockets this enormous plun-
der found its way—whether they were military men,
or whether they were legislators or ex-legislators,
was never known, and cannot now be investigated ;
though it may well be suspected that they were all
" politicians " in the American sense of the word.

Popular elections in all free countries, Great
Britain not excepted, are commonly, if not inevitably, attended by practices more or less corrupt—
especially when the constituencies, whether large or
small, are composed, for the most part, of men
condemned to daily manual labour and sordid engrossing pursuits, without leisure, taste, or opportunity for the acquisition of political knowledge.   There
is seldom a time in America when an election of
some kind or other is not proceeding, under the
manipulation of a local " caucus," that regulates
the action of the voters who elect the candidates,
who are nominated—but who are not allowed to
nominate themselves—for office in the several States,
or in the more important Legislature of the Congress at Washington.   Of all these multifarious
elections, the chief and most engrossing is that for
the Presidential office, which takes place every four
years, and which, it may be said without exaggeration, engrosses the attention of party managers, and

distracts the attention of men of business, for at
least two years out of the four.   It is felt by most
Americans to be in itself and in its preliminaries
a nuisance in all its stages, more especially in its
last, to say nothing of the cost of time, of attention, and of labour imposed upon busy men by
these constantly recurring contests.   Their cost in
money is enormous.   The money is wrung from
the reluctant pockets of party men of both political factions throughout the whole vast extent of the
Union—from Maine to Florida, and from Massachusetts and Rhode Island to California and Oregon.
Uninformed Americans, who talk of the exorbitant
expenses and the splendid Civil List necessary to
maintain a constitutional or other monarch in
befitting state and dignity, as compared with the
modest stipend allowed to the Chief Magistrate of
their vast Republic, forget how much it cost to
elect him.   The cost may be surmised, but has
never yet been accurately—though it has often been
approximately—estimated, at an amount every four
years greatly in excess of the Civil List for the
same period of the British Sovereign.   Publicity
in all free countries where a newspaper press is in
flourishing existence, is a highly expensive luxury.
The number of newspapers in the United States

may be roughly designated as "legion"; and every one of them expects to receive the advertisements of one or both of the candidates, Democratic and Republican, for the coveted Presidency. As newspaper proprietors throughout the United States generally, if not invariably, combine the business of general printers with the literary and political business of journalism, the number of bills, placards, and printed appeals to the public which are affixed to the walls, and lavishly distributed through the post-office, may be counted by millions—during the two years that the election is virtually in progress. The very large sums thus to be disbursed find their way into the pockets of innumerable prosperous and unprosperous journals throughout the Union, and influence more or less the opinions of their proprietors and writers.

The hire and lighting of public rooms in every one of the large cities—and in the great majority of the smaller towns and villages—for the purposes of public meetings, constitutes another large item of expense which has to be provided for. To this must be added the very considerable sums paid for the hire of bands of music that, as the day of election approaches, parade the streets of the great cities at all hours, to keep up the spirits of the candidate's friends, and proportionately to discourage his opponents by the noise and blare of his pretensions. The raising of this money is one of the greatest scandals of the political life of America. Voluntary offerings for the maintenance of the cause, by its rich or ambitious friends, no doubt contribute large sums to the fund; but the great bulk of the money is raised by a compulsory assessment upon the salaries of every official, great or small, who has owed his place to his party, under the penalty, in case of refusal, of expulsion from its ranks. The same assessment is made upon the "outs" as is made upon the "ins"; for the "outs" invariably expect to be the "ins" if the candidate be successful—and hopes must pay as well as realisations. Such is the law of the "wire-pullers" who conduct unseen, but by no means unfelt, the political destinies of the Republic.

These assessments are made by the irresponsible and self-appointed leaders of each party, on a scale varying from five to ten, or even twenty, per cent of the annual income of the offices, however humble or however elevated such offices may be. To the victors belong the spoils, is the immoral doctrine laid down by General Jackson, which is accepted as truth by all parties. The victors who enjoy the spoils for four years are expected—and compelled, by agencies more powerful than the law itself—to contribute out of the " spoils " a stipulated percentage to the support of the party that achieved the victory for them, and that expect to achieve it again by the same efforts. The evil is widely spread and keenly felt, not only by the immediate sufferers, but by a very large portion of the thoughtful men in America, who hold themselves aloof from professional politics as they would from the plague, and who think that, in the public interest, place-holders should be appointed for life, or during good behaviour, as they are in other countries. This much-needed reform has not yet found wide acceptance among the ultra-democracy —whether it be of the Republican or the Democratic party—though it forms what is called a " plank " in the platform of the smaller body of truly independent men who do the thinking of the Republic.

The great and fundamental error of ultra-democracy in all countries—and especially in the United States—is, that it teaches and allows the power of voting to be a *right* with which a man is born, and not a *privilege* to be acquired by him, or conceded to him, not for his own benefit, but for that of the community. In Great Britain——though, under the influence of Radical *doctrinaires* and unscrupulous and ignorant demagogues, we are rapidly approaching to manhood suffrage, with an extension to womanhood suffrage in due time——the inherent right of any one to vote is not acknowledged.

Manhood and womanhood suffrage would be excellent if men and women were invariably good and wise, and knew the true interest of the State as well as their own ; and the Americans act upon the supposition that, as far as adult men are concerned, they are all philosophers, statesmen, and patriots. But we have not yet arrived at that faith in Great Britain. We still think it wise and expedient to deny that the exercise of the voting power is anything but a privilege to be conferred on certain conditions for the benefit of the public and not of the individual, and to be withheld in like manner for satisfactory and adequate public reasons. Law cannot say that the good and wise alone shall vote in the government of their fellows, because Law is utterly unable to distinguish and to declare who are the good and the wise, and to grant them privileges accordingly. But Law can take cognisance of physical if not of intellectual facts, and can decree that, if a man occupies a house and pays annual rent for it, and contributes according to his means, directly or indirectly, to the necessary expenses of the Government which protects him in his life and liberty, he is, though perhaps neither a very good nor a very wise man, entitled to the privilege of helping to elect a representative to act on his behalf in the councils of the State.

In giving him this privilege, the State makes him one of the trustees of the national interest. In so doing, it confers no inalienable right upon him, but merely endows him with a privilege which he may forfeit if he becomes a pauper or a criminal, or ceases to be a householder and a contributor to the national revenues. It is not so under the system of what is sometimes called Universal, but that ought to be called Manhood, suffrage, which is established in America and France, and is gradually extending itself into Great Britain. To teach the people—whether white or black—that the suffrage is a right which it is unjust and tyrannical to withhold from them, is to instil into the minds of the ignorant and needy among them that it is a right which they may turn to pecuniary and other personal advantage at the expense of the men of a superior class in society who are so eager in asking for its exercise in their favour. The corruption that springs from this source is by no means peculiar to the United States; but it may be stated with perfect truth, and without exaggeration, that it is much more prevalent in that country, where the suffrage is unrestricted—except by sex and nonage, insanity and crime—than it is in countries where the suffrage is a privilege that may be earned, and that may also be forfeited.

One of the foremost dangers to the stability of the American Union, and to the perpetuation of the public liberties, springs from the acknowledgment of the rights of millions of black men to the suffrage. Before the close of the great Civil War in 1865, when Abraham Lincoln, as a measure of expediency, or, as he deemed it, of military necessity, abolished slavery by a stroke of his pen, the negro population of the Southern States amounted to less than four millions, and of the Northern and Western States to less than half a million. In 1884, the negroes in the Southern States numbered upwards of seven millions. The negro population all over the United States is calculated to increase at the rate of thirty-five per cent in ten years, and the white population, inclusive of the European immigration, at the rate of less than twenty-eight per cent during the same period. In the three southern States of South Carolina, Mississippi, and Louisiana, the negro population amounts to 56.4 per cent of the whole, and the white population only to 43.6. In other southern States the negro majority is not quite so large; but if to the three States above named are added Virginia, North Carolina, Georgia, Florida, and Alabama, the census gives the proportion of blacks to whites as 48.8 per cent, or nearly one-half—that promises to be more than one-half when the next returns are taken.

Of the 7,000,000 of negroes—all the adult males among whom are entitled to the privilege of voting —no less than 6,000,000 or upwards are unable to read or write. Should the present rate of increase be maintained both among the white and black races, the negroes in the South will form a large majority, and in the course of a century will considerably outnumber the white people in the whole Union, unless immigration from Europe—which is not likely—should maintain the now existing preponderance. In any case, the white Americans— if they do not wish to be governed by a majority of black citizens, enjoying equal political privileges and powers with themselves—will have to consider whether manhood suffrage, irrespective of race and colour, is the form of ultra-democratic government that will suit their idea of liberty, or conduce to the stability of the institutions on which they pride themselves. The germs of a war of races—one of the most hideous of all possible wars—may be concealed beneath the voting power now unwisely granted to an ignorant and but slightly teachable population.

Another great and more immediate danger arises from the venality of the multitude, and from the constantly recurring nuisance of popular elections —especially that for the Presidential office, which every four years renders a political convulsion and a revolution far more imminent than thoughtful Americans like to confess. But perhaps the greatest danger of all lies in the ingrained, inappeasable, unconquerable desire of the people of the Northern and Western sections, aggravated and intensified by the conquest of the Southern States, to make the Republic one and indivisible, and to minimise, and ultimately to abolish, State Rights, so dear to the hearts and the judgment of the founders of the original Union in the days of Washington. The desire is for ascendancy and dominion rather than for liberty,—a passion which

is the vice of all great democracies. The extent of
their territories, the magnitude of their revenues,
the rapid growth of their population, and the
marvellous development of their wealth and enterprise, open their eyes to the perception of the
fact that they dwarf in these respects all the old
States of Europe except Great Britain, which, in
these respects, only keeps pace with her vigorous
American offshoot by the vastness of her dominions
in Canada, Asia, Africa, and Australia.

Great Britain is the first power in the world, and
the United States desire to become so—*vice* the
mother-country relegated into the second rank.
This, disguise it as they may, is the leading
passion in American hearts—a passion which cannot be gratified until the Republic becomes " one
and indivisible." It was more to indulge this
passion for unity of dominion, as we think has
been made apparent in these pages, than for any
innate love of the negro, or any real abhorrence of
the immoral and cruel system which enslaved
him, that they ignored State Rights—the real
corner-stone of their liberty, if they would but
know and confess it—that they waged war upon
and ultimately conquered the South, by dint of
superior wealth and numbers. The question of

negro slavery is dead and buried, never more to
be revived; but other questions remain, and will
be developed in due time to cause political conflict, that may not perhaps admit of peaceful conclusions.   The material interests of California and
Oregon on the one side of the continent, and of
Massachusetts and New Hampshire on the other,
are not the material interests of Louisiana and
the Carolinas; and the battle of a high prohibitive
tariff, for the protection of native industry, may
be fought out to as dire conclusions as were imminent under the guiding hand of Mr Calhoun in
South Carolina in 1832, and as are still imminent
between the manufacturing and the agricultural
interests in the two great sections of the Union.
And should civil strife arise on this question, or
any other of equal importance, and disunion be
again threatened—as in the case of negro slavery—
the passion for dominion will once more assert itself, unless the darling object of American ambition
be abandoned, and the Americans learn that liberty
is better worth having than the subjugation of a
brother.

It has become proverbial to assert, as we have
already observed in these pages, that " war is a game
which, were their subjects wise, kings would not play

at." But ancient and modern history alike teach us that the game is one which unbridled democracies, when their passions are stirred or the lust of dominion gets the mastery over them, are as ready to play as ever kings have been. The American Democracy has more than once tasted the blood of conquest, and enjoyed its flavour. It provoked, in the last generation, a war with Mexico, and wrested large provinces from that State: one province, that of Texas, as extensive as France; and California, another not quite so large, but of far greater value. It has expressed, on more than one occasion when its passions were excited or its cupidity was aroused, a desire to annex Canada, even at the risk of a war with Great Britain; and still cherishes the wish, and awaits the opportunity, to pick a quarrel with Spain for the possession of Cuba, and with Great Britain for the possession of the West India Islands. The greed of territory, that receives a certain amount of pabulum in the creation of new States in the vast and as yet thinly-peopled territories—that stretch between the western slopes of the Rocky Mountains and the Pacific Ocean—is gratified but not satiated. When these embryo commonwealths are digested and assimilated, as they will be in a few years, the pampered and unappeased appetite will turn with hungry ferocity to weak and unoffending Mexico, with all the greater intensity because the expansion northwards of the mighty Republic will be stopped by unconquerable Canada.

The absorption of Mexico is not likely to lead to any European complications that would render difficult or impossible the aggression of the American Union.   But the case of Cuba is far different, and may involve other European countries besides Spain. An attack upon this island, in addition to its other attractions in American eyes, has in those of the North—which conquered the South, on the plea of its maintenance of negro slavery—the charm of a new crusade for the abolition of that pernicious institution.   Cuba, while it remains a Spanish colony, may support slavery; but as a conquered State, finally annexed to the American Union, the doom of slavery within its borders would be pronounced by the President for the time being, supported by the Washington Legislature, amid the sympathies of Great Britain and France, and of all Europe, Russia not excepted.   The subject has long been familiar to the American mind as one that demands action, and that will most certainly receive it, sooner or later—if not in the present generation, in the next.

All other questions that imperil the peace and the liberty of the American people sink into insignificance compared with the growing lust of dominion, and the tendency to the concentration of political power at the expense of the free local governments. This is the latent and inherent disease in the system, which, unchecked, must inevitably lead to the downfall of the ultra-democracy that knows not how to restrain itself, and that, in the day of some overwhelming calamity, will seek and find a master or tyrant, and a restrainer. Such has been in all ages and in all countries the doom of an unbridled Democracy. Such must be its doom in America, unless its people take warning in time, and learn to profit by the bitter experience of the past, and shape the present and the future in such a manner as to prove to all men that a brighter and more beneficent era has dawned upon the world in a new hemisphere than ever shed light upon the old. But this dream of a possible Utopia afar off, will not blind the eyes of thoughtful observers in other countries to the superior advantages and greater safety of a wise liberty, guarded and fenced around by the prudent restraint which separates liberty from licence; and that, if it cannot eradicate popular ignorance, can at all events render it innocuous, by denying it political privileges and power over the fate and fortunes of wiser people, and of the great country to which both the wise and the foolish belong.

INDEX.

www.ingramcontent.com/pod-product-compliance
Lightning Source LLC
Chambersburg PA
CBHW030948110726
47900CB00004B/1178